AF608234

The Provisions of the Decree *Spiritus Sancti Munera*:

THE LAW FOR THE EXTRAORDINARY MINISTER OF CONFIRMATION

The writing of this dissertation was conducted under the direction of the Very Rev. Clement V. Bastnagel, S.T.L., J.U.D., as major professor, and was approved by the Rev. Meletius M. Wojnar, O.S.B.M., S.T.L., J.C.D., and the Rev. John J. McGrath, A.B., LL.B., J.C.D., as readers.

THE CATHOLIC UNIVERSITY OF AMERICA
CANON LAW STUDIES
No. 397

The Provisions of the Decree *Spiritus Sancti Munera:*

THE LAW FOR THE EXTRAORDINARY MINISTER OF CONFIRMATION

A DISSERTATION

Submitted to the Faculty of the School of Canon Law of The Catholic University of America in Partial Fulfillment of the Requirements for the Degree of Doctor of Canon Law

BY

REV. HENRY J. DZIADOSZ, M.A., S.T.L., J.C.L.
A Priest of the Diocese of Norwich

THE CATHOLIC UNIVERSITY OF AMERICA PRESS
WASHINGTON, D. C.
1958

Nihil Obstat:

CLEMENS V. BASTNAGEL, S.T.L., J.U.D
Censor Deputatus

Washingtonii, die 28 maii, 1958.

Imprimatur:

✠ BERNARDUS J. FLANAGAN, D.D., J.C.D.
Episcopus Norvicensis

Norvici, die 31 maii, 1958.

Printed by
THE WICKERSHAM PRINTING CO.
Lancaster, Pennsylvania

Veni, Sancte Spiritus, et emitte caelitus lucis tuae radium.
Veni, pater pauperum, veni, DATOR MUNERUM, *veni, lumen cordium.*

DEDICATED TO THE BELOVED MEMORY OF
MY FATHER AND MOTHER

FOREWORD

A little more than ten years have elapsed since the appearance of a pontifical pronouncement which marked a momentous milestone in the history of the discipline of the Church governing the administration of the sacraments. So far-reaching were the provisions of this document that some have compared it to the epochal decrees of St. Pius X on daily Communion and the age for the reception of first Holy Communion. The decree *Spiritus Sancti munera* by its extensive augmentation of the list of extraordinary ministers of confirmation, effective January 1, 1947, amply ameliorated the spiritual status of numerous souls who otherwise might have departed from this world without the munificent benefits of the sacrament of confirmation.

Though the decree was warmly and enthusiastically welcomed throughout the Christian world and has proved to be a bountiful blessing, diffidence on the part of some pastors and priests in charge of souls may have somewhat tempered the full fruition of its magnanimous provisions. Unfamiliarity with the rubrics of the liturgical rite of confirmation, uncertainty about the manifold canonical stipulations for the valid and lawful use of the faculty, and a latent reluctance to "infringe" upon the immemorial prerogative of bishops may have contributed in part to the creation of an unwarranted and undesirable passivity in the actual exercise of this sublime function. It is hoped that the present reappraisal of the provisions of the decree against the background of history and in the light of current developments, along with an understanding discernment of the practical problems which might confront the priest-minister in the administration of confirmation to those who are in danger of death, will result in a gratifying increase in the use of this extraordinary faculty.

By a public expression of heartfelt gratitude and prayerful devotion to the blessed memory of His Holiness, Pope Pius XII, who promulgated the decree, the present writer simply reflects the sentiments of present and future generations. *Spiritus Sancti munera* together with *Christus Dominus* and *Sacram Communionem,* which created a new discipline for the Eucharistic fast and granted permission for evening Mass, as well as *Maxima redemptionis* which introduced salutary revisions in the liturgical observance of Holy Week, give eloquent testimony to the indomitable energy of a supremely solicitous Shepherd of souls whose noble soul returned to its Maker on the 9th of October, 1958.

The writer also welcomes the opportunity to extend his deep appreciation to the Most Reverend Bernard J. Flanagan, D.D., J.C.D., the Bishop of Norwich, not only for the opportunity to pursue graduate studies in Canon Law at the Catholic University of America but also for his continued fatherly interest and inspiration. He wishes to thank his fellow priests in the diocese of Norwich for their kind encouragement, his classmates for the treasured privilege of association with them, the members of the Faculty of the Graduate School of Canon Law for their scholarly guidance, and finally, the Reverend Clement V. Bastnagel, J.U.D., whose superintendence and immediate direction in behalf of the writer aided him immeasurably in the composition of this dissertation.

TABLE OF CONTENTS

SECTION C

PART II

CANONICAL COMMENTARY

CHAPTER III

CHAPTER IV

CHAPTER V

CHAPTER VI

PART I

DOCTRINAL AND HISTORICAL SYNOPSIS

CHAPTER I

DOCTRINAL ASPECT OF THE DECREE

ARTICLE 1—NATURE AND EFFECTS OF CONFIRMATION

In the very opening words of the decree *Spiritus Sancti munera* the Sacred Congregation for the Discipline of the Sacraments concisely appraised the dignity and spiritual value of the sacrament of confirmation when it asserted that this sacrament confers the treasured gifts of the Holy Spirit,[1] supernatural habits which dispose the soul to answer promptly the inspirations of God and which are commonly enumerated as wisdom, understanding, counsel, fortitude, knowledge, piety and fear of the Lord.[2] With striking succinctness and expert expression the preamble to the canonical provisions of the decree delineated the fundamental teaching of the Church on this marvellous mystery of sanctifying redemption, which is an admirable aid in the bitter and fierce struggle against the wickedness of the devil and the allurements of the flesh and the world as well as a means of augmenting grace and all virtues on earth and acquiring a greater increase of glory in heaven. Through the remarkable gifts which confirmation confers the recipient is clothed with an abundance of grace and adorned with the insignia of a soldier of Christ, so that he becomes equipped for every good work.[3]

The sacrament of confirmation is generally defined by theologians as a visible sign instituted by Christ our Lord in virtue of which a baptized person through the anointing and imposition

[1] "Spiritus Sancti munera sacramento Confirmationis conferri catholica doctrina proclamat."—*Acta Apostolicae Sedis, Commentarium Officiale* (Romae, 1909-1929; Civitate Vaticana, 1929-) XXXVIII (1946), 349 (hereafter cited as *AAS*).

[2] "And the spirit of the Lord shall rest upon him: the spirit of wisdom, and of understanding, the spirit of counsel, and of fortitude, the spirit of knowledge, and of godliness. And he shall be filled with the spirit of the fear of the Lord."—Isaias, XI: 2-3.

[3] *Spiritus Sancti munera, AAS,* XXXVIII (1946), 350.

of the hand along with the prescribed formula of words is strengthened in grace and signed as a soldier of Christ.[4] That confirmation confers grace is an article of faith, formally defined implicitly in two declarations of the Council of Trent, namely in the declaration that confirmation is truly and properly a sacrament[5] and in the declaration that every sacrament gives grace.[6] Though it is theologically certain that confirmation does not intrinsically (*per se*) confer first grace, since the Church teaches that only baptism and penance directly effect the remission of mortal sins, it is at least equally certain that in addition to an increase of sanctifying grace confirmation confers a grace of a special nature, whereby through the Holy Spirit the soul is strengthened and perfected.[7] Thus, as St. Thomas noted, an important effect of confirmation is the full and complete giving of the Holy Spirit.[8] In a descriptive definition he referred to confirmation as the sacrament of the fullness of grace,[9] the sacrament of the perfected age of the spiritual life.[10] This special sacramental grace has been variously described by theologians as *"collatio Spiritus Sancti," "donum Spiritus Sancti," "gratia augmentativa," "gratia confirmativa," "gratia perfectiva,"* and *"gratia roborativa."*[11]

[4] Zubizarreta, *Theologia Dogmatico-Scholastica ad Mentem S. Thomae Aquinatis* (4. ed., 4 vols., Vitoria, 1949), IV, n. 269, p. 147.

[5] Conc. Trident., sess. VII, *de confirmatione,* can. 1; also *de sacramentis in genere,* can. 1.—Denzinger-Bannwart-Umberg-Rahner, *Enchiridion Symbolorum Definitionum et Declarationum de rebus fidei et morum* (30. ed., Friburgi Brisgoviae: Herder, 1955), nn. 871 and 844 respectively (hereafter cited as Denzinger-Rahner, *Enchiridion*).

[6] Sess. VII, *de sacramentis in genere,* can. 6.—Denzinger-Rahner, *Enchiridion,* n. 849.

[7] Doronzo, *De Baptismo et Confirmatione* (Milwaukee: Bruce Co., 1947), pp. 339 ff.

[8] ". . . in hoc sacramento datur plenitudo Spiritus Sancti ad robur spirituale."—*Summa Theologiae,* IIIa, q. 72, a. 2, *in corp.*

[9] "Confirmatio est sacramentum plenitudinis gratiae."—*Summa Theologiae,* IIIa, q. 72, a. 1, ad 2 et ad 4.

[10] "In confirmatione autem homo accipit quasi quandam perfectam aetatem spiritualis vitae."—*Summa Theologiae,* IIIa, q. 72, a. 1, *in corp.*

[11] Doronzo, *op. cit.,* p. 347.

Another effect of confirmation is its imprinting of the character of a Christian soldier. It has been defined that in three sacraments, namely, baptism, confirmation, and holy orders, there is impressed upon the soul a character which is a spiritual and indelible sign because of which these sacraments can only be received once.[12] The character of confirmation is a distinctive sign in virtue of which the Christian must struggle not only against the invisible powers of Satan but also against visible enemies, such as persecutors of the church.[13] It will also serve in heaven as an added crown of glory.[14]

Confirmation, therefore, is a sacrament which is both a moral necessity and an invaluable asset in the spiritual development of the follower of Christ. Throughout the centuries the Fathers and Doctors of the Church have enhanced its majesty by considering it a complement to baptism, which is the sacrament of spiritual regeneration.[15] Baptism has been called the sacrament of the Trinity, confirmation, the sacrament of the Holy Spirit;

[12] Conc. Trident., sess. VII, *de sacramentis in genere,* can. 9, also cited in sess. XXIII, *de ordine,* cap. 4.—Denzinger-Rahner, *Enchiridion,* nn. 852 and 960 respectively.

[13] *Summa Theologiae,* IIIa, q. 72, a. 5, *in corp.* et ad 1 *um.*

[14] *Summa Theologiae,* IIIa, q. 72, a. 8, ad *4um.*

[15] Herman notes that the concept of confirmation as a sacrament which gives strength to fight against the onslaughts of the devil and to profess publicly one's faith in Christ is foreign to Oriental theology. There the stress is placed upon confirmation as the plenitude of the spiritual life, the complement or perfection of baptism. This perhaps explains why the priests of the Eastern rites have seen the need of possessing the power to confirm infants immediately after baptism.—"Confirmation dans l'Orient moderne," *Dictionnaire de Droit Canonique* (commencé sous la direction de A. Vellien et E. Magnin, continué sous la direction de A. Amonieu, publié sous la direction de R. Naz, Paris: Letouzey et Ané, 1924-), IV, 122. Cf. "Ten Years' Work on Baptism and Confirmation, 1945-1955" by J. Crehan in *Theological Studies,* XVII (1956), 494-515. The author (pp. 513-514) advocates a return to the concept of confirmation as the complement of baptism as it was known in Tradition, which referred to the act of confirming as *"perficere baptizatum."* For the development of the theological notion of strength for spiritual warfare and public confession of faith from the time of William of Auvergne through St. Thomas, see *The Effects of the Sacrament of Confirmation* (Washington, D. C.: 1940) by J. Gillis, pp. 61-139.

baptism, the sacrament of the building of the temple of God, confirmation, the sacrament of the consecration of the temple of God, the filling of the temple with the presence of the Deity; baptism, the sacrament of regeneration, confirmation, the sacrament of adulthood; baptism, the sacrament of faith conferred, confirmation, the sacrament of faith confirmed; baptism, the sacrament of spiritual ablution, of initiation, confirmation, the sacrament of spiritual anointing and consummation; baptism, the sacrament of formation in the Christian society, confirmation, the sacrament of strengthening in the militia of Christ, and, finally, baptism has been referred to as the sacrament of faith, and confirmation as the sacrament of strength.[16]

Article 2—Age for the Reception of Confirmation

The present discipline of the Latin Church calls for the administration of confirmation to those who are about seven years of age.[17] An answer from the Pontifical Commission for the Authentic Interpretation of the Canons of the Code, given on June 16, 1931, indicated that this regulation is of a mandatory, and not simply of an advisory, character.[18] However, for good and serious reasons, such as immemorial custom and danger of death, the reception of confirmation can be lawfully anticipated.[19]

[16] Doronzo, *op. cit.*, p. 352.

[17] *Codex Iuris Canonici Pii X Pontificis Maximi iussu digestus, Benedicti Papae XV auctoritate promulgatus, Praefatione, Fontium Annotatione et Indice Analytico-Alphabetico ab Emo Petro Card. Gasparri Auctus* (Romae: Typis Polyglottis Vaticanis, 1917; reimpressio, 1934), canon 788 (hereafter reference is made simply to the number of the canon).

[18] *AAS*, XXIII (1931), 353.

[19] Canon 788; cf. also the reply of the Sacred Congregation for the Discipline of the Sacraments, June 30, 1932, *AAS*, XXIV (1932), 271-272. Ideally, the reception of confirmation should precede the first reception of the Holy Eucharist. Thus, the Congregation states in part, ". . opportunum esse videatur et conformius naturae et effectibus sacramenti confirmationis, pueros ad sacram mensam prima vice non accedere nisi post receptum confirmationis sacramentum, quod est veluti complementum baptismatis, et in quo datur plenitudo Spiritus Sancti." Pope Leo XIII, on June 26, 1897, in response to an enquiry made by the Archbishop of Marseilles commended the practice of confirming children before they receive

The undue protraction of the administration of confirmation, on the other hand, is not to be tolerated. The same Commission mentioned above absolutely refused to sustain the mandate of a local ordinary which forbade the reception of confirmation until the party has reached the age of ten years. On March 26, 1952, in reply to an enquiry whether a mandate of the local ordinary forbidding that the sacrament of confirmation be administered to children who have not yet reached the age of ten years should be sustained, the Commission emphatically replied, *"Negative!"* [20]

---

the Eucharist, ". . . sic confirmati adolescentuli ad cupienda praecepta molliores fiunt, suscipiendaeque postmodum Eucharistiam aptiores."—"Epistula Abrogata ad Episc. Massilien." in *Leonis XIII Pontificis Maximi Acta* (23 vols., Romae: ex Typographia Vaticana, 1881-1905), XVII (1898), 205-206.

[20] *AAS,* XLIV (1952), 496. For a thorough treatment of the age for the reception of confirmation cf. Bennington, *The Recipient of Confirmation,* The Catholic University of America Canon Law Studies, no. 267 (Washington, D. C.: The Catholic University of America Press, 1952), chap. VII, pp. 76-93. He concludes: "To require a minimum age of twelve or fourteen for the reception of confirmation in order to keep children in attendance at religious instruction is not justifiable even on the basis of expediency." —*Op. cit.,* p. 127, n. 10. In an article, "Confirmation at Eleven Plus, a View from Ireland," *The Clergy Review,* XLI (1956), 201-206, Tynan shows that confirmation at the dawn of adolescence (the age of ten or eleven plus) rather than at the age of the use of reason is not only contrary to the mind and law of the Church but not even good religious psychology or catechetical discipline. The article is written in answer to a suggestion made by George Andrew Beck, Bishop of Brentwood, who had been transferred to the see of Salford, that the sacrament of confirmation be linked with the secondary school. "If the initiation to secondary school were accompanied by the reception of confirmation, and the first year in the secondary school devoted to this theme, a profound effect might be produced in the minds of the boys and girls thus entering into a privileged group and acquiring special status in the Church." See "The School and the Parish," *The Clergy Review,* XL (1955), 584. McCarthy, in his work *Problems in Theology, I: The Sacraments* (Dublin: Browne and Nolan Limited, 1956, Westminster: Newman Press) defends the practice in Ireland of postponing confirmation for a few years after the age of discretion has been reached, the purpose of which is to secure sufficient and adequate catechetical instruction. In his analysis of the two decisions of the Commission for the Authentic Interpretation of the Canons of the Code, as cited above, he concludes: "The recent reply of the Code Commission (1952) might then be described as a somewhat extensive interpretation of

canon 788, inasmuch as it states that an order of the local Ordinary forbidding the administration of Confirmation to children under the age of ten may not be upheld. Canon 788 now emerges as mandatory from two standpoints. In 1931 it was declared to be mandatory as fixing about seven years as the minimum age for Confirmation for the normal case in the Latin Church. The recent reply implies that it is also mandatory as fixing about seven years—meaning at least under ten years—as the age beyond which the local Ordinary cannot order the postponement of Confirmation. In other words local Ordinaries cannot henceforth issue a mandate prescribing ten completed years as the minimum age for the reception of this sacrament. There is nothing in the reply to prevent the prescription of a minimum age provided it is under ten years."—*Op. cit.*, p. 78. The present writer cannot agree with this conclusion.

CHAPTER II

HISTORICAL ASPECT OF THE DECREE

The present decree *Spiritus Sancti munera* along with subsequent declarations of the Holy See shines forth in sparkling splendor as indisputable proof of the Church's concern to administer confirmation to as many souls as possible. Faced with the startling statistics of a high mortality rate among infants and children and of the great number of adults who die without the sacrament of confirmation,[1] the Holy See considered it urgent to reappraise its discipline concerning the administration of this august sacrament in order to provide such a large number of the faithful with the opportunity of receiving confirmation.[2] Up to this time the teaching and practice of the Church on the minister of confirmation were embodied in the first two paragraphs of canon 782:

§ 1.—The ordinary minister of confirmation is solely a bishop.[3]

§ 2.—The extraordinary minister is a priest to whom the power has been granted either by the common law or by a special indult of the Apostolic See.

The historical foundation for this doctrine and policy presents an interesting study. Indeed, it must have influenced the deliberations of the officials of the Congregation which issued the

[1] The decree uses the expressions, *"permultos pueros," "adultis non paucis," "immodicus christicolorum numerus"—AAS,* XXXVIII (1946), 350.

[2] *AAS,* XXXVIII (1946), 351.

[3] This paragraph states a defined doctrine of faith, namely canon 3, *de confirmatione,* of the 7th session of the Council of Trent. Since this statement involves a matter of faith rather than of discipline, it should be noted that one must apply this to the body of beliefs professed by members of the Eastern rites. Occasionally commentators confuse the issue when they contrast the custom of the Oriental Church, where simple priests confirm immediately after baptism, with the statement that in the Latin Church the ordinary minister of confirmation is the bishop. Actually in both the Oriental and the Latin Churches the only ordinary minister of confirmation is the bishop.

decree *Spiritus Sancti munera.* Before making any final decisions, they obtained the opinions of many prudent and experienced consultors and also reviewed and compared all previous documents pertaining to the law on the minister of confirmation.[4]

The aim of the present writer in this historical conspectus is to reproduce the more important incontrovertible texts which have a bearing on the history of the extraordinary minister of confirmation in the discipline of Western Church, i.e., the Latin rite.[5] The chief sources which will be the object of a more detailed analysis are the *Decretum* of Gratian and the *Decretals of Gregory IX* along with the observations of the various glossators and commentators, the seventh session of the Council of Trent, and the subsequent documents issued by the Popes and Congregations which were concerned with the extraordinary minister of confirmation. Inasmuch as the documents of the early centuries have been minutely examined in other studies related to the subject under discussion, the writer chooses to present only a cursory historical treatment of the period preceding the *Decretum* of Gratian.

SECTION A—THE PERIOD UP TO THE COUNCIL OF TRENT

ARTICLE 1—SCRIPTURE AND THE PRACTICE OF THE CHURCH IN THE EARLY CENTURIES

There are two main instances for tracing the idea of the minister of confirmation in the New Testament. The one concerns the inhabitants of Samaria, who had only been baptized in the Lord Jesus by Philip the Deacon. That these converts might receive the Holy Spirit, Peter and John came from Jerusalem to lay hands upon them.[6] The other is the record of St. Paul's visit to Ephesus. There he found some disciples of John the Baptist.

[4] *AAS,* XXXVIII (1946), 351.

[5] Among the majority of the peoples of the Eastern rites the custom prevails that a simple priest in the regular rounds of his sacerdotal duties confers confirmation as an extraordinary minister immediately after baptizing the children. One can only conclude that this is done in virtue of at least an implicit authorization of the Holy See.

[6] Acts of the Apostles, VIII: 5-17.

First Paul baptized them in the name of the Lord Jesus, and then laid hands upon them, after which the Holy Spirit came upon them.[7] These two texts of themselves and in themselves do not prove that the administration of confirmation was reserved to any special order, bishop or priest. Nor do they exclude the idea of the extraordinary minister.[8] Nevertheless, in the light of Christian tradition and practice, they might be and have been cited in proof of the bishop's exclusive prerogative as the minister of confirmation.[9]

In the early days of Christianity the bishop alone administered all the sacraments.[10] Baptism and confirmation, usually associated together as the initiation rite, were functions which were reserved to him. He alone offered Mass, he alone preached, managed the temporal goods, and applied disciplinary and juridical measures. Priests could exercise priestly functions, but they needed a commission from the bishop in the form of a mandate for each particular function. One might say that the priests and deacons exercised the functions of their respective offices only in the name and by the authority of the bishop.[11]

In his epistle to the Christian community of Smyrna, Ignatius of Antioch († ca. 107) warned that it was not permitted without

[7] Acts of the Apostles, XIX: 1-7.

[8] Quinn, *The Extraordinary Minister of Confirmation According to the Most Recent Decrees of the Sacred Congregations* (Rome: Catholic Book Agency, 1951), p. 5; Coleman, *The Minister of Confirmation,* The Catholic University of America Canon Law Studies, no. 125 (Washington, D. C.: The Catholic University of America Press, 1941), pp. 9-11.

[9] Quinn, *op. cit.,* pp. 6 ff. Coleman (*op. cit.,* p. 11, footnote 8) gives a number of references to illustrate and substantiate this statement.

[10] Cf. Chardon, "Histoire des Sacraments," in *Theologiae Cursus Completus* (annotavit vero simul et edidit J. P. Migne, 28 vols., Parisiis, 1863-1866), XX, 126-135, and 192-199.

[11] Alzog, *Manual of Universal Church History* (translated from the 9. and last German ed. by F. J. Pabisch and Rev. Thos. S. Byrne, 3 vols., Cincinnati: Robert Clark & Co., 1874), I, p. 391. For an analysis of the early history of parish discipline cf. Bastnagel, *The Appointment of Parochial Adjutants and Assistants,* The Catholic University of America Canon Law Studies, no. 58 (Washington, D. C.: The Catholic University of America, 1930), pp. 3-21.

authorization from the bishop either to baptize or to hold an *agape.*[12] Tertullian (ca. 160-223) also stressed the necessity of episcopal permission for the administering of baptism in his work *De Baptismo,* written between the years 200-206, while he was still a Catholic.[13] However, as the number of the faithful grew and the Church spread from the city into the rural areas, pastoral powers, including the administration of the sacraments, were exercised by the priests. The Roman and the African Churches adopted the policy of reserving confirmation to the bishops.[14] The Oriental, Spanish and Gallic Churches did not. As a matter of fact, numerous documents from the Church in Spain and Gaul testify to the administration of the sacrament of the Holy Spirit by priests in the absence of the bishop, or, with his permission, in his presence.[15] For the Spanish Church one may point to canon 20 of the first Council of Toledo (400):

> . . . Statutum vero est, diaconum non chrismare, sed presbyterum, absente episcopo; praesente vero, si ab ipso fuerit praeceptum.[16]

The same thought is repeated in the *Capitula* of St. Martin of Braga, composed after 563 by Bishop Martin. Canon 52 states that a priest in the presence of the bishop should not sign the

[12] "Non licet sine episcopo neque baptizare, neque agapen celebrare."—Migne, *Patrologiae Cursus Completus, Series Graeca* (161 vols., Parisiis, 1857-1866), V, 713.

[13] "Superest ad concludendam materiolam de observatione quoque dandi et accipiendi Baptismum commonefacere. Dandi quidem habet ius summus sacerdos, qui est episcopus; dehinc presbyteri et diaconi, non tamen sine episcopi auctoritate."—Migne, *Patrologiae Cursus Completus, Series Latina* (221 vols., Parisiis, 1844-1864), I, 1217 (hereafter cited as *MPL*).

[14] Lennerz, in his work *De Sacramento Confirmationis* (2. ed., Romae, 1949), has compiled texts in which one can see reflected the practice of the Roman Church: n. 19, Pope St. Cornelius (251-253); n. 20, *Liber Pontificalis* of Pope St. Sylvester I (314-335); nn. 22 and 23 from the Gelasian and Gregorian *Sacramentaries.*

[15] Mostaza, *El Problema del Ministro Extraordinario de la Confirmación* (Salamanca, 1952), pp. 10-50. The author reaches this conclusion from his analysis of the pertinent texts.

[16] Mansi, *Sacrorum Conciliorum Nova et Amplissima Collectio* (53 vols. in 60, Parisiis, 1901-1927) III, 1002 (hereafter cited as Mansi).

infants unless he is given permission by the bishop.[17] In the Gallic Church, canon 2 of the I Council of Orange (441), though the exact reading of the text varies, contains the thought that priests should confirm the person who had to bc baptized in necessity.[18]

Among the texts of the first five centuries on the question of the minister of confirmation, the most important document is that of Pope Innocent I (401-417), which was issued on March 19, 416, in answer to a question proposed by Bishop Decentius of the diocese of Gubbio. A recent writer noted that Innocent's letter enshrines the first papal resistance to the 'presumed' administration of confirmation by any priest.[19]

> De consignandis vero infantibus manifestum est, non ab alio, quam ab episcopo fieri licere. Nam presbyteri, licet sint sacerdotes, pontificatus apicem non habent. Hoc autem pontificibus solis deberi, ut vel consignent vel paracletum Spiritum tradant, non solum consuetudo ecclesiastica demonstrat; verum et illa lectio Actuum Apostolorum quae asserit Petrum et Joannem esse directos, qui iam baptizatis traderent Spiritum Sanctum. Nam presbyteris, seu extra episcopum, seu praesente episcopo, cum baptizant, chrismate baptizatos ungere licet, sed quod ab episcopo fuerit consecratum; non tamen frontem ex eodem oleo signare, quod solis debetur episcopis cum tradunt Spiritum paracletum.[20]

The tenor of the text is evident—only the bishop should confirm. However, attention must be drawn to the fact that the Pope did not deny that priests have the power to confirm. Rather he stated, *"non licere,"* which can presuppose an implicit distinction between invalid and unlawful. For a priest to confirm was certainly unlawful, especially since this was against the Roman practice and custom. One might say that this text indicated that confirmation was *"ordinarie saltem"* reserved to the bishop.[21]

[17] Mansi, IX, 856.

[18] Mansi, VI, 435.

[19] Ellard, "How Fifth Century Rome Administered Sacraments" in *Theological Studies,* IX (1948), 3-19.

[20] Mansi, III, 1029.

[21] Pistoni, *De Confirmatione a Ministro Extraordinario* (Liberia Editrice Vaticana, 1947), p. 4.

This document also has other features which are interesting to note, particularly in the light of later development. The phrase explaining why it was unlawful for priests to confirm, namely, *"pontificatus apicem non habent,"* was adopted and used quite frequently in the Pseudo-Isidorian decretals.[22] Likewise, already in the time of Pope Innocent I an appeal was made not only to custom but even to Scripture in justification of the bishop's exclusive power of confirming. But despite this, one can safely say that no document from apostolic times to the eighth century denied the priests the potential power of confirming.[23] As a matter of fact, it was during this period, namely in 594, that power for confirming was granted to simple priests by Gregory the Great. This document, because of the tremendous influence it exerted in the centuries which followed, will be studied in detail in the discussion of Gratian's teaching.

Article 2—The Period from the Eighth Century to Gratian

During the subsequent centuries there gradually developed a stringent insistence that the bishop was the *only* minister of confirmation. This was particularly true of the discipline in the West, where the Popes did not tolerate any contrary custom that might have recognized priests as the usual ministers of this sacrament. Two chief factors contributed to the dissemination of this doctrine, the fight against the chor-bishops and the Photian difficulty.

There was a concerted effort on the part of the compilers of false decretals to destroy the canonical institute of chor-bishops by bitterly inveighing against them and considering them as having only the order of the priesthood. As one glossator later on commented, *"Isti autem chorepiscopi aliquid habebant supra presbyteros, sed non bene determinat quid."* [24] This attitude was

[22] The spurious text of Pope Leo I to the bishops of Germany and Gaul, supposedly written between 440-461, in explaining why chor-bishops could not confirm concluded: "Quoniam, quamquam consecrationem habeant, pontificatus tamen apicem non habent."—Hinschius, *Decretales Pseudo-Isidorianae* (Lipsiae, 1835), p. 628 (hereafter cited as Hinschius).

[23] Mostaza, *op. cit.*, p. 50, conclusion (e).

[24] *Glossa Ordinaria,* ad c. 4, D. 68, s.v. *inter episcopos.* For a general

evidenced in the spurious letter attributed to Pope St. Leo the Great (440-461), supposedly written to all the bishops of the regions of Germany and Gaul.[25]

This text was used by Gratian when he strove to show the distinction between bishops and chor-bishops. The former were appointed for urban jurisdictions, the latter primarily in rural areas.[26] The bishop had the right to consecrate and confer holy orders, whereas the chor-bishops could confer only minor orders.[27] Among the various functions denied to the chor-bishop was that of giving the Holy Spirit through the imposition of hands to the baptized or converted heretics. The reason adduced by the false decretal written under the name of Pope Leo I was that they lacked the fullness of the priesthood.[28]

Another factor which made the very mention of the priest-minister of confirmation not only indiscreet but also gave grave cause for suspicion of heresy and revolt against the Church was the great controversy with the schismatical Eastern Church and Photius under Pope St. Nicholas I (858-867).[29]

Ignatius, Patriarch of Constantinople, had incurred the wrath of Prime Minister Bardas and in the year 858 was either forced to resign under pressure or was outright deposed by Emperor

---

background on the controversy with the chor-bishops, cf. Quinn, *op. cit.*, pp. 24-27.

[25] Jaffé, *Regesta Pontificum Romanorum ab condita Ecclesia ad annum post Christum natum MCXCVIII* (2. ed., correctam et auctam suspiciis G. Wattenbach, curaverunt S. Loewenfeld, F. Kaltenbrunner, P. Ewald, 2 vols., Lipsiae, 1885-1888) no. 551 (CXCIII); (hereafter cited as Jaffé, new number, with old number in parentheses); Hinschius, p. 628.

[26] Chor-bishop etymologically signifies a bishop of the country or village as distinguished from the city bishop. Cf. *Dictionnaire de Droit Canonique*, III, 686-689, for the history of this institute in the Oriental Church; *ibid.*, pp. 689-694, in the Western Church.

[27] *Dictum Gratiani,* c. 4, D. 68.

[28] C. 4, D. LXVIII.

[29] The historical aspect of the Photian difficulty is treated by Quinn, *op. cit.*, pp. 27-29. Cf. also Hughes, *A History of the Church* (3 vols., Vol. II, revised edition, New York: Sheed & Ward, 1949) II, 169-173; Dvornik, *Le Schisme de Photius, Histoire et Légende* (Paris: De Latour-Maubourg, 1950).

Michael, the Drunkard.[30] In his place Michael raised Photius, an imperial secretary, who, because he was a layman, had first to receive ordination and consecration. Gregory Asbestas, Archbishop of Syracuse, who had been excommunicated by Ignatius, performed the ceremony. Nicholas I refused to sanction the maneuver, particularly since it was done without the consent of the Holy See.[31] In a letter to Photius and Emperor Michael on March 18, 862, the Pope refused to consider Ignatius as deposed.[32] In a synod held in 863 the Pope decided in favor of Ignatius and excommunicated Photius, denouncing him in very strong language.[33] Emperor Michael sent a bitter letter in 865, which was ably answered by Pope Nicholas, and incidentally is to be considered an excellent defense of the Roman primacy.

Another volatile situation which confronted the Church during this period was the Bulgarian question. Because of the country's strategic geographical location, Constantinople was anxious to annex it to its jurisdiction. Just about the time when Photius was intruded into the patriarchical see, the Bulgarians made an appeal to Constantinople for missionaries. Photius sent them Greek priests, who in 864 baptized Emperor Boris (852-889) and many of his followers. A little later, Boris, fearing Byzantine political domination more than German, wrote to Pope Nicholas I and asked for Latin clergy, though he soon switched back to the Greeks. In a series of answers to the questions proposed by the Emperor, Nicholas I issued an outstanding pastoral and canonical treatise, *Nicolai Responsa ad Consulta Bulgarorum.*[34]

The two papal legates reconfirmed those who had been invalidly confirmed by Photius' priests. This occasioned a bitter encyclical by Photius, who in 867 assailed the claims of Rome and condemned all Latin Catholics as heretics. A Greek synod

[30] After a critical evaluation of the conflicting testimony, Dvornik (*op. cit.*, pp. 77-89) concluded that Ignatius was not deposed by force, but that he resigned to avoid greater evils.

[31] Dvornik, *op. cit.*, p. 123; Mansi, XV, 168-170.

[32] Dvornik, *op. cit.*, pp. 148-149; Mansi, XV, 174-178; 178-186.

[33] Cf. Dvornik, *op. cit.*, p. 152, for the canons of this synod.

[34] Dvornik, *op. cit.*, p. 172; Mansi, XV, 400-434.

declared Pope Nicholas excommunicated. Photius was forced to resign when a usurper, named Basil, murdered Emperor Michael and his powerful minister, Bardas. However, Photius was reinstated in 877.[35]

The pertinent observations pertaining to the sacrament of confirmation are these: after Photius had broken with the Church, he sent a number of priests to do missionary work in Bulgaria; Pope Nicholas I ordered his representatives to reconfirm those who had received the sacrament from the hands of the schismatical priests sent by Photius from Constantinople. Benedict XIV (1740-1758) in his *De Synodo Dioecesana* discussed the whole controversy. He contended that Nicholas I wished to have the Bulgarians confirmed again because (1) the priests who conferred the sacrament were imbued with the error of Photius, that is, they thought that they had equal power with the bishop to confirm by ordinary right; (2) these priests had been delegated by Photius who was a traitor and an intruder, a pseudo-patriarch who did not have the rights of the legitimate patriarch, and (3) Bulgaria belonged to the Western patriarchate, and therefore the delegation which had been expressly or tacitly conceded by the Holy See to priests in the patriarchate of the East by no means authorized them to do the same thing in Bulgaria.[36] Herman adds another reason, namely, that there was doubt concerning the validity of the chrism consecrated by an unlawful patriarch.[37]

Since the feelings on these two issues, namely, the suppression of the chor-bishops and the struggle with Photius, were quite strong, it is not difficult to understand the great influence that would be exerted upon the principal canonical collections before

[35] Cf. Neill-Schmandt, *History of the Catholic Church* (Milwaukee: Bruce Publishing Co., 1957), pp. 171-173; also chap. 4, "Nicolas, Photius et Boris," pp. 144-195 of Dvornik's scholarly treatise.

[36] Benedictus XIV, *De Synodo Dioecesana* (2. ed., 2 vols., Romae, 1806), Tom. I, lib. 7, c. 9, sectio 3.

[37] *Dictionnaire de Droit Canonique,* IV, 126. According to Herman, it is certain that, whatever may have been the reasons for the action of Nicholas I, today the Holy See has granted by privilege this ancient faculty to the Catholic Bulgarian priests.

the time of Gratian. Inevitably this trend of thought came to be reflected in the *Decretum* of Gratian, particularly in the third part, *de Consecratione.*

Article 3—Gratian and the Famous Concession of Gregory the Great

The first lengthy reference to the minister of confirmation in the treatise of Gratian does not occur as an *ex professo* made treatment of the subject. It is found in the oft-referred-to Distinction 95 of the first part, where he examined the question of obedience and submission of the priests to the bishops. Gratian there tried to reconcile the prohibitions of "Pope Leo I" and Pope Gelasius with the famous concession granted in the year 594 by Pope St. Gregory I (590-604). This distinction became the primal object of the glossators' commentaries.

a.—Historical Background

In 593 Pope Gregory wrote to Januarius, the Bishop of Cagliari, a city on the island of Sardinia, that it was not permitted to priests to anoint on the forehead.

> Presbyteri baptizatos infantes signare in frontibus sacro crismate non presumant. Sed presbyteri baptizatos ungant in pectore ut episcopi postmodum confirment in fronte.[38]

This ruling which forbade priests to confirm must have created quite a wave of dissent and disagreement, especially in that part of the world, for in May of the following year the Pope reversed his prohibition and granted a concession for priests to confirm wherever bishops were not present. It is with this canon that Gratian began his Distinction 95, providing it with the rubric, *"Ubi episcopi desunt, baptizatos in frontibus presbyteri crismate tangant."* [39]

b.—Distinction 95 of Gratian

In the first chapter of Distinction 95 Gratian († ca. 1157) set

[38] C. 120, D. IV, *de cons.;* Jaffé, n. 1281 (1st ed., n. 914, not 714 as given by Friedberg, *Corpus Iuris Canonici* (editio Lipsiensis secunda, ex Officina Bernhardi Tauchnitz, 1879-1881), I, p. 1399, ftnt. 1498).

[39] C. 1, D. XCV.

down the full text of Gregory's letter, which begins with the word *'Pervenit.'*

> It has come to our attention that some have been scandalized that we have forbidden priests to touch with chrism those who have been baptized. We indeed acted according to the ancient usage of our Church. But if anyone is completely saddened by this regulation, we grant, wherever there is a lack of bishops, a concession for priests to anoint the baptized with chrism, even on the forehead.[40]

Two points should be noted in this text. Pope Gregory explained his initial action by stating that his prohibition was made *"secundum veterem usum nostrae ecclesiae,"* that is, the prevalent practice of the Roman Church. Secondly, the Pope in allowing the priests of Cagliari to confirm seemed to grant more than just a permission; rather, it was more in the line of a concession, a special faculty, as the word *'concedimus'* seems to indicate.

In the *Dictum* and second chapter which follow, Gratian quoted two regulations that were contrary to Gregory's liberal concession, first, the spurious text of *Quamvis Corepiscopis,* attributed to Pope Leo I, which said that priests and chor-bishops could not confirm, a text which already has been discussed, and secondly, the prohibition of Pope Gelasius (492-496), the great champion for the rights of the Church and the defender of the authority of the hierarchy, who wrote on March 11, 494, to all the bishops in Sicily to correct the abuses whereby priests were attempting to overstep their own power by attributing to themselves episcopal prerogatives, especially that of sealing.[41]

How could Gratian reconcile these two apparently opposite regulations on the practice of conferring confirmation? He explained in the *dictum* which follows that Gregory's concession was to be understood as having been granted for one particular occasion for a particular serious reason, namely to pacify certain

[40] Jaffé, n. 1298 (933).

[41] "Presbyteros ultra suum modum tendere prohibemus, nec episcopali fastigia debita sibimet audacter assumere, non conficiendi chrismatis, non consignationis pontificalis adhibendae sibimet arripere facultatem."—Jaffé, n. 636 (391), or Mansi, VIII, 39. It is interesting to note in passing that the regulation of Pope Gelasius preceded Gregory's concession by 100 years.

inimical elements and to remove scandal.[42] The regulations of Popes Leo and Gelasius, on the other hand, were more common and in general use, except where the custom of some permitted the priests to confirm the baptized in extreme necessity. One might say that the prohibitions of Leo and Gelasius were understood to apply when bishops were available and there was no pressing and immediate need. The concession of Gregory, however, could be used in emergencies.[43]

C.—THE COMMENTARY OF THE GLOSSATORS ON DISTINCTION 95

The glossators introduced their analysis of Distinction 95 by asking whether priests could anoint children on the forehead, i.e., confirm them. Though the answer was "no," the concession in the letter *Pervenit* of Pope Gregory immediately arose as an objection to disprove this assertion. Therefore, they used the word *'concedimus'* in the text of Gregory's letter as a springboard, so to speak, from which to plunge into the discussion regarding the Pope's delegation of this power. A priest who confirmed on his own authority effected nothing, for the sacrament was neither administered by the minister nor received by the recipient.[44]

But could the Pope delegate a priest to confirm? Various answers of the commentators and teachers were then given. Some taught that by delegation from the Holy Father a priest could confer any of the sacraments he has already received. Thus, a deacon might be delegated to confer the diaconate, but not priestly orders; he could not be delegated to offer the Holy Sacrifice of the Mass, since Christ spoke only to the priests when He said, "Do this in commemoration of me." Others held that

[42] This attitude, i.e., that this was a special delegation, by way of dispensation, not by way of the common law, was consistently reflected in the comments of the glossators. Hostiensis († 1271), for example, in referring to Gratian's Distinction 95, emphasized that Gregory allowed this:

1. *propter scandalum;*

2. *ex speciali indulgentia;*

3. *ad tempus.*—*Commentaria in V Libros Decretalium* (6 vols. in 4, Venetiis, 1581), ad c. 4, X, *de consuetudine,* I, 4.

[43] *Dictum Gratiani* post c. 2, D. XCV.

[44] ". . . presbyter chrismando si sua auctoritate hoc facit, nihil agit."—*Glossa Ordinaria,* s.v. *concedimus.*

the Pope could not delegate anyone to confirm, and that those who acted under Gregory's concession did so invalidly. Did the Pope then actually grant permission to do something which was unlawful and sinful? [45] They sought to answer this objection by saying that he did it against his will because of the exceedingly great scandal.[46]

The glossators asked whether a bishop could delegate that which belongs to the episcopal order. He could delegate that which pertains to jurisdiction, e.g., he could delegate a priest to receive or reconcile a penitent. But even in the field of jurisdiction he was limited, since among his jurisdictional powers there were certain ones which he could not delegate except to a cleric, e.g., to depose or correct a cleric. That which pertains to orders, on the other hand, he could not delegate. Guido de Baysio († 1313), known as "the Archdeacon," in his commentary on Distinction 95, presented an interesting explanation of this limitation:

> Quia quae sunt ordinis quasi ossibus adhaerent ut separari non possint, sicut nec anima a corpore.[47]

Article 4—Gratian and the Pseudo-Isidorian Texts

The specific treatment of the sacrament of confirmation can be found in the 5th distinction of the 3rd part of Gratian's *Decretum.* Chapter 1 stated that after baptism the Christian was to receive confirmation:

> Omnes fideles per manus impositiones *episcoporum* Spiritum Sanctum post baptismum accipere debent.[48]

This text was taken from a spurious document supposedly written by Pope Urban I (222-230).[49]

[45] "In hoc videatur eis dare licentiam peccandi."—*Glossa Ordinaria,* s.v. *concedimus.*

[46] ". . . nec dabat eis occasionem mali quia invitus hoc concedebat."—*Glossa Ordinaria,* s.v. *concedimus.*

[47] *Rosarium seu in Decretorum Volumen Commentaria* (Venetiis, 1577), in c. 1, D. XCV.

[48] C. 1, D. V, *de cons.*

[49] Jaffé, n. 87 (LXXXI); Hinschius, p. 146.

After a discussion in chapter 2 of the gifts which the Holy Spirit confers in baptism, and of those which He confers in confirmation, chapter 3 proceeded to explain in what sense confirmation, the sacrament of the imposition of hands, was greater in dignity than baptism. The basis of the argumentation was a spurious text attributed to Pope St. Melchiades, supposedly written between the years 310-314, to the bishops of Spain.[50] In answer to an enquiry, the Pope explained that, although both sacraments are great, confirmation must be held in greater veneration because its administration is reserved to bishops alone:

> . . . scitote, utrumque magnum esse sacramentum, et, sicut unum maioribus, id est *summis pontificibus* est accommodatum, quod a minoribus perfici non potest, ita et maiori veneratione venerandum et tenendum est.

Upon these texts the glossators made practically no comment at all.

Chapter 4, however, which stated that the sacrament of the imposition of hands could be perfected only by bishops, became the object of discussion. Gratian quoted a spurious text, attributed to Pope Eusebius (ca. 309), as a letter written to the bishops of the districts of Campania and Tuscany:

> The sacrament of the imposition of hands is to be held in great veneration because it can be conferred only by bishops. It is common knowledge that in the time of the Apostles it was not conferred except by the Apostles, and it cannot and must not be conferred except by those who are their successors. If it is ever presumed otherwise, it is considered invalid and useless, not to be reckoned among the sacraments of the Church.[51]

This text introduced a new aspect of the problem, namely, the historical. Since the Apostles were the only ones who confirmed, so the argument ran, their successors were the only ones who could do so in the present. In the words of the quoted text, *"si aliter praesumptum fuerit, irritum habeatur."*

In the remaining chapters of Gratian's treatise on confirmation there were expressions which reflected a solidly established

[50] Jaffé, n. 171 (CXXIX); Hinschius, p. 245.

[51] Jaffé, n. 165 (CXXIII); Hinschius, p. 242.

conviction that the bishop is the only minister of this sacrament.[52] It seems surprising that Gratian did not even entertain the question of anyone other than a bishop as the minister of confirmation, or make a single allusion to the first part of the *Decretum,* where in Distinction 95 he had considered a priest without episcopal orders as the extraordinary minister of confirmation.[53]

The frequent use of texts from the Pseudo-Isidorian decretals presents a problem which must be solved. It is generally held that these forged decretals were composed in the middle of the ninth century with a view to enhancing the position of local episcopal ordinaries. They portrayed a tendency to accomplish a canonical reform by attempting to borrow authority from the past, even by having spurious documents accepted as law. The forgers made their texts believable by changing manuscripts, by altering the texts, by composing new texts from the old sources, and by fitting them to change their meaning. It was only in the 15th-16th centuries that the authenticity of these decretals was called into question. Should the teaching of Gratian then be

[52] "Novissime a *summo sacerdote* per manus impositionem Paraclitus traditur baptizato . . . signatur enim baptizatus cum chrismate per sacerdotem in capitis summitate; per *pontificem* vero in fronte."—c. 5, D. V, *de cons.*; ". . . numquam erit Christianus nisi in confirmatione *episcopali* fuerit crismatus."—c. 6, D. V, *de cons.*; "Ut *episcopi* non nisi ieiuni per impositionem manuum Spiritum Sanctum tradant . . ."—c. 7, D. V, *de cons.*; "ab eisdem *episcopis,*" and "qui a *pontifice* confirmatus fuerit."—cc. 8 and 9, D. V, *de cons.*

[53] This discrepancy lends weight to the conclusions of textual critics of Gratian's *Concordia discordantium canonum* that most likely this monumental masterpiece was not composed and published in one magnificent thrust. In a scholarly treatise entitled, "New Studies on the Roman Law in Gratian's Decretum," Kuttner makes reference to the discoveries of external signs of textual and transcriptional disturbances made by Mme. Rambaud and Abbe Guizard in a number of Paris manuscripts with regard to the transmission of both the *tractatus de poenitentia* and the *tractatus de consecratione.* He observes that serious discrepancies in the manuscript tradition of *de consecratione* should be viewed in conjunction with the well known fact that this treatise (part III) differs from the rest of Gratian's work by the absence of all *paragraphi,* i.e., by altogether abandoning the dialectical procedure of *Concordia discordantium canonum.*—*The Jurist Seminar,* XI (1953), 17.

completely rejected? This would be rather unscientific, since it must be remembered that the false decretals were not the sole source of legislation on the sacrament of confirmation. These documents must have at least been in keeping with the traditional teaching of the time. If they had not contained doctrinal matter on the minister of confirmation which was already accepted, they would scarcely have gained any credence at all.

Article 5—The Glossators and the Decretal *Quanto* of Innocent III

In their analysis of Gratian's Distinction 95 the glossators made reference to a document which engendered a similar discussion. This was a letter of Innocent III (1198-1216). This important piece of legislation was included in the *Decretals of Gregory IX*, promulgated September 5, 1234, in the papal bull *Rex Pacificus*.[54] Nicholas de Tudeschis (1386-1453), known as Abbas Siculus or Panormitanus, summarized the *casus* very succinctly by declaring that customary usage cannot bring it about that any cleric who is not a bishop can exercise those prerogatives which are reserved to the episcopal order.

In 1199, the second year of his pontificate, Pope Innocent III wrote to his legate at Constantinople to reprobate the custom which prevailed in that city, where simple priests of the Latin rite were conferring the sacrament of confirmation on the faithful, in imitation of the Greek practice.

> It has come to our attention that some priests without episcopal orders (*sacerdotes simplices*) are presuming to administer to the faithful those sacraments whose administration from apostolic times has been properly reserved to the bishops alone, such as the sacrament of confirmation. By signing with chrism the newly baptized, only the bishops can confer this sacrament through the imposition of hands. Customary usage is urged by these priests as an excuse for their sinfulness . . . . Wherefore, we command that you most strictly forbid all priests of the Latin rite who live in Constantinople to ever presume in their bold temerity or reckless rashness to do that.

[54] C. 4, X, *de consuetudine,* I, 4.

The Pope then concluded by saying that, since confirmation is not necessary for salvation, even though the faithful are surely not to neglect or spurn its reception, it is better that confirmation be not administered at all rather than that it be administered by those who rashly presume to confer what is forbidden to them and thus expose the sacrament to invalidity.[55]

The Pope expressed a firm persuasion regarding the apostolic origin of the episcopal prerogative to administer confirmation. This same conviction was conveyed in a letter which was sent in February, 1204, to the Archbishop of Tirnovo, the primate of the Bulgarians.[56] It should also be noted that Pope Innocent expressly forbade all continuance of the custom of confirming as it had been practiced by priests of the Latin rite. He did not include the priests of the Oriental rite who resided in Constantinople.[57]

The glossators, who regarded this decretal as providing fertile soil for the seed of canonical speculation, once again introduced the question whether the Pope can delegate a priest to administer the sacrament of confirmation. Gregory's action obviously implied that possibility, since *"ab esse ad posse valet illatio."* Otherwise the Pope would have to be accused of deception and error.[58]

Still another concept was introduced with reference to the

[55] Potthast, *Regesta Pontificum Romanorum, inde ab anno post Christum natum MCXCVIII ad annum MCCCIV* (2 vols., Berolini, 1874-1875), n. 868; *MPL,* CCXIV, 772.

[56] "Per frontis chrismationem manus impositio designatur, quae alio nomine dicitur confirmatio, quia per eam Spiritus Sanctus ad augmentum datur et robur. Unde quum ceteras unctiones simplex sacerdos vel presbyter valeat exhibere, hanc non nisi summus sacerdos, id est episcopus, debet conferre, quia de solis Apostolis legitur, quorum vicarii sunt episcopi, quod per manus impositionem Spiritum Sanctum dabant, quemadmodum Actuum Apostolorum lectio manifestat."—Potthast, *op. cit.,* n. 2138; *MPL,* CCXV, 215. This letter is included in the *Decretals of Gregory IX* under the title which deals with sacred anointings. Cf. c. 1, X, *de sacra unctione,* I, 15.

[57] "Decretalis autem Innocent III solos respicit sacerdotes Latinos."—Benedictus XIV, *De Synodo Dioecesana,* Tom. I, lib. 7, c. 9, sectio 3.

[58] *Glossa ordinaria,* ad c. 4, X, *de consuetudine,* I, 4, s.v. *reservata.*

content of Pope Innocent's letter. If the Pope forbade a delegated priest to confirm, the consequent action of this priest was to be regarded as invalid.[59] What if the Pope forbade a bishop? In this case, so argued Hostiensis, the bishop would at least confer the character, since by his office he had the right which the priest obtained purely through a delegation. When the priest lost that, he had nothing, since whatever he had was conferred by way of a delegation.[60]

Pope Innocent IV (1243-1254), in his commentary on the 4th chapter of the 4th title of the first book in the *Decretals of Gregory IX,* mentioned, but without officially approving it, a contrary opinion, which concluded that the Pope, inasmuch as he has complete control over the administration of the sacraments, could, by means of a formal decree, take away even the power of confirming which the bishop holds. Because of the clarity of the text and its timeliness in view of current discussions concerning the extent of the power of the Church over the sacraments, it is here quoted in full:

> Si dominus papa a primo conferret presbytero potestatem chrismandi, et postea auferret nihil conferret sic; sed si prohiberet episcopo chrismare et, contempta prohibitione, confirmaret, imprimeretur caracter. Ratio diversitatis quia episcopus potest confirmare ex officio et ordine; sacerdos alius ex delegatione et adminiculo habiti sacramenti; mandato ergo sublato, nihil potest; alii dicunt quod si papa prohiberet episcopum chrismare quod postea chrismando non confert caracterem; licet enim papa non possit tollere sacramentum confirmationis, potest tamen contra illud, ut in forma et in personis et in diebus a quibus et in quibus conferri debeat, suas constitutiones facere et si potest circa personas conferentes aliquid statuere, ergo certae personae vel etiam episcopo potest potestatem auferre chrismandi.[61]

[59] "Item nihil confertur a sacerdotibus si chrismaret in fronte baptizatos et ita pro non dato habetur quod datur qui dare non potest de iure."—*Glossa ord., ibid.,* s.v. *reservata;* "sed hoc notandum quod si (Papa) delegaret sacerdoti et postea prohiberet, nihil conferret."—Hostiensis, *Commentaria,* in c. 4, X, *de consuetudine,* I, 4.

[60] *Loc. cit.*

[61] Innocentius IV, *In V Libros Decretalium Gregorii IX* (Venetiis, 1570), in c. 4, X, *de consuetudine,* I, 4.

Article 6—The Scholastic Theologians

In reviewing the texts heretofore cited, one is bound to note that there was a preponderance of testimony to the prevalent doctrine that the conferring of the sacrament of confirmation is a prerogative of the bishop. However, there was also ample proof that at times priests did act as extraordinary ministers. Already in the time of Gratian and Gregory IX, the principle of the power of the Pope to delegate a simple priest for confirming was generally well established and accepted as a fairly common opinion. Indeed, one might say that the action of Gregory I forced them to postulate this premise. They assented to it, not, however, without insisting on the extraordinary circumstances surrounding the concession of this power. In such a case of delegation, the glossators mentioned the necessity of an "*adminiculum habiti sacramenti*" in the person delegated.

This general attitude was reflected in the scholastic teaching on the minister of confirmation. The characteristic feature of the early Scholastic period was the continual insistence on the fact that the administration of this sacrament was reserved in a special way to the bishop. Hugh of St. Victor († 1141), the author of the *Summa Sententiarum,* and Peter Lombard († 1160), the "*Magister Sententiarum,*" appealed to the text of the *Acts of the Apostles* in support of their doctrine. Other theologians—St. Bruno of Segni († 1123), Honorius of Autun († early 12th cent.), Robert Pullen († ca. 1146), Peter of Poitiers († 1161), Hugh of Rouen († 1164), Roland Bandinelli († 1181), Gandulphus of Bologna († before 1200), Alan of Lille († 1203), Magister Simon († 1215), Sicard of Crimona († 1215), William of Auxerre († 1231), Geoffredus de Trano († 1245)—repeated the same doctrine, varying only in the degree of emphasis they placed upon it.[62] Very little attention was given to the possible administration of confirmation by a simple priest.

Later scholastic theologians, however, brought a fuller and

[62] Cf. O'Doherty, *The Scholastic Teaching on the Sacrament of Confirmation,* The Catholic University of America Studies in Sacred Theology (Second Series), no. 23 (Washington, D. C.: The Catholic University of America Press, 1949), p. 48. This author cites the passages wherein the opinions of these theologians can be studied.

more detailed treatment to this problem. St. Albert the Great († 1280), surnamed the *"Doctor Universalis,"* denied that confirmation could be conferred by a simple priest, since the proper nature of the sacramental sign of confirmation did not admit a minister who possessed only limited or restricted powers. He explained the concession granted to the clergy of Sardinia by Pope Gregory the Great either as the toleration of an abuse or as a temporary permission to bestow a special blessing on those who were to be confirmed.[63] Alexander of Hales († 1245), the *"Doctor Irrefragabilis,"* taught that a simple priest cannot confirm on his own authority, though he can do so in virtue of an authorization which the Pope is empowered to grant. St. Bonaventure († 1274), known as the *"Doctor Seraphicus,"* accepted the doctrine of his teacher, Alexander of Hales.[64]

St. Thomas († 1274) rejected the above mentioned opinion of Albert the Great on the basis that it was not fitting to presume that the Sovereign Pontiff would permit or even tolerate the simulation of a sacramental rite, not even with a view to the avoidance of scandal. In his commentary on the *Four Books of the Sentences* he wrote:

> Sed non videtur conveniens ut talem simulationem in dispensatione sacramentorum induxisset Gregorius, vel sustinuisset: quia dispensatio pertinet ad veritatem doctrinae, quae non est propter scandalum dimittenda.[65]

The Angelic Doctor furnished two explanations for showing that it was possible for the Holy See to commission a simple priest for confirming. In his commentary on the treatise of Peter Lombard, he distinguished between the real body, the *"corpus verum,"* and the mystical body, the *"corpus mysticum,"* of Christ. In virtue of sacerdotal ordination, both the priest and the bishop have the fullness of power in relation to the *corpus verum.* The bishop, however, has superior power in relation to the *corpus mysticum.* The Pope, in virtue of his supreme power

[63] *Commentarium in IV Sententiarum* in *Opera Omnia* (38 vols., Vives: Parisiis, 1890-1899), XXIX, dist. VII, a. 4.

[64] Cf. O'Doherty, *op. cit.*, p. 51.

[65] *In IV Sent.*, dist. VII, q. 3, a. 1.

over the *corpus mysticum,* can concede to some the faculty to confirm, inasmuch as confirmation perfects a person *in actu corporis mystici* and does not have any relation to the *corpus verum.*[66]

In the 3rd part of his *Summa Theologiae,* where he treated of the minister of confirmation, St. Thomas held that it is essential (*de necessitate huius sacramenti*) that this sacrament be given by a bishop, since confirmation is the final completion of baptism, and in every work the final completion is reserved to the supreme act or power. However, in answer to the first objection, namely that Gregory allowed priests to confirm, and thus changed that which is essential to the sacrament, St. Thomas stated:

> The Pope has the plenitude of power in the Church, in virtue of which he can commit to certain lower orders things which belong to the higher order; thus he allows priests to confer minor orders, which belongs to the episcopal power. And in virtue of this fullness of power the Pope, Blessed Gregory, allowed simple priests to confer this sacrament as long as the scandal was duly obviated.[67]

The Scholastics after St. Thomas continued their discussions on the possible delegation of an extraordinary minister for confirming. The greatest challenge to those who refused to admit such a possibility was the concession made by Gregory the Great. Various explanations were given for his action. Some said that Gregory as a man made a mistake, *"non docendo vel definiendo, sed operando";* others, that the priests of Cagliari were more than simple priests, namely consecrated bishops without episcopal jurisdiction; and still others maintained that the Pope was speaking of some ceremonial rite rather than of confirmation. To Scotus (1266-1308) was attributed the opinion: *"D. Gregorium per illam concessionem constituisse illos presbyteros, eosque quodamodo episcopos effecisse, quoad istum actum."*[68] The

[66] *Loc. cit.*

[67] *Summa Theologiae* IIIa, q. 72, a. 11.

[68] Suarez, quaestio LXXII, "De Sacramento Confirmationis," article 11, "Utrum hoc sacramentum per solos episcopos detur," disputatio XXXVI, sectio 2, no. 10—*Opera Omnia* (28 vols., Parisiis, 1856-1861), XX, 682.

teaching of these divergent schools of thought were often referred to by the theologians and bishops later present at the Council of Trent.[69]

Article 7—The Official Attitude of the Holy See

Side by side with the scholastic speculations, there was being formulated in the official documents of the Holy See a concept of far-reaching effect. Reference was made to the bishop as the *ordinary* minister of confirmation.

Pope Innocent IV (1243-1254) was one of the last Popes to insist on maintaining the Roman custom and practice that *only* bishops were recognized as ministers of confirmation. He expressed this in a letter, *Sub Catholicae,* written on March 6, 1254, to the Bishop of Frascati, legate of the Apostolic See, to settle a dispute which was being waged between the Archbishop of Nicosia along with his suffragan Latin bishops, on the one part, and the Greek bishops of Cyprus, on the other. In paragraph 3, n. 4, the Pope stated:

> Soli autem Episcopi consignant chrismate in frontibus baptizatos, quia huius unctio non debet, nisi per episcopos exhiberi. Quoniam soli Apostoli, quorum vices gerunt Episcopi, per manus impositionem, quam confirmatio, vel frontis chrismatio repraesentat, Spiritum Sanctum tribuisse leguntur.[70]

On September 23, 1351, Pope Clement VI (1342-1352) issued a document which marked an important trend in the doctrine on the extraordinary minister of confirmation. Known as *Super quibusdam,* and written to Consolator, the Patriarch of the Armenians, this questionnaire to test the orthodoxy of that great ecclesiastic brought out three very important issues: (1) the

[69] For a more extensive treatment of the teachings of the Pre-Tridentine theologians, 13th-16th centuries, cf. Mostaza, *El Problema del Ministro Extraordinario de la Confirmación,* chap. 4, "Pensamiento de los Teologos Antetridentinos," pp. 103-159.

[70] *Codicis Iuris Canonici Fontes,* cura Emi Petri Card. Gasparri editi (9 vols., Romae [postea Civitate Vaticana]: Typis Polyglottis Vaticanis, 1923-1939; Vols. VII-IX, ed. cura et studio Emi Iustiniani Card. Serédi), n. 34 (hereafter cited as *Fontes*).

bishop is the sole minister *ex officio* of confirmation, i.e., he alone administers it *ordinarie;* (2) the Pope who has the fullness of power can delegate priests who are not bishops to confirm, and (3) confirmations conferred without this papal delegation—episcopal delegation alone not being sufficient—are invalid and are to be repeated. The highlights of this text read as follows:

> Rursus . . . responsiones dedisti, quae nos inducunt ut a te sequentia requiramus . . . , secundo, si credis quod sacramentum confirmationis per alium quam per episcopum, non potest ex officio ordinarie ministrari—Tertio, si credis, quod solum per Romanum Pontificem, plenitudinem potestatis habentem, possit dispensatio sacramenti confirmationis presbyteris qui non sunt episcopi committi.—Quarto, si credis, quod chrismati per quoscumque sacerdotes, qui non sunt episcopi, neque a Romano Pontifice super hoc commissionem seu concessionem aliquam receperunt, iterum per episcopum vel episcopos sint chrismandi.[71]

The Council of Constance, which opened November 15, 1414, and came to a close April 22, 1418, after forty-five sessions, considered the major current heresies, namely those of Hus († 1415), and Wycliffe († 1384). At the eighth session, held May 4, 1415, it condemned 305 propositions taken from the writings of John Wycliffe, which were ordered to be burned. One of these propositions touches upon the minister of confirmation:

> Confirmatio iuvenum, clericorum ordinatio, locorum consecratio reservantur Papae et episcopis propter cupiditatem lucri temporalis et honoris.[72]

Although the Council of Constance had condemned the errors of the Wycliffites and Hussites, there still remained sympathetic supporters of these errors, particularly in England and Bohemia. Thus, the suppression of heresy was to be one of the main goals of the Council of Basle, the 17th general council, which was destined to follow a stormy and violent course. On the day on

[71] *Fontes,* n. 42. What precise theological note is to be attached to this document remains a moot question. Cf. Mostaza, *op. cit.,* pp. 167-168.

[72] Mansi, XXVII, 1208, n. 28. For general background regarding this Council, cf. Schroeder, *Disciplinary Decrees of the General Councils* (St. Louis: B. Herder Book Co., 1937), pp. 443-455.

which the Council was to have opened, March 4, 1431, only one delegate was present. Subsequent sessions were marked by a pronounced defiant and rebellious attitude of the members of the Council against Pope Eugene IV (1431-1447), who on November 12th issued a bull authorizing the dissolution of the Council. This bull was withdrawn on December 15, 1432.

The question of deciding upon a suitable place for the negotiating of a reconciliation with the Greeks engendered another controversy which widened the rift until by a decree of December 30, 1437, or January 1, 1438, the Pope transferred the Council to Ferrara. Those who remained at Basle thus became a body of schismatics. In January, 1439, because of the financial straits of the Pope and a concomitant offer by the Florentines to donate a large sum of money to the Papal States, the Council was transferred to Florence, where the 17th session was held on February 26, 1439, in the papal palace.

On July 6th, the famous Bull, *Laetentur coeli,* was solemnly published in the cathedral. It announced the reunion of the Western and Eastern Churches. On November 22nd of the same year Eugene IV published his *Decretum pro Armenis,* which was part of the Bull *Exultate Deo.* It declared that the bishop is the ordinary minister of confirmation, though it noted at the same time that on occasions the Holy See has granted concessions to simple priests to administer this sacrament with chrism blessed by the bishop. Very noncommittally this historical fact of the granted papal dispensation was introduced with the word *legitur.* The Council was transferred to Rome for two sessions. The second session was held on August 7, 1445, and with it the Council of Florence came to an end.

Paragraph 11 of the Bull *Exultate Deo* contained an important statement on the minister of confirmation:

> Secundum sacramentum est confirmatio. . . . Ordinarius minister est episcopus. Et cum ceteras unctiones simplex sacerdos valeat exhibere, hanc nonnisi episcopus debet conferre, quia de solis Apostolis legitur, quorum vicem tenent episcopi, quod per manus impositionem Spiritum Sanctum dabant, quemadmodum Actuum Apostolorum lectio manifestat. . . . Legitur tamen aliquando per Apostolicae Sedis dispensationem, ex rationabili et urgente admodum causa,

simplicem sacerdotem chrismate per episcopum confecto, hoc administrasse confirmationis sacramentum.[73]

The reference to the bishop as the ordinary minister of the sacrament by Eugene IV was to be taken up again by the Council of Trent. To be noted also is the fact that a *rationabilis et urgens causa* was needed for the granting of this dispensation.

During this entire period there were very few official records of any concession allowing an individual priest to administer confirmation in the Western Church. However, it seems that in the 15th century [74] Franciscan priests, sent to places in the north and east where there were no bishops, were given the faculty to administer the sacrament of confirmation.

Eugene IV, in his *Sacrae Religionis,* issued on January 29, 1445, conceded to the Franciscan missionaries working among the inhabitants of Scythia, Moldavia and the seven lower regions of the Sicilies the faculty to administer confirmation.[75] Pope Nicholas V (1447-1455) on February 10, 1448, in the Bull *Ineffabilis,* and Leo X (1513-1521) in the Bull *Alias felices,* made similar concessions.[76]

SECTION B—THE SEVENTH SESSION OF THE COUNCIL OF TRENT

After the completion of its sixth session, the Council of Trent set forth as its chief agenda the sacraments of the Church. On the 17th of January, 1547, a general meeting was held to list all

[73] *Fontes,* n. 52; Denzinger-Rahner, *Enchiridion,* n. 697.

[74] In a *monitum* which Prospero Lambertini, later Pope Benedict XIV, as Secretary of State, prepared for Pope Clement XII (1730-1740) in connection with a petition from South America, Nicholas IV (1288-1292) and John XXII (1316-1334) were cited as having granted concessions to missionaries.—*Thesaurus Resolutionum Sacrae Congregationis Concilii* (167 vols., Urbini, 1739-1741; Romae, 1741-1908), II, 188 (hereafter cited as *Thesaurus*).

[75] ". . . baptismatis, chrismatis seu confirmationis, extremae unctionis et alia sacramenta ecclesiastica ministrare."

[76] Waddingus, *Annales Minorum seu Trium Ordinum a S. Francisco Institutorum,* (3. ed. curavit Joseph Maria Fonseca, 27 vols., Ad Claras Aquas, 1931-1934) XI, n. 209, pp. 238-239; XI, n. 286, p. 329; XVI, n. 116, p. 138. Lennerz, *De Sacramento Confirmationis,* nn. 186, 187, 188, pp. 108-109.

the Protestant errors concerning the sacraments in general, and concerning baptism and confirmation in particular. Fourth on the list of errors concerning the sacrament of confirmation was the false teaching contained in the *Libellus Reformationis ad Colonienses,* namely that not only the bishop but any priest whatsoever is the minister of confirmation.[77]

Article 1—Opinions of the Theologians

The assembly of theologians, thirty-three in number, from the ranks of regulars and seculars, began the discussions on the 20th of January with the last paper read on the 29th of that month. They were given the following instructions: (1) to examine each proposition individually in order to determine whether it was historical or erroneous, and to adduce the reasons and evidence for its needed condemnation by the Council; (2) to show the reasons why some of the propositions given were not to be condemned; (3) to explain the opinions of the Fathers and the teaching of the Councils of previous centuries, and to show which and how many of the propositions had already been condemned, and which still awaited condemnation, and (4) to bring to the attention of the Council any subject matter pertinent to the main topics if it had not been included and at the same time seemed worthy of censure and condemnation. The theologians were then warned to exclude extraneous matter, all controverted points not *de fide, "de quibus, salva fide, in utramque partem disceptari potest,"* and to avoid long and complicated argumentations.[78]

The first to speak, Richard Le Mans, O.F.M., prominent professor at the Sorbonne in Paris, noted that the article on the minister of confirmation had never been condemned as such.[79]

[77] "Confirmationis minister non est solus episcopus sed quivis sacerdos." —*Concilium Tridentinum: Diariorum, Actorum, Epistularum, Tractatuum Nova Collectio,* edidit Societas Goerresiana (13 vols., Friburgi Brisgoviae: B. Herder, 1901-) Tomus V (acta post sessionem tertiam usque ad concilium Bononiam translatum collegit, edidit, illustravit Stephanus Ehses), p. 838 (hereafter cited as *C. Tr.*).

[78] *C. Tr.*, V, 844.

[79] *C. Tr.*, V, 845.

He cited texts which indicated that the bishop is the sole minister of confirmation along with texts which revealed the contrary.[80] Melchior Alvarez Bosmedianus of Spain also felt that the proposition was not totally erroneous.

> . . . quoad confirm. art. 4, quoad primam partem non est damnandum, quia verus, neque quoad secundam partem, ut cap. *Pervenit,* dist. 95, et in cap. *Quando, de consuetudine,* Panormitana. Tamen Gregorius cap. 26, lib. 3, sui registri aliud sentit.[81]

Some of the theologians considered the proposition as false. In this group were numbered Alphonsus Salmeron, S.J., of Spain,[82] Francis Herrera of Spain,[83] Andrew Navarra of Spain,[84] Anthony Solisius of Spain, who indicated that the practice of the Church in accord with which only bishops confirmed was recorded in apostolic times, and hence must have emanated from Christ,[85] and Augustine de Sena, O.C., who appealed to the 8th and 19th chapters of the *Acts of the Apostles* to prove that only bishops used to confer this sacrament.[86]

A large group of the theologians considered the proposition as heretical inasmuch as it had already been condemned. Included

[80] In the former category were listed c. 5, D. V, *de cons.*; the decretal *Quanto* of Innocent III, c. 4, X, *de consuetudine,* I, 4; the letter of Pope Innocent III to the Primate of the Bulgarians; the Council of Florence. In the latter category he mentioned the first book of Gratian, Distinction 95.—*C. Tr.,* V, 845. All these texts have been discussed in the previous articles.

[81] *C. Tr.,* V, 855. The editor, Stephen Ehses (1855-1926), in ftn. 3 on this page pointed out that the reference to *Quando* was obscure; if the theologian referred to the decretal *Quanto,* the opposite held true, for there the custom was reprobated (cf. article 5, Section A, of this Chapter, pp. 24 ff.). He then added: "Quid per *Panormitanam* significetur iurisperitis relinquo. Forsan laudatur ille glossator Panormitanus sive Abbas Siculus."

[82] *C. Tr.,* V, 850.

[83] *C. Tr.,* V, 853.

[84] ". . . quartus falsus, cum sit solus episcopus minister sacramenti confirmationis."—*C. Tr.,* V, 856.

[85] *C. Tr.,* V, 859.

[86] ". . . soli episcopi conferebant hoc sacramentum."—*C. Tr.,* V, 860.

were Sebastian de Castello, O.F.M. Conv.,[87] George (not Gregory) of St. James, O.P., of Portugal,[88] James Laynez, S.J., of Spain, Jerome of Oleastor, O.P., of Portugal, John Consilii, O.F.M., of France, John (Louis?) Carvialus, O.F.M., of Spain, Francis Salazar, O.F.M., of Spain and Lawrence Fulginius, O.F.M. Conv.[89] Both Louis Vitriarius, O.F.M. Conv., of Verona, and Bartholomew Miranda, O.P., of Spain, felt that the proposition should be condemned absolutely without any restriction.[90]

Despite this apparently strong opposition, a number of theologians felt that the proposition which states that the bishop is not the sole minister of confirmation could not be condemned outright without reservation. They proposed a rewording of the text with further explanations. In the forefront of this school of thought was Gaspar de Regibus, O.P., of Spain, whose opinion was incorporated in the summary which followed the discussions.[91] Peter Paul Caporella, O.F.M. Conv., mentioned Gregory's dispensation, which was granted in virtue of the Pope's supreme power, and which enabled the priest to confirm, not in virtue of his own authority but as with delegated authority.[92] Ambrose of Verona, an Augustinian, who discussed only the subject of confirmation, proposed that the proposition be condemned in the way that it was done at the Council of Florence.[93] This suggestion was to exert a powerful influence on the subsequent discussions and the final formulation of the canon. Andrew

87 ". . . damnatur a conc. Florent. et *de cons.,* dist. 5."—*C. Tr.,* V, 847.

88 ". . . etiam damnatus in conc. Florent." However, he added: "Tamen potest committi causa confirmationis ab episcopo Romano sacerdoti, ut Gregorius Papa fecit."—*C. Tr.,* V, 849.

89 The opinions of these theologians are recorded in *C. Tr.,* V, on pages 850, 851, 853, 858, 862, 862.

90 " Quartus erroneus et damnandus est. Innocentius I *ad Decentium,* cap. 3, Eusebius *ad Episcopos Companiae* eum damnant."—*C. Tr.,* V, 849. With reference to Louis Vitriarius, cf. *C. Tr.,* V, 846.

91 *C. Tr.,* V, 849.

92 "Quia Pontifex habet plenitudinem potestatis, et cum dispensat, non facit sacerdos sua auctoritate, sed tamquam delegatus."—*C. Tr.,* V, 851.

93 "Igitur non est simpliciter damnandus, sed prout fecit conc. Florentinum, id est regulariter."—*C. Tr.,* V, 851.

Verga, O.F.M., of Spain, combined the opinions of Caporella and Ambrose thus:

> ... item haereticus est de ministris in quo condemnari potest, quod sacerdos propria auctoritate possit confirmare; sed auctoritate Pontificis posset quod tenet Alexander de Ales, Cardinalis de Turrecremata, Gregorius, et videtur idem sentire Concilium Florent. cum dicit, "Huius sacramenti ordinarius administrator est episcopus." [94]

Lawrence Mazzochius, O.S.M., suggested the modifying of the term *Minister* with the word *ordinarius*.[95] Jerome of Lombardy, O.F.M., mentioned that the final proposition should take into consideration the fact that the Pontiff can delegate priests.[96]

Finally, to conclude this survey, it should be added, as a point of historical interest, that twelve theologians made no allusions to the question of the minister of confirmation.[97]

In the summary which followed the discussion of the theologians there was unanimity on three of the four condemned propositions on confirmation.[98] All were agreed that these propositions had been and deserved still to be condemned. However, on the fourth proposition, namely, the erroneous declaration that the bishop is not the sole minister of confirmation, there was a feeling that this error should not be condemned as

[94] *C. Tr.*, V, 855.

[95] "Tamen non est damnandus ita simpliciter, sed cum particula ordinarius."—*C. Tr.*, V, 860.

[96] ". . . articulus 4, falsus, sed cum declaratione damnandus quia Pontifex dispensare potest cum presbytero."—*C. Tr.*, V, 860.

[97] Aurelius Philippentius, O.S.A., de Roccacontra (p. 862), Gregory of Padua, who spoke only on baptism (p. 852), Nicholas of Taborelli, O.C., of France (p. 852), Sigmund de Diruta, O.F.M. Conv. (p. 854), Vincent Leo of Sicily, O.C. (p. 854), John the Baptist of Monte Calvo, O.F.M. Conv. (p. 856), Peter Sarra of Spain (p. 857), John Anthony Delphinus, O.F.M. Conv. (p. 859), Francis Visdomini, O.F.M. Conv. (p. 861), John the Baptist of Orvieto, O.S.M. (p. 861) and Gentianus Hervetus, from Paris, (p. 862).

[98] "(1) confirmationem non esse sacramentum; (2) confirmationem esse a patribus institutam et non habere promissionem gratiae Dei; (3) confirmationem esse otiosam caeremoniam et olim fuisse catechesim, quae adolescentiae proximi fidei suae rationem coram ecclesia exponebant."—*C. Tr.*, V, 838.

such, but rather with certain qualifications. The summary reads as follows:

> Aliqui cuperent hunc articulum non damnari simpliciter, sed cum aliqua declaratione, quia concilium Toletanum, canon 20, concedit in casu necessitatis potestatem confirmandi sacerdoti, ut fecit Gregorius et refert concilium Florentinum et tenent Alex de Ales, Turrecremata, Panormitanus et alii doctores. Item Melchiades Papa. Propterea censent reducendum ad formam dicti concilii Florentini, quod addidit 'ordinarium ministrum,' etc. Reliqui autem simpliciter damnari censent, quoniam cum sacerdos simplex dispensatus confirmat, non sua sed delegata sibi potestate fecit. . . .[99]

Article 2—Opinions of the Bishops

The Fathers of the Council began their deliberations on the subject of the general nature of the sacraments and on baptism and confirmation in particular on the 8th of February, 1547.[100] The findings of the theologians were divided into: (1) those articles which completely were to be condemned as heretical; (2) those which indeed were to be condemned but *"cum aliqua declaratione"*; (3) thost which were to be passed by without any condemnation, and (4) those which the theologians had added to the original list of condemned propositions. The Fathers were asked to comment accordingly.[101]

A study of the minutes of the general sessions shows that the greater number of the bishops present went on record as being opposed to the suggested change of the theologians in the proposition which pertained to the minister of confirmation. Understandably they wanted a strong emphasis on the prerogatives of the episcopacy, and, therefore, they repeatedly insisted that the bishop is the sole and exclusive minister of confirmation. Typical of many was the declaration of the Archbishop of Sassari in Sardinia, Salvator Alexius:

[99] *C. Tr.*, V, 866.

[100] These deliberations were interrupted daily by the discussions of the theologians on the Eucharist, since Lent was approaching, and many of the theologians had to leave to fulfill preaching commitments.

[101] *C. Tr.*, V, 896.

Quoad confirmationem non placet adnotatio, quod episcopus dicitur ordinarius minister, sed dicatur solus.[102]

Some of the bishops added to their opposition interesting explanations, many of which had been proposed by the various Scholastic theologians. Benedict de Nobilibus, Bishop of Acci in Corsica, branded as false the suggestion that, since the Pope can with one word constitute a man a priest, he should be able to empower him to confirm.[103] Balthasar de Heredia, Bishop of Bosa in Sardinia, in order to substantiate his position, explained the famous concession of Pope Gregory the Great as constituting a consecration of the delegate as bishop *ad hanc causam*.[104] Other evaluations of Gregory's action ranged from a judgment that it was a mere toleration of the practice[105] to a severe condemnation as an error and a dissimulation.[106] Both the Bishop of Aquino and the Bishop of Castellamare, John Fonseca, insisted that the exclusive prerogative of the bishop to confirm

102 *C. Tr.*, V, 986. Some other comments: Olaus the Great, Archbishop of Upsala (p. 903); Mark Vigerius, Bishop of Senigallia: "Simpliciter damnetur quod episcopus non sit solus minister" (p. 903); Quintius de Rusticis, Bishop of Mileto: "Solus episcopus est minister confirmationis" (p. 907); Dionysius the Greek, Bishop in Crete: "Episcopus est solus minister" (p. 907); Eliseus Theodinus, Bishop of Sora, which was united with the diocese of Aquino in 1818: ". . . ad solum episcopum pertinet confirmare" (p. 908); Jerome de Bononia, Bishop of Siracusa (p. 927); Richard Musso, Bishop of Worcester, now suppressed in England: ". . . episcopus solus est minister confirmationis" (p. 927); Cornelius Musso, Bishop of Bitonto, united in 1818 with Ruvo: ". . . damnetur sine ulla declaratione" (p. 927), and many others, including Peter Cardinal Pacheco, Bishop of Jaen in Spain (p. 924).

103 "Cum Papa possit facere sacerdotem unico verbo, ut tenet Angelus in *lib. I de sentent.* passim, multo magis videtur posse demandare hanc curam presbytero ut confirmet, quod tamen falsus est. Solus enim episcopus est minister confirmationis ut Act. Apost. 8 et declaratur in concilio Constaniensi."—*C. Tr.*, V, 904.

104 *C. Tr.*, V, 922.

105 Francis Navarra, Bishop of Badajoz: ". . . Gregorius toleravit contrarium propter scandalum, et est casus specialis."—*C. Tr.*, V, 930.

106 Gallazzo of Fiarimonte, Bishop of Aquino: "Gregorius erravit."—*C. Tr.*, V, 930; John Salazar, Bishop of Lanciano: ". . . non fuit permissio sed dissimulatio propter scandalum."—*C. Tr.*, V, 927.

was of divine origin.[107] John the Baptist Cicada, Bishop of Albenga, gave an etymological explanation of why only bishops confirm—the very word 'confirm' implies the action of a superior.[108]

The minority opinion, on the other hand, which favored a less stringent declaration on the minister of confirmation, based its arguments fundamentally on the need of protecting the power of the Pope to commission a simple priest to confirm. The grant made by Pope Gregory was a clear precedent for the exercise of this power. Tomasso Campeggio, Bishop of Feltre, stated the case thus:

> . . . ultimus de confirmatione, cum episcopus non sit ex institutione divina solus minister confirmationis, aliter Gregorius non potuisset super eo dispensare, dicatur quod episcopus ordinarius sit confirmationis minister, ut dixit concilium Florentinum.[109]

Both the Bishop of Oporto, Balthasar Lympo, and the Bishop of Alife, Sebastian Pighini, repeated the basic assertion of this school of thought, namely, that the definition should read to make the bishop the ordinary minister of confirmation, since the Pope can dispense in the case of necessity.[110] Though only relatively few bishops maintained this view,[111] the superior generals

[107] ". . . quoad confirmationem, no. 4, haereticus, quia solus episcopus est minister confirmationis, *etiam de iure divino* et Papa non potest super ea dispensare, et Gregorius erravit adeo quod sacerdos dispensatus a Papa, ut confirmans possit, confirmans nihil agit."—*C. Tr.*, V, 930; Bishop Fonseca: ". . . de confirmationis ministro damnetur simpliciter, quia solus episcopus est minister confirmationis *a Deo institutus*. Innocentius I id asserit aperte."—*C. Tr.*, V, 924.

[108] ". . . etiam ex vi verbi confirmatio ad superiorem pertinet, quasi presbyteri baptizent, episcopi confirment ut superiores."—*C. Tr.*, V, 931.

[109] *C. Tr.*, V, 903.

[110] Bishop Lympo: ". . . in 4 de confirmatione placet consilium theologorum, quod dicatur ordinarius minister episcopus, ut factum est in concilio Florentino, quia Pontifex potest in munus demandare sacerdoti."—*C. Tr.*, V, 922; Bishop Pighini: ". . . Pontifex super ea potest dispensare in casu necessitatis."—*C. Tr.*, V, 933.

[111] Among these can be listed Sebastian Lecavela, Archbishop of Naxos in Greece—*C. Tr.*, V, 897; Philos Roverella, Bishop of Ascoli Piceno—*C.*

of the leading religious orders, with the exception of the Superior of the Carmelites[112] spoke on behalf of a modified definition which would recognize the power of the Pope to delegate.[113]

The discussions of the Fathers of the Council of Trent were completed on the 21st of February, thirteen days after their commencement. The prevalent opinion held that the proposition which stated that the bishop is not the *only* minister of confirmation should be condemned without any reservation or modification, i.e., *simpliciter.*[114]

Article 3—Discussion on the Revised Formula

On the 26th of February the various propositions were presented in their final form. Apparently an attempt was made to circumvent the thorny issue of the bishop as the sole minister of confirmation, and so the canon was presented as a denial that any and every priest can confirm: *"Si quis dixerit, quemlibet sacerdotem esse ministrum confirmationis, anathema sit."*[115] Needless to say, this compromise did not escape the close scrutiny of the Fathers of the Council, who deliberated in general sessions which opened on the 1st of March. Almost immediately Cardinal Pachecus insisted that the canon be revised to read: *"Si quis dixerit non esse episcopum ministrum, sed quemlibet sacerdotem, etc."*[116] Robert Wauchope, Archbishop of Armagh, who was the

---

Tr., V, 903; John Campegius, Bishop of Parenzo—*C. Tr.*, V, 924; Anthony de Numais—*C. Tr.*, V, 907; Louis Simonetta, Bishop of Pisa—*C. Tr.*, V, 925.

[112] *C. Tr.*, V, 970.

[113] Lucian de Octonibus from Ferrara, representing the Order of St. Benedict—*C. Tr.*, V, 936; Bonaventure Pius, Superior General of the Order of Friars Minor Conventual—*C. Tr.*, V, 959; Francis Romaeus, Superior General of the Order of Friars Preachers—*C. Tr.*, V, 960; Jerome Seripando, Superior General of the Order of the Hermits of St. Augustine—*C. Tr.*, V, 967; Augustine Bonucius, Superior General of the Order of the Servants of Mary—*C. Tr.*, V, 967.

[114] *C. Tr.*, V, 972.

[115] *C. Tr.*, V, 985.

[116] *C. Tr.*, V, 987.

tenth to speak, suggested a rewording of the canon to make the bishop the *proper* minister of confirmation.[117] Braccius Martellus, Bishop of Fiesole, then championed the cause of those who wanted a strict definition by insisting that the bishop be regarded as the *solus minister*.[118] Though there were variations on the main theme,[119] the general refrain became an insistence that the canon contain a reference to the bishop as the minister of confirmation, *"in 3 fiat mentio episcopi."* Following the suggestion of Thomas Casellus, Bishop of Bertinoro, that the bishop be referred to as the *ordinarius minister*, the tide of episcopal opinion turned to favor the final formulation of the canon in the terminology of the Council of Florence.[120] Thus, when the last meeting was held on March 2nd to draft the final formulation, it was decided to revise the third canon to read that the bishop, and not any simple priest, is the ordinary minister of confirmation:

> 3 aptatur ut dicatur, episcopum esse ordinarium ministrum et non quemvis simplicem sacerdotem.[121]

Article 4—Conclusion of the Seventh Session

On the 3rd of March, 1547, amid impressive solemnities, in the presence of 2 presiding Cardinal Legates, the Cardinal of Spain, 9 archbishops, 51 bishops, 2 procurators, 2 abbots, 5 superiors general and 30 theologians,[122] the seventh session of the Council

117 *C. Tr.*, V, 987.

118 *C. Tr.*, V, 988.

119 The Bishop of Oporto supported the Archbishop of Armagh to make the bishop the proper minister—*C. Tr.*, V, 988; the Bishop of Lanciano wanted to add to the original, "et negaverit ad solum episcopum hoc munus pertinere, anathema sit."—*C. Tr.*, V, 989; the Bishop of Saluzzo, Philip Archintus, ". . . si quis dixerit non modo episcopum, sed quemlibet sacerdotem esse ministrum confirmationis, anathema sit."—*C. Tr.*, V, 989.

120 "Nonnulli dixerunt, tertium aptandum iuxta decretum concilii Florentini."—Summary of Massarelli, secretary of the Council. Cf. *C. Tr.*, V, 991.

121 *C. Tr.*, V, 993.

122 Theiner, *Acta Genuina SS. Oecumenici Concilii Tridentini sub Paulo III, Julio III et Pio IV, PP.MM.* (2 vols., Zagabriae Croatiae, 1874), I, 465.

of Trent was brought to a close with definitive proclamations on the general nature of the sacraments as well as on baptism and confirmation, which included a canon on the minister of confirmation. In its final form the canon stated:

> Si quis dixerit, sanctae confirmationis ordinarium ministrum non esse solum episcopum [123] sed quemvis simplicem sacerdotem, anathema sit.[124]

Through an adroit wording of the text the divergent schools of thought, as expressed by the Fathers of the Council, were reconciled. The prerogatives of the episcopacy were protected and preserved with the door left open to admit special cases wherein a priest could become the extraordinary minister of this sacrament. Hefele (1809-1893) summarized the effects of this definition when he concluded:

> Thus the goal sought by the Council was attained—the claim of the Protestants attributing to any priest the power of conferring confirmation was condemned. Without taking away the extraordinary power of simple priests, the canon defined as a dogma of faith that the bishops are the sole ordinary ministers of confirmation.[125]

Though the Council of Trent did not formally take up the question of the extraordinary minister of confirmation, by implication it included this matter in its definition. The assiduous avoidance of the expression *solus minister* and the explicit emphasis upon the form *ordinarius minister* indicate sufficiently an implicit admission of the institution of an extraordinary minister. This conclusion can be corroborated by the words of a canon in a later session, the twenty-third, which pointed out that the

[123] It is interesting to speculate concerning the discussions which must have taken place privately among the bishops between the 2nd and 3rd of March to have the canon include the word *solus*.

[124] *C. Tr.*, V, 996.

[125] *Histoire des Conciles d'apres les Documents Originaux,* traduite en français par Dom H. Leclerq (11 vols. in 21, Librairie Letouzey et Ané: Paris, 1907-1952) Tom. X, première partie (Les Decrets du Concile de Trente, par A. Michel), p. 231.

power by which a bishop confirms is not a power which priests hold in common with him.[126]

SECTION C—THE OFFICIAL DOCUMENTS OF THE HOLY SEE AFTER THE COUNCIL OF TRENT

Article 1—The Sacred Congregation of the Council

After the Council of Trent a certain reluctance to grant faculties to simple priests for conferring confirmation persisted in the attitude of the Holy See. This is especially noticeable in the decisions of the Sacred Congregation of the Council.

On February 28, 1643, in a decision sent to Portugal, the Congregation decreed that a Benedictine abbot who was not blessed could not confirm seculars or regulars; if he had done so, he needed absolution.[127] On June 26, 1655, the Congregation decided that the abbots of the Order of St. Bernard and St. Benedict in Portugal could not confirm; if they sought to do so, they incurred a censure, and the ones who had been presented to them for confirmation needed to be confirmed anew.[128]

The concern now was not so much about the possibility of granting this extraordinary faculty, but rather about the urgency and seriousness of the cause required. The Bishop of Terracina, whose diocese included the territory of Zuisa, an island in the Tyrrhenian Sea, requested that the faculty to confirm be granted to the head missioner on the island. The petition stated that this place had not been visited by a bishop for more than forty years, because of the danger from the marauding pirates. On Jan. 25, 1659, a negative decision was given by the Congregation. A number of years later, the Archbishop of the Philippines requested the faculty of delegating priests, both secular and regular, to confirm because of the large size of the diocese and the

[126] Conc. Trident., sess. XXIII, *de sacramento ordinis,* can. 7: "Si quis dixerit, episcopos non esse presbyteris superiores; vel non habere potestatem confirmandi et ordinandi, vel eam quam habent, illis esse cum presbyteris communem, . . . anathema sit."—Denzinger-Rahner, *Enchiridion,* n. 967.

[127] *Fontes,* n. 2640.

[128] *Fontes,* n. 2743.

great number of people, *"propter amplitudinem dioecesum et populorum frequentiam."* The answer, given on January 28, 1668, was negative, because the case seemed not sufficiently urgent.[129]

The following case is interesting because of the manner in which it was handled.

On Saturday, June 13, 1722, the Fathers of the Sacred Congregation of the Council met to consider the petition of the Jesuits who were doing missionary work in Chile. The latter requested the faculty of administering confirmation, since many of the Christians were dying without this sacrament. So great were the distances from the episcopal see that in one instance during an entire century only one episcopal visitation had been made by a certain Bishop Didacus Monterus, who returned to his diocese completely exhausted from the hazards and exertions incidental to his journey.

In their deliberations the members of the Congregation noted three points: (1) the Holy father can entrust a simple priest with the faculty of conferring the sacrament of confirmation; (2) examples are not lacking of such grants made by the Popes; (3) a great and urgent cause is required, not an absolutely necessitating cause. However, when they considered some of the former decisions made by their predecessors, the response stated: *"scribatur episcopis iuxta instructionem."* [130]

Apparently this letter was never written, for when the Congregation convened on January 24, 1733, to consider another request made by the Bishop of Chile to empower the Jesuit Rector of the seminary to confirm, it was stated that there was no record of any execution of the previous instruction.[131] This time the officials decided to write to the Apostolic Nuncio to determine whether conditions were such as described by the petitioners. In a session held on April 3, 1734, the letter of the Nuncio was accepted. In it he had verified that in many places confirmation could not be administered by the bishop without

[129] *Thesaurus,* II, 186.

[130] *Thesaurus,* II, 187-190.

[131] *Thesaurus,* VI, 15.

great peril and danger to life, "*sine ingenti periculo ac discrimine vitae.*" He also added that it was impossible to ask for an auxiliary, inasmuch as the bishop could barely support himself. The Congregation of the Council decreed: "*Ad Emum Praefectum iuxta mentem.*" [132]

Article 2—Papal Documents

Though the Sacred Congregation of the Council was rather slow and hesitant about granting the faculty empowering simple priests to confirm, the number of direct papal delegations began to increase. This was especially true in the reign of Pope Benedict XIV (1740-1758), a strong advocate of this privilege. In his *De Synodo Dioecesana* he had concluded that it was no longer lawful to argue whether or not the Pope can grant simple priests the power to confirm:

> Quare non videtur hodie fas esse potestatem, de qua olim disceptabatur, summo Pontifici abiudicare. Quoniam ut ait Veracrux: De Pontificis potestate, postquam dispensavit, dubitare, instar sacrilegii est. Et magis ad rem Sotus: Non est dubitandum, quin simplex sacerdos ex commissione Papae possit sacramentum confirmationis exhibere. Et qui de hoc iam modo haesitaret, ecclesiasticis sanctionibus adversaretur. Etenim, quamvis haec conclusio ex sacris litteris non plane colligatur, sufficere tamen debet orthodoxis, quod Gregorius (addimus nos, et alii Pontifices) illam fecerit dispensationem.[133]

A *dubium* had been presented whether the custodian and guardian of the Holy Sepulchre had the necessary faculty to confer the sacrament of confirmation in virtue of certain privileges and special delegation of the Holy See. Pope Innocent XIII (1721-1724), in a constitution *Cum ad infrascriptam,* issued on September 13, 1721, granted this favor specifically.[134] Ex-

[132] *Thesaurus,* VI, 244. Quinn, *The Extraordinary Minister of Confirmation* (p. 42), concluded that the faculty was granted.

[133] Tomus I, lib. 7, cap. 7, no. 6.

[134] "Eidem Ioanni Philippo Custodi, et Guardiano eiusdem Sancti Sepulchri durante eius officio, et pro locis Terrae Sanctae tantum, ubi non erunt Episcopi Ritus Latini, in propria Dioecesi residentes, potestatem, et facultatem conferendi Sacramentum Confirmationis huiusmodi. Oleo, et Chris-

actly the same delegation, couched in the same terminology, was granted by Pope Benedict XIV on January 9, 1741, to a certain Paul a Laurino.[135] In 1732 Pope Clement XII (1730-1740), in an apostolic letter *Creditae Nobis,* granted to the Abbot General *Nullius* of Monte Vergine the faculty to confirm his subjects.[136]

On December 24, 1743, Pope Benedict XIV issued an encyclical letter *Demandatam* to the Patriarch of the Greek Melkites at Antioch and to all the Catholic bishops of the same rite subject to the Patriarch Cyril, who had presented the Holy See with a list of questions and apparent grievances which the Holy Father sought to settle. In paragraph 14 the Pope allowed the Custodian of the Holy Land to reconfirm *sub conditione* the Greeks who had been confirmed by simple priests and who sought the sacrament again. This power could be exercised only if there was not present any Greek Catholic resident bishop, or at least only with his permission.[137]

To settle certain doubts about the rites of the Coptic Church proposed by a Frater Jacobus of the Friars Minor Capuchin, head of the Mission in Egypt, Benedict XIV issued an instruction *Eo quamvis tempore* on May 4, 1745. The first *dubium* inquired whether the missionaries could confer confirmation immediately after baptism upon the children of the Copts, who were scandalized that the two sacraments were not conferred concomitantly. The Pope noted that to confirm belongs to the bishop, *"episcopis huius sacramenti administrandi ordinaria potestas commissa est," "hoc munus episcopale,"* but, nevertheless, if conditions warranted the granting of a concession to the missionaries, the matter would be favorably considered by the Holy See.[138]

This document is important because it gave official pontifical

---

mate etiam antiquis, si nova haberi non possint per Catholicum Antistitem gratiam et communionem Sedis Apostolicae habente[m], benedictis, dicta auctoritate, tenore praesentium concedimus, et delegamus."—*Fontes,* n. 279.

[135] *Fontes,* n. 305.

[136] This is mentioned in a decision of the Sacred Congregation of Bishops and Regulars, March 30, 1855.—*Fontes,* n. 1972.

[137] *Fontes,* n. 338.

[138] *Fontes,* n. 357.

approbation to the practice by which priests of the Eastern rite administer confirmation immediately after baptism. Benedict XIV noted that Rome has not expressly forbidden this practice, but rather has tolerated it "*ex indulgentia.*" He explained that the policy of the Holy See to delegate this faculty was neither recent nor infrequent. It was exercised whenever the needs of the people demanded it and there was danger that they would die without confirmation because of the shortage or lack of bishops or the tremendous distances.[139] In paragraph 9 of this document is found the expression *minister extraordinarius,* which may well be the first time that this expression appeared in a papal document.

Another explicit reference in an official document to the expression *extraordinarius minister* appeared in a letter of Benedict XIV, *Ex tuis precibus,* of November 16, 1748. The chief subject under consideration was the power of the Pope to delegate a priest, in this case an abbot, to consecrate a church. To substantiate his arguments, the Pope drew a parallel with the power of a Pope to delegate priests to confirm:

> Enim vero, quamvis Sacramenti Confirmationis administratio ita soli conveniat Episcopo, ut nullus Antistes simplicem sacerdotem, qui baptizatos confirmet, possit delegare; multis tamen Praedecessorum Nostrorum exemplis docemur, eiusmodi munus Sacerdotibus, et praecipuis quibusdam Abbatibus, esto nullo charactere Episcopali insignitis, fuisse collatum; modo extraordinarius Confirmationis Minister, Oleo, cui Episcopus pridem benedixit, utatur.[140]

139 "Huiusmodi delegatio nec nova nec inusitata videri debet. . . . Cum enim saepe contingerit, Christifideles Pastoris solatio esse destitutos, et Episcopis ob distantiam locorum impossibile vel difficile admodum fuerit, populorum necessitatibus praesentes fieri; in hanc partem Episcopalis ministerii vocati sunt sacerdotes, dummodo uterentur chrismate ab episcopo rite benedicto et consecrato: ne alias contingeret, fideles rem sanctitatis plenam cunctando negligere, vel decedere sine hoc sacramento divinis muneribus cumulato, et ad nostram sanctificationem instituto."—*Fontes,* n. 357 § 8. These were precisely the reasons which motivated the Sacred Congregation to issue the 1946 decree.

140 *Fontes,* n. 393, # 1. The terminology is also used in the ninth paragraph: ". . . simplices sacerdotes in extraordinarios Confirmationis, ac minorum Ordinum Ministros pluries fuisse designatos, satis probavimus in

Anno vertente, issued June 19, 1750, was to serve the purpose of clarifying some of the doubts and misunderstandings which might have persisted since the 1745 instruction, discussed above. In this document Pope Benedict frequently referred to his treatise on the minister of confirmation in his *De Synodo Dioecesana.* In paragraph 5 he used a very interesting substitute expression for extraordinary minister. In his explanation of the necessity for a Latin priest to use chrism blessed by the bishop he stated: "*. . . si a summo Pontifice constituatur minister extra ordinem sacramenti confirmationis.*"[141]

It should be noted that, although Pope Benedict XIV was liberal in his granting of the concession to confirm, he was equally insistent on the necessity of a papal delegation for the valid conferring of this sacrament. On May 26, 1742, he issued a constitution, *Etsi pastoralis,* governing the faith and practices of the Italo-Greeks, many of whom had fled the persecutions of their native land. In the third paragraph the Pope ordered the reconfirmation of the infants who had been presented for confirmation to the Greek priests, since this faculty had not been given by him or his predecessors. As a matter of fact, it had been specifically revoked by Pope Clement VIII (1592-1605) in the instruction *Sanctissimus,* given August 31, 1595.[142]

The text of Benedict's orders reads as follows:

> Episcopi Latini infantes, seu alios in suis Dioecesibus baptizatos a Presbyteris Graecis *absolute* chrismate in fronte consignatos confirment; cum neque per Praedecessores

---

praelaudato Tractatu Nostro, *De Synodo Dioecesana.*" The Sacred Congregation of the Council in a decision, given on December 11, 1897, also used the phrase when it declared that the abbot *Nullius* of the monastery of the Holy Trinity in Cava could not confirm outside his territory, even with the permission of the bishop. The reason given was this: ". . . namque Abbas simplex sacerdos est minister confirmationis extraordinarius, tantum a Summo Pontifice delegatus, sed aliqua gravi instante causa."—*Fontes,* n. 4305.

141 *Fontes,* n. 407.

142 "Presbyteri Graeci, baptizatos chrismate in fronte non consignent. . . . § 1. Episcopi Latini infantes, seu alios baptizatos a Presbyteris Graecis de facto chrismate in fronte consignatos confirment."—*Fontes,* n. 179.

> nostros, neque per Nos Graecis Presbyteris in Italia, et Insulis adiacentibus, ut infantibus baptizatis sacramentum confirmationis conferant, facultas concessa sit, aut concedatur; quin imo usque ab anno 1595 a fel. rec. Clemente VIII Praedecessore nostro fuit Presbyteris Italo-Graecis expresse interdictum, ne baptizatos chrismate consignent.[143]

In the fourth paragraph of the same document the Pope noted that those who had been confirmed *"a simplice sacerdote"* need not be compelled, at the cost of scandal, to receive this sacrament from the bishop. The reason for this was not that the sacrament had been validly received, but rather that the sacrament was not necessary for salvation.[144] In his conclusion Benedict urged that the faithful be warned that it is a serious sin to neglect to receive this sacrament.

An interesting letter was sent by the Secretary of the Sacred Congregation of Bishops and Regulars to the Bishop of Mazara del Vallo in Sicily, on August 3, 1789. On the 15th of May, he had been granted a very unusual indult, which authorized him to entrust his vicar general with the administration of confirmation. The bishop wrote back with the request that he be allowed to extend the indult to empower some other priest to confirm, since the vicar general was feeble and in ill health. When this matter was brought to the attention of the Holy Father, the first reaction of Pope Pius VI (1775-1799) was to comment that the bishop should have been satisfied with the first indult, especially since it was unique in Sicily and all Italy. However, in virtue of his merits and physical disabilities, and also because of the vast expanse of the diocese, many parts of which were inaccessible,[145] the bishop was allowed to designate the canon of first dignity in the cathedral chapter *"pro tempore"* to administer confirmation

143 *Fontes*, n. 328, § III.

144 This incident seems to parallel very closely the difficulty between Pope Nicholas I and Photius about the confirmations administered in Bulgaria. Pope St. Pius X (1903-1914) in his letter *Ex quo*, issued December 26, 1910, discussed and condemned some of the errors which prevented reunion with the dissident Orientals. He stated that the thesis which holds that confirmation conferred by any priest is valid can never be reconciled with true Catholic doctrine.—*AAS*, III (1911), 117-127; *Fontes*, n. 691.

145 ". . . della vastità della sua diocesi per luoghi anche inaccesabili."

in the diocese according to the instructions of the original indult.[146]

It was this same Pontiff, Pius VI, who in the first year of his pontificate on April 10th issued a letter, *Cum sicut accepimus,* in which he allowed the bishop of Mazara del Vallo to delegate *"de speciali gratia"* one priest on the Islands of Pantellaria and Favignana to which access was difficult because of the dangers from the Turks, to confirm, even with old chrism, as long as it had been blessed by a bishop in communion with the Holy See. The Pope's action was motivated by his concern for souls. It is interesting to note that it was not specified that the priest have any special ecclesiastical dignity. The document simply instructed the bishop to select a priest, *"tibi benevisum, moribus gravem, ac pietatis, et religionis zelo praeditum."* [147]

These papal documents exerted considerable influence on the contemporary canonists and theologians who had continued their discussion on the extraordinary minister of confirmation. Honoré de Tournely (1658-1729) considered the opinion that a simple priest by delegation could validly confer the sacrament of confirmation as the more common opinion.[148] He summarized his teaching on the minister of confirmation thus:

> The minister of confirmation is to be distinguished into the ordinary, that is, one who functions *ex officio,* and the extraordinary, that is, one who functions *ex dispensatione.* The ordinary minister of confirmation has the full and complete power of validly conferring the sacrament in virtue of his orders or character, which power cannot be impeded by any superior authority. Only the bishop is such a minister. The extraordinary minister, namely a simple priest, has an inchoative and incomplete power in virtue of his orders. In order to be validly exercised, this power must be completed and perfected through a legitimate dispensation, much in the

[146] *Anacleta Juris Pontificii,* Recueil des dissertations sur différent sujets de droit canonique, de liturgie, de théologie et d'histoire (28 vols., Roma, Parisiis, Bruxellis, 1855-1891), XII (1873), 208.

[147] *Fontes,* n. 468.

[148] *Cursus Theologicus Scholastico-dogmaticus* (14 vols., Venetiis, 1755-1765) Vol. X, *Praelectiones Theologicae de Sacramentis Baptismi et Confirmationis,* p. 263.

same manner that the power of absolving from sins which is conceded to the priest at ordination is incomplete and tied up so that it cannot be validly exercised (outside of the case of necessity) unless jurisdiction has been granted by the bishop.[149]

It is not within the scope of this historical study to evaluate at this point the relative value or validity of the theological explanation of the nature of this delegation or dispensation granted by the Holy See, in virtue of which a simple priest is empowered for confirming.

Article 3—The Sacred Congregation for the Propagation of the Faith

One of the earliest indults empowering simple priests to confirm was granted by the Congregation for the Propagation of the Faith on January 18, 1767.[150] The use of episcopal vestments by those *"quibus ab Apostolica Sede extraordinaria Sacramentum Confirmationis administrandi facultas conceditur"* was forbidden by this Congregation in a response issued April 23, 1774.[151]

On May 4th of the same year, the Congregation issued detailed instructions to be followed by simple priests who confirmed in virtue of delegation from the Holy See. The practice among missionaries must have been quite extensive, even at this early date, to warrant the publication of such a document. The preface reflected the general teaching of the Church:

> Etsi iuxta Sacrosancti Tridentini Concilii definitionem solus episcopus sit ordinarius huius sacramenti minister, *solet*, tamen, quandoque iustis de causis Sedes Apostolica simplici sacerdoti, tamquam extraordinario ministro, facultatem tribuere illud conferendi.[152]

[149] *Op. cit.*, X, 253.

[150] Reference was made to this indult at a synod held by the Vicariate of Soochow in 1803, chap. III, no. 2.—*Acta et Decreta Sacrorum Conciliorum Recentiorum, Collectio Lacensis* (7 vols., Friburgi Brisgoviae, 1870-1892), VI, 599.

[151] *Collectanea S. Congregationis de Propaganda Fide* (2 vols., Romae; Typographia S. C. de Propaganda Fide, 1907), I, no. 502 (hereafter cited *Collectanea*); *Fontes*, n. 4564.

[152] *Collectanea*, I, n. 503; *Fontes*, n. 4565.

The priest was admonished to inform the faithful that he confirmed only in virtue of a special indult.[153]

In a letter written on September 11, 1841, to the Apostolic Vicar of Korea, who had reported that sometimes this admonition was not followed, the Sacred Congregation assured him that, nevertheless, the sacrament was validly conferred, although the instruction of course was to be religiously and scrupulously followed.[154] On July 29, 1841, this same Congregation, with the approval of Pope Gregory XVI (1831-1846), had issued an indult, granting the faculty of administering confirmation, to the rulers of a vacant diocese in mission territories of China, with the power of subdelegating. Once again it was stated that the concern for souls was the chief motive for this grant.[155]

On March 30, 1851, Pius IX (1846-1878) granted the faculty of confirming to a certain Prefect of the missions who, in turn, could further grant it to certain priests.[156] On July 5, 1860, the Sacred Congregation granted to a Vicar Apostolic the faculty of delegating a simple priest to administer the sacrament of confirmation in his territory, provided that he himself was absent or legitimately impeded, and that there was no bishop available.[157]

In addition to the territory subject to the Congregation for

[153] ". . . eisque praesertim denuntiet, quod nullus alius nisi solus episcopus confirmationis ordinarius minister est; se vero paratum esse illam conferre iure per S. Sedem delegato."—*Loc. cit.*

[154] *Collectanea,* I, n. 940; *Fontes,* n. 4796.

[155] *Collectanea,* I, n. 933; *Fontes,* n. 4792.

[156] *Collectanea Constitutionum Decretorum, Indultorum ac Instructionum Sanctae Sedis ad Usum Operariorum Apostolicorum Societatis Missionum ad Exteros* (Parisiis: Typis Georges Chamerot, 1880), n. 307. On March 21, 1851, the Sacred Congregation for the Propagation of the Faith issued a warning to a certain Vicar Apostolic that the faculty of confirmation was to be used only in a case of necessity. Baptism and confirmation were not to be administered at the same time unless there was the danger of death. Cf. *Fontes,* nn. 4833 and 4834. "Simultanea collatio baptismatis et confirmationis in pueris admittenda non est, nisi forte in mortis periculo iuxta praxim."—*Fontes,* n. 4834.

[157] *Collectanea,* I, n. 1196; *Fontes,* n. 4850, ". . . dummodo vel sis absens, aut legitime impeditus."

the Propagation of Faith, there were many parts of the world, especially in the Latin Americas, which after the creation of a hierarchy, after the establishment of dioceses, etc., were taken out of the jurisdiction of this Congregation, but nevertheless were still faced with the problems of tremendous territory, primitive means of communication, and difficult methods of transportation. On March 4, 1903, the Holy Office considered the request of the Bishop of Concepcion in Chile, who petitioned for the faculty of delegating a priest to confer confirmation within the limits of his diocese. The reason given was that in his diocese there were a million souls, and it was impossible for the bishop to reach all of them. On the 5th of March, Pope Leo XIII (1878-1903) approved the response as follows:

> R.—Iuxta decretum 9 Maii 1888 quod ita se habet: "Supplicandum SSmo pro facultate subdelegandi unum vel alterum presbyterum, concedenda per Sacram Congr. Negotiis Ecclesiasticis Extraordinariis praepositam non solum Episcopis petentibus, sed etiam aliis qui in similibus circumstantiis reperiantur, durante eorum munere."[158]

Article 4—Preliminary Studies of the Vatican Council

Had the Vatican Council run its full course, a great deal of light might have been shed on the question of the extraordinary minister of confirmation, since the practice of the Oriental Church was to have been closely scrutinized and analyzed. Listed under the topics *De Fide* in the prospectus suggested for consideration was the following statement:

> Mos vi cuius in Oriente confirmatio a simplicibus presbyteris simul cum baptismo confertur, effecit, ut orientales catholici generatim minus accuratas habent notiones circa ministrum ordinarium et extraordinarium illius sacramenti, atque adeo circa distinctionem substantialem unius sacramenti ab alio. Qua de causa, commissioni theologicae propositum fuit, ut vellet hac super re, in capite doctrinali revocare catholicas veritates ratione habita Orientalium, quin tamen necesse sit eos nominari.[159]

[158] *Collectanea,* II, n. 2161.

[159] Mansi, L, 106*.

Of the approximately 764 Council Fathers present, 60 of them were of the various Oriental rites, 541 of them were from the dioceses of Europe and 48 from the United States.[160]

June 30, 1867, Pope Pius IX, in a document which began "*Periucunda,*" officially announced his intention to convoke an oecumenical council which would open on the feast of the Immaculate Conception, December 8, 1869.[161] The bull of convocation was promulgated a year later on the feast of the apostles Peter and Paul, June 29, 1868.[162] Six commissions were established, each with a cardinal at the head, to prepare the subject matter which was to be submitted by the Holy See for the scrutiny and vote of the Council Fathers. One of the commissions was that for the churches of the missions and the Oriental rites with Cardinal Barnabo at the head and including fourteen distinguished consultors.[163] On the 8th and 13th of September, 1868, respectively, letters of invitation to participate in the Vatican Council were sent to the Oriental bishops who were not in communion with the Holy See and to Protestants and other non-Catholics.[164]

The dogmatic constitution on the Catholic faith, *Dei Filius,* was promulgated with its canons in the third general session held on *Quasimodo* Sunday, April 24, 1870.[165] The fourth general session, held on the 18th of July, 1870, promulgated the constitution, *De Ecclesia Christi,* wherein the primacy and infallibility of the Roman Pontiff were defined.[166] Because of the invasion of Rome, September 20, 1870, by the hostile forces of

[160] Cf. Guérin, *Concile Oecuménique du Vatican* (Bar-le-Duc: Louis Guérin, 1872), p. 2.

[161] *Pii IX Pontificis Maximi Acta* (9 vols., Romae: ex typographia Bonarum Artium; ex typographia Vaticana, 1854-1878), IV, 292-295.

[162] Mansi, L, 194*-199*.

[163] Their names can be found in the *op. cit.,* of Guérin, p. 15.

[164] Mansi, L, 199*-203*, the letter to the schismatic Oriental bishops; 203*-206*, the letter to the Protestants.

[165] Mansi, LI, 429-436.

[166] Mansi, LII, 1330-1334.

the army of united Italy, which made further free deliberations impossible, Pius IX decided to prorogue the Vatican Council until a more opportune time to be decided by the Holy See. October 20, 1870, the Pope issued the decree *Postquam Dei munere* which reads in part as follows:

> . . . idcirco Nos, eo res adductas magno cum animi Nostri moerore perspicientes, ut Vaticanum Concilium tali in tempore cursum suum omnino tenere non possit, praevia matura deliberatione, motu proprio eiusdem Vaticani Oecumenici Concilii celebrationem usque ad aliud opportunius et commodius tempus per hanc Sanctam Sedem declarandum, apostolica auctoritae tenore praesentium suspendimus et suspensam esse nunciamus, Deum adprecantes auctorem et vindicem Ecclesiae Suae, ut submotis tandem impedimentis omnibus Sponsae Suae fidelissimae ocius restituat libertatem et pacem.[167]

That the Council had planned a definition on the extraordinary minister of confirmation is quite clear from the decision, made and approved by all, to define the necessity of a pontifical delegation for a priest to confirm:

> . . . Cum satis explorata non sit penes Orientales pontificiae delegationis neccesitas ad hoc, ut sacerdotes chrismare valide et licite possint, omnibus visum fuit exprimendum esse a concilio oecumenico sacerdotes hoc sacramentum administrare ex delegatione Romani Pontificis.[168]

October 25, 1869, at the 26th preliminary session and at the 27th session, October 28, 1869, discussions were conducted on the *votum* of Professor Rossi, *"De Ministro Extraordinario Confirmationis Apud Orientales."*[169] In February 1870, the following outline was drawn up to include the most salient features of the principles which would clarify the teaching of the Church on the extraordinary minister:

> Quamvis ordinarius minister sacramenti confirmationis sit episcopus, legitur tamen aliquando per apostolicae sedis dis-

[167] *Pii IX P.M. Acta,* V, 254-255.

[168] Mansi, L, 109*.

[169] Mansi, L, 59*-71*.

> pensationem ex rationabili et urgenti admodum causa simplicem sacerdotem chrismate per episcopum confecto hoc administrasse sacramentum, quemadmodum in missionibus interdum contigit et apud fideles orientalis ritus fieri solet, quibus a presbyteris eiusdem ritus sacramentum confirmationis valide confertur; iis tamen exceptis ecclesiis et locis, in quibus extraordinariam hanc facultatem expresse et totaliter apostolica sedes revocavit. Quo autem usus eiusdem facultatis modum non excedat ac meminerint presbyteri se extraordinarios tantum ministros esse huius sacramenti, decernimus illicitum ex nunc fore eisdem presbyteris orientalibus absque proprii episcopi venia hoc sacramentum administrare fidelibus illis, quos, licet solemniter baptizatos, eveniat nondum sacro chrismate fuisse linitos. Optamus, vero, et vehementer hortamur episcopos, ut hos quantum fieri potest, per se confirment, ac nonnisi ex necessitate huiusmodi veniam presbyteris concedant.[170]

Two facts are especially to be noted: 1) that the bishop is the ordinary minister of confirmation was presumed by the Council as a dogma already defined; 2) the priests of the Eastern rites were urged to remember that, though they be the customary ministers of confirmation, they are only its extraordinary ministers.

Article 5—The Code of Canon Law

In view of the decrees and documents which emanated from the Holy See since the eighteenth century, it is safe to say that the doctrine on the extraordinary minister of confirmation was well established at the time when the Code of Canon Law was being drawn up. Wernz (1842-1914), who prophetically anticipated the provisions of the *Spiritus Sancti munera* by more than thirty years, wanted to include a canon by which pastors would be given the faculty of confirming persons who are in danger of death.

The Commission requested that this be made part of the common law, but, for reasons unknown, this matter was omitted in the final formulation of canon 782.[171] Instead, the canon listed

[170] Mansi, LIII, 893.

[171] Zerba, *Commentarius in Decretum Spiritus Sancti Munera* (Libreria Editrice Vaticana: Typis Polyglottis Vaticanis, 1947), pp. 33-34.

cardinals, abbots *nullius,* prelates *nullius,* vicars apostolic and prefects apostolic as those who enjoyed the power of conferring confirmation as an extraordinary minister in virtue of the law itself. All these ministers, with the exception of the cardinals, can use their power only within the limits of their territory and during their term of office.[172]

Article 6—Post-Code Legislation

On the feast of Pentecost, 1934, the Sacred Congregation for the Discipline relating to the Sacraments issued a new instruction to be followed by the simple priest when he administers the sacrament of confirmation in virtue of a delegation from the Holy See.[173] The purpose of this instruction was to correlate and incorporate the various decisions and legislation theretofore issued by different departments of the Roman curia. It was drawn up as the result of a decision reached in a plenary session on the 31st of March, 1928.

In this document the history of the practice of the Church since the Code was reviewed. The shortage of bishops and the extraordinary conditions in Latin America had prompted the Holy See *"gravi et urgente exstante causa"* to delegate simple priests to confirm. To preserve the honor, distinction and eminence inherent in this sacrament, the delegated priest was to hold some ecclesiastical dignity.[174] The document further noted

[172] Canon 782, § 3.

[173] *AAS,* XXVII (1935), 11-22.

[174] This is evident in the renewal by Pope Pius XI (1922-1939) of the faculties given by Pope Leo XIII for the priests of the dioceses of Latin America. "Item Ordinarii locorum deputare possunt, ad sacramentum confirmationis administrandum, sacerdotes quantum fieri potest in aliqua dignitate ecclesiastica constitutos, vel munere Vicarii foranei fungentes; numquam vero simplices sacerdotes commorantes illis in locis in quibus praedictum Sacramentum administrandum erit."—*AAS,* XXI (1929), 555. On April 28, 1939, in a decree from the Sacred Consistorial Congregation, the permission of Pope Pius XI was extended for another ten years with one notation, namely, that the expression *"Ordinarii locorum"* did not include the vicar general without a special mandate of the bishop.—*AAS,* XXXI (1939), 224. The decree *Spiritus Sancti munera* evidently had no

that in 1924, as a result of requests made by the Bishop of Namur in Belgium and by others, the Congregation had considered the following *dubium:*

> An praxis deputandi sacerdotes episcopali charactere carentes ad Sacramentum Confirmationis administrandum, etiam in posterum servanda sit intra limites hactenus praefinitos, vel potius, instantibus gravibus et urgentibus causis, extendenda sit ad alias regiones etiam in Europa in casibus particularibus.[175]

The answer to the first part was affirmative, and to the second part negative. In the explanation which followed, the Congregation expressed its determination not to extend to the dioceses of Europe the indults which had been granted to the dioceses of South America. The ordinaries of Europe were advised to petition for auxiliary or coadjutor bishops.[176]

Thus, although this instruction did not reveal any pronounced change of attitude towards the granting of the faculty to empower priests to confirm as extraordinary ministers, it did indicate an increase in the number of petitions from all parts of the world. Evidently the provisions of the Code in determining the conditions and requisites for the extraordinary minister of confirmation did not meet the exigencies of the Catholic world. The fact that many were dying without the spiritual and sacramental benefits of confirmation caused grave concern to the ordinaries as well as the Holy See. In answer to the searching question of

---

bearing on this special privilege, inasmuch as the letter was renewed by the same Congregation until December 31, 1959.—*AAS,* XLI (1949), 190.

[175] *AAS,* XXVII (1935), 14.

[176] "Mens vero EE. PP. fuit quod nihil esset immutandum in disciplina Ecclesiae, quam hactenus servavit et vetuit immutari H. S. C., factis tantummodo nonnullis exceptionibus pro aliquibus regionibus in Americae Meridionali, ubi servari non potest ius commune ob extraordinaria rerum et personarum adiuncta. Equidem simplex sacerdos est minister extraordinarius Sacramenti Confirmationis per deputationem Sedis Apostolicae. Quodsi ex aliis regionibus exhibeantur huiusmodi petitiones, S. Congregatio suadeat Episcopis oratoribus ut recurrant ad S. Sedem pro obtinendo Episcopo Auxiliari seu Coadiutore, vel opem petant, pro huiusmodi Sacramento administrando, ab Episcopis finitimarum dioecesium."—*AAS,* XXVII (1935), 14.

how to provide for the spiritual needs of so many Christians, infants and adults, when their life was endangered by grave illness and when consequently it was not unlikely that they would die unconfirmed if the canon law on the extraordinary minister was strictly to be complied with,[177] the Sacred Congregation for the Discipline of the Sacraments, with the approbation *in forma specifica* of Pope Pius XII, issued the momentous decree *Spiritus Sancti munera,* officially entitled, *Decretum de Confirmatione Administranda Iis, qui ex Gravi Morbo in Mortis Periculo Sunt Constituti,* which considerably augmented the ranks of extraordinary ministers of confirmation. In a decree dated December 18, 1947, the Sacred Congregation for the Propagation of the Faith granted to all local ordinaries under its jurisdiction the power to give by apostolic indult to all priests subject to them and having the care of souls the faculty to administer confirmation under certain conditions.[178] The Sacred Congregation for the Oriental Church issued a decree on May 1, 1948, which extended the power so that a priest of the Latin rite can use his faculty for a subject of the Oriental rite who is placed under the authority of the local Latin ordinary—provided it was clear that confirmation had not been administered immediately after baptism.[179] Some particular indults have also been issued including one for the Church in the United States. All these documents will be the object of a canonical commentary which follows. Whether future developments will call for more pages to be written in the history of the extraordinary minister of confirmation remains a question which only time and subsequent provisions of the Holy See can determine.

SUPPLEMENT—THE MINISTER OF CONFIRMATION IN THE EASTERN CHURCH RITES

Though it is beyond the scope of this historical analysis to trace the discipline of the Oriental Churches in relation to the

[177] *AAS,* XXXVIII (1946), 351.

[178] *AAS,* XL (1948), 41.

[179] *AAS,* XL (1948), 422-423.

minister of confirmation, a few observations may contribute to a better understanding of the basic problems which pertain to the extraordinary minister of this sacrament.

It must be admitted that in many, not all, Oriental rites the priest is empowered to administer confirmation immediately after baptism. What is the source of this faculty? The best answer to this question can be found through a study of the classic treatise of Pope Benedict XIV, namely, his *De Synodo Dioecesana.*[180]

To ascertain precisely the period of the beginning of this practice among the Greeks and other members of the Eastern rites is difficult. However, long before the Photian schism it was common for simple priests to confirm children and adults immediately after baptism.[181] Though some might argue that this practice was condemned by Rome, Benedict XIV declared that no pontifical document could be produced to indicate such a universal prohibition. Indeed, these priests could be said to enjoy a privilege which had at least tacitly been granted by the Holy See:

> Ceterum in aliis locis, in quibus Chrismatio data a Sacerdotibus Graecis, non est a Sede Apostolica expresse improbata, ea pro valida est habenda, ob tacitum saltem privilegium a Sede Apostolica illis concessum: cuius quidem privilegii praesumptionem inducit ipsamet conniventia et tolerantia Romanorum Pontificum, qui praedictum Graecorum morem scientes non contradixerunt, nec umquam illum damnarunt; sicuti post Goarium et alios, recte rationatur Arcudius, *de Concord. Eccles. Occident. et Orient.*, lib. 2, *de confirm.*, cap. 15, p. 96, inquiens: "Tutissimum est

[180] Tom. I, lib. 7, cap. 9.

[181] It seems that the greater emphasis among the Orientals was upon the reservation to the Patriarch of the right to consecrate the *myron,* the chrism. The actual use of it was secondary, since the dependence of the priest upon the bishop was already sufficiently vindicated. Cf. R. Souarn, "De Presbytero Orientali Confirmationis Ministro," *Jus Pontificium,* XI (1931), 133-143; cf. also DeClercq, *Histoire des Conciles d'après les documents originaux,* tome XI, *Conciles des Orientaux Catholiques, première partie de 1575 a 1849* (Paris: Librairie Le Touzey et Ané, 1949), pp. 431-432.

> dicere Graecorum Presbyteros, per suos Patriarchas et Antistites, eiusmodi facultatem a summo Pontifice obtinuisse, a quo omnis iurisdictio, quasi a capite in alios, veluti membra, immediate vel mediate derivatur et diffunditur." [182]

It is therefore established that the priests of the Eastern rites [183] confirm in virtue of a Papal delegation, if not express, then at least tacit. However, when there is certain proof that the faculty has been taken away by the Holy See, the confirmation which a simple priest may have sought to administer under those circumstances is to be considered invalid.[184] Pope Benedict XIV then urged the following method of procedure, which is still followed today. It is necessary to find out whether the practice has been abolished or tolerated by the Apostolic See. If the former is true, the sacrament of confirmation must be administered anew; if the latter is true, the first administration is to be considered valid. If a positive doubt prevails as to the existence or non-existence of at least a tacit delegation, the case must be submitted to the Holy See for final adjudication.

In concluding his treatise, Benedict cited cases in indication of where and how this principle had been applied. In a synod of

[182] *De Synodo Dioecesana, ibid.*, sectio 3. This statement, "ceterum . . . damnarunt," which was confirmed in the instruction *Anno vertente* of 1750, no doubt will be incorporated verbally or at least substantially by the commission for the redaction of the Oriental Code of Canon Law in its canons pertaining to the priests of the Eastern rites as the extraordinary though usual minister of confirmation.

[183] The statement is limited to the Catholic priests. Whether the dissidents possess this power is a disputed point upon which there has not been any definite pronouncement. In response to questions asked on various occasions the Holy Office has responded that it is not expedient to reconfirm those who had been confirmed by schismatic priests unless the converts are to be promoted to tonsure and orders, or if their parents seek reconfirmation. In these cases the confirmation is to be conferred secretly and conditionally. Cf. *Collectanea,* I, n. 1095, response of Holy Office, July 5, 1853; II, n. 1381, Holy Office, March 16, 1872; II, n. 1515, Holy Office, April 2, 1879; II, n. 1630, Holy Office, January 14, 1885.

[184] There are records that such action was taken by Pope Nicholas I against the Photian priests in Bulgaria (cf. article 2 of Section A, pp. 15 ff.), by Pope Innocent IV against the priests on Cyprus (cf. article 7 of Section A, p. 30), and by Popes Clement VIII and Benedict XIV against the Italo-Greeks (cf. article 2 of Section C, pp. 49-50).

the Maronites, held at the time of Gregory XIII (1572-1585),[185] it was declared that a person of that rite would be free to seek confirmation from a bishop, since it was not certain that the priests of Jerusalem, to which the Maronites were subject, ever had even a tacit privilege from the Holy See. In a national synod held in 1736 and approved by Pope Benedict XIV in 1741, all priests of this same Rite of Orientals were forbidden to confirm if they lacked episcopal orders.[186] On the other hand, a provincial synod of the Ruthenians, held in 1720, decreed that confirmation given by a simple priest would be held as valid, since it was certain that a tacit delegation had been granted by the Holy See.[187] In like manner, other Eastern rite groups have certified the power of their priests for confirming. These decisions have become incorporated in their particular body of law.[188] Herman concluded as a result of his research on the subject of the minister of confirmation that actually the sacrament of confirmation is administered by the priest in all of the Catholic Oriental rites with the exception of: (1) the Greeks on the isle of Cyprus—Innocent IV, *Sub Catholicae,* 1254; (2) Italo-Greeks and Italo-Albanians—Clement VIII and Benedict XIV, *Etsi pastoralis,* 1742; (3) the Maronites, although the patriarch has the power to grant this faculty by delegation only to perideuts and Chor-bishops; (4) the Malabar-Christians who in the synod of Diamper introduced the Latin practice; (5) among the Catholic Ethiopians there seems to be a dispute which needs be settled by a decision of the Holy See.[189]

To place the entire question of the discipline on confirmation

[185] DeClercq, *op. cit.*, pp. 3-15.

[186] *Ibid.*, pp. 215-273; the minister of confirmation, n. 15, p. 229, n. 2, p. 230.

[187] *Ibid.*, pp. 159-181; the minister of confirmation, n. 1, p. 164, also footnote 2, p. 164.

[188] Cf. the summary as given by DeClercq on pages 432-433. The legislation of the synods from the year 1850 to 1949 can be found in the second part of DeClercq's very scholarly study, *Conciles des Orientaux Catholiques* (Paris: Librairie LeTouzey et Ané, 1952). The summary for this period appears on page 1022.

[189] *Dictionnaire de Droit Canonique,* IV, 126.

among the Orientals in its proper perspective, it must be clearly understood that the priests of the Eastern rites enjoy a privilege and that the revocation of this privilege by the Holy See would make the contrary actions not only unlawful but also invalid, since the priest cannot validly confer this sacrament without having obtained a delegation from legitimate superior authority.[190]

190 *Ibid.*, p. 125.

PART II

CANONICAL COMMENTARY

CHAPTER III

PRELIMINARY NOTIONS

ARTICLE 1—JURIDIC NATURE OF THE DECREE *Spiritus Sancti munera*

To determine the precise canonical nature of the decree *Spiritus Sancti munera* is indeed a task which cannot be discharged with a few facile observations. Though many of the commentators have been satisfied with calling it a decree, an indult or a privilege without reflecting on its effect in the interpretation of the provisions of the decree, some have seriously grappled with the problem and proposed various solutions. Bergh calls it a general indult without any limit of time or of place.[1] Quinn classifies the decree as a general indult of the Holy See which has the force of law.[2] Pistoni calls it a papal faculty in the nature of a habitual faculty of canon 66, § 1, and applies the rules of rescripts and laws to its interpretation.[3] He also considers it a derogation of the law by which bishops in the Latin Church enjoy the prerogative to confirm. In doubt, therefore, the decree must be interpreted strictly as an incursion into the vested rights of others.[4]

Onclin refers to the decree as a decree-law, *"un décret-loi,"* a universal law of the Church drawn up according to the prescriptions of the Motu proprio *Cum iuris canonici* of Benedict XV (1914-1922), confirmed by the Pope and properly promulgated.[5] Conway points out that the new decree is not a mere

[1] "Administration de la confirmation aux fidèles dangereusement Malades" in *Nouvelle Revue Théologique,* LXIX (1947), 84 (hereafter listed as *NRT*).

[2] *The Extraordinary Minister of Confirmation According to the Most Recent Decrees of the Sacred Congregations,* p. 76.

[3] *De Confirmatione a Ministro Extraordinario,* p. 82.

[4] Cf. canon 50.

[5] "L'administration du Sacrement de la Confirmation en cas de danger de mort" in *Ephemerides Theologicae Lovanienses,* XXV (1949), 333 (hereafter listed as *ETL*).

indult granting certain privileges to certain persons; it is a general law of the Universal Church with the same solemnity and force as a canon of the *Code*.[6] He cites Cappello as his authority.[7] Regatillo considers the decree a law,[8] as does Mostaza, who takes note of the lack of unanimity among commentators on this point and then declares himself in favor of the school which regards the decree as a law; hence the primary principles of interpretation will be those which govern the interpretation of laws.[9]

There are two basic factors which contribute to the seemingly insurmountable task of determining the formal aspect of the decree, whether it is a new law, a derogation from the law, an exception to the law, an indult, a faculty or a privilege contained in a rescript, or perhaps a canonical combination of these. The first difficulty stems from the variable usage of the terms involved, most of which are nowhere specifically defined in the *Code*. Canon 4 mentions indults with no further explanation, canon 66, § 1, describes faculties as privileges *praeter ius*, and the whole fifth title of the first book (canons 63-79) deals with privileges but refrains from handing down a definition.[10] The second difficulty springs from the necessity of taking into consideration certain canonical provisions which already exist in virtue of the canons of the *Code* that pertain to the minister of confirmation.

One fundamental fact can be fairly well ascertained in the discussion on the juridic nature of the decree *Spiritus Sancti munera*. Under whatever formal aspect one chooses to regard the decree, one must at least admit that it has the binding force of a pontifical law, even though it was issued by the Sacred

[6] *Problems in Canon Law* (Dublin: Browne and Nolan, Limited, 1956, published here by Newman Press, Westminster, Maryland), p. 144.

[7] *Periodica*, XXXV (1946), 382: "Hoc decretum habet vim legis universalis pro tota Ecclesia latina."

[8] *Ius Sacramentarium* (2. ed., Santander: Sal Terrae, 1949), p. 58.

[9] *El Problema del Ministro Extraordinario de la Confirmación*, p. 347.

[10] Van Hove, *De Privilegiis—De Dispensationibus* (Mechliniae-Romae: H. Dessain, 1939), n. 9, p. 12; n. 11, p. 14.

Congregation for the Discipline of the Sacraments. Since the promulgation of the new Code of Canon Law, the Congregations are basically the administrative departments of the Church.[11] Pope Benedict XV in the Motu proprio which he issued on September 15, 1917,[12] set down the fundamental principle of present day legislation in regard to the value of the decrees issued by the sacred congregations. The sacred congregations were explicitly denied true legislative power.[13]

They no longer were to be capable of themselves to issue decrees which formally or equivalently would have the force of law. Their main function was to take care that the laws of the *Code* would be religiously observed and at times to issue opportune instructions which would serve to clarify the precepts of the *Code* and make them more effective. The fact that the decrees of the sacred congregations have the approbation of the Roman Pontiff [14] does not of that very fact change their nature from administrative decrees to pontifical laws. This approbation is usually given *in forma communi* or *in forma specifica.* Though confirmation *in forma communi* certainly adds greater weight and force to the contents of the enactment, the decree retains its original status, namely, an administrative act of the respective congregation. By virtue of the second type of confirmation, *in forma specifica,* the decree becomes the special act of the Roman Pontiff himself. It proceeds from the plenitude of his power and becomes a law, having the force of a papal constitution.[15]

[11] Cicognani, *Canon Law* (authorized English translation, 2. ed. revised, Philadelphia: The Dolphin Press, 1935), pp. 77, 78, 79.

[12] *AAS,* IX (1917), 483-484; also in the preface of the Gasparri edition of the Code.

[13] "Sacrae Romanae Congregationes nova decreta generalia iamnunc ne ferant, nisi qua gravis Ecclesiae universae necessitas aliud suadeat."—Preface to *Code,* p. LI.

[14] Canon 244, § 2; Gratiae quaevis ac resolutiones indigent pontificia approbatione. . . .

[15] Cf. Schmidt, *The Principles of Authentic Interpretation in Canon 17 of the Code of Canon Law,* The Catholic University of America Canon Law Studies, no. 141 (Washington, D. C.: The Catholic University of

Various expressions connote the type of approbation. The following formulae indicate an approbation conceded *in forma communi: "facto verbo cum Sanctissimo," "a S. Congr. ex audientia SSm̃i"* or *"SSm̃us D.N. resolutionem Em̃orum Patrum approbavit et confirmavit."* On the other hand, approbation granted *in forma specifica* is indicated by formulae such as the following: *"ex motu proprio," "ex certa scientia," "de apostolicae auctoritatis plenitudine declaramus, statuimus, etc.," "non obstante quacumque lege seu consuetudine in contrarium," "ab ipso Papa in audientia."* [16]

The commentators are unanimous in declaring that the decree *Spiritus Sancti munera* has specific approbation.[17] The terms which connote specific approbation are evident in the decree itself.[18] The very fact that the Holy Father declared that the decree should have the force of law,[19] established a definite date

America Press, 1941), article 5 of chapter 3, "The Competence of the Sacred Congregations for the Interpretation of Law," pp. 76-108; also Cicognani, *op. cit.*, pp. 80, 86.

[16] Cf. Sheehy, *The Sacred Congregation of the Sacraments, Its Competence in the Roman Curia,* The Catholic University of America Canon Law Studies, no. 333 (Washington, D. C.: The Catholic University of America Press, 1954), p. 114, footnote 11. The authorities cited are Cappello, Cocchi, Maroto and Beste.

[17] Bergh, "art. cit.," *NRT,* LXIX (1947), 83; Cappello, *De Sacramentis* (5 vols., Vol. I, 6. ed., Taurini-Romae: Marietti, 1953), I, n. 201 *bis,* p. 183; Crosignani, "De Extraordinario Confirmationis Ministro" in *Divus Thomas,* XXIV (1947), 92; Onclin, "art. cit.," *ETL,* XXV (1949), 334; Pistoni, *op. cit.*, p. 86; Quinn, *op. cit.*, p. 75; Mostaza, *op. cit.*, p. 346; Smiddy, *A Manual for the Extraordinary Minister of Confirmation,* p. 30; Zerba, *Commentarius in Decretum "Spiritus Sancti munera,"* p. 36. The statement by Cappello in the cited article in the *Periodica* (1946), p. 382, summarizes and explains the common opinion of all these commentators: "Decretum est vere et proprie pontificium, licet editum a S. Congregatione de Sacramentis, cum approbatum fuerit in forma specifica, a S. Pontifice eiusque iussu rite promulgatum, additis rubris 'contrariis quibuslibet etiam speciali mentione dignis, minime obstantibus.'"

[18] ". . . ab Ipso certa scientia et matura deliberatione . . ."—*AAS,* XXXVIII (1946), 352; ". . . contrariis quibuslibet etiam speciali mentione dignis, minime obstantibus . . . ," p. 353.

[19] ". . . vim legis habere incipiat"—p. 353.

for it to acquire juridical force,[20] and ordered it to be published and promulgated in the *Acta Apostolicae Sedis,* gives more than ample proof that this decree binds as a law.

Onclin analysed the Motu proprio of Benedict XV cited above, and concluded that a sacred congregation in one instance has the power to promulgate a law, namely, if a serious universal need of the Church should demand it. In this case the Motu proprio declared:

> III. If in the course of time, the good of the whole Church will demand that a new general decree be drawn up by some sacred Congregation, that congregation shall draw it up; but if it disagrees with the prescription of the *Code,* the Pope is to be informed of the difference. After the decree has been approved by tht Pope, the same congregation is to refer it to the Commission whose duty it will be to adapt the canon and canons according to the text of the decree.[21]

This pressing need for new legislation to extend the number of extraordinary ministers of confirmation was sufficiently urgent to empower the congregation to promulgate a new law. Indeed the decree itself expressed this urgent motivation.[22] Thus, Onclin argued, since there was a sufficiently grave cause for the decree as demanded in the Motu proprio, the new decree must be considered as a law.[23]

One factor, however, seems lacking in the estimation of the present writer. There was no accompanying official declaration on the part of the Commission for the Authentic Interpretation of the Canons of the Code regarding the manner in which this new law was to amend the *Code.* Was it to be an extension of canon 782, § 2, or canon 782, § 3, or was it to stand as a separate canon in itself?

20 ". . . a die la Ianuarii, 1947"—*loc. cit.*

21 Preface to the *Code,* p. LI.

22 ". . . necessarium visum est huic S. Congregationi remedium aliquod exquirere ac suppeditare hac gravissima de causa, ut tam notabili fidelium numero offeratur occasio confirmationis suscipiendae."—*AAS,* XXXVIII (1946), 351. The Holy Father himself by a special mandate commissioned the congregation to draw up the decree, p. 352.

23 "Art. cit.," *ETL,* XXV (1949), 333.

Whatever explanation may be adopted, one can safely say that this decree has the authority of a general law. Indeed it is the conclusion and contention of this writer that this decree not only has the force of law but actually was issued *per modum legis* in virtue of a special mandate of the Roman Pontiff, that is, with his special approbation and duly authorized promulgation.[24]

If this were the sole issue at stake, one could dismiss the problem and state that the decree *Spiritus Sancti munera* is a pontifical, universal law. To do so, however, would perforce lead to certain apparently untenable conclusions. Thus, Regatillo denies that the power of pastors to confirm in danger of death is a privilege and maintains that it is an ordinary power attached by law to an office in the sense of canon 197.[25]

Bergh declares that it would be canonically correct to speak of power delegated by law (*potestas a iure delegata*).[26] Thus the decree would seem to be an extension of canon 782, § 3, which enumerates those who can confirm as empowered *a iure*. However, just previous to the above quoted statement, Bergh speaks of the decree's being presented to us as an application of canon 782, § 2, in virtue of which *indults* of the Holy See can constitute extraordinary ministers of confirmation.[27] As will be shown later, the present writer is in accord with the line of reasoning which makes the decree an extension of the second, not the third, paragraph of canon 782.

To eliminate over-simplification of the problem, which would result in an incomplete evaluation of the juridic nature of the decree, one must, consequently, introduce two other concepts, the canonical concept of indult and of privilege.

Commonly understood, an indult is a temporary concession granted by a superior.

> Indultum est quaelibet largitio favorabilis aliquem determinatum actum ponendi, et eatenus a privilegio differt, quod

[24] Quinn (*op. cit.*, footnote 30, pp. 75-76), denies that the decree was issued *ad modum legis*.

[25] *Op. cit.*, p. 58.

[26] "Art. cit.," *NRT*, LXIX (1947), 84.

[27] *Loc. cit.*

ad tempus tantum tribuitur, dum, e contra, privilegium est largitio permanens.[28]

As noted previously, the term 'indult' does not have a precise meaning. It could be the equivalent of a particular privilege granted for a limited time, or a negative privilege which exempts one from the observance of a law. Michiels notes that some authors feel that the term 'indult' signifies the manner of the specific act by which privileges are conceded in opposition to privileges granted by law, custom, or acquired by way of legal prescription.[29] Vermeersch—Creusen refer to indults as the *"fons uberrimus privilegiorum."* [30]

In relation to the present discussion Onclin made a very pointed and appropriate distinction. In the formal sense an indult is an administrative act by which the Holy See grants a favor; in the material sense it is the favor itself.[31] Since an indult usually is of a temporary nature, the decree *Spiritus Sancti munera* cannot be considered such under a formal aspect, since the concession as granted is not limited either by time or by place, and was given as a pontifical law with the specific approbation of the Holy Father. However, the decree can be considered as an indult under the material aspect.

The wording of the decree necessitates the introduction of the concept of indult, for therein it is stated, ". . . ex generali Apostolicae Sedis indulto tamquam ministris extraordinariis facultas tribuitur. . . ." [32] This evidently was done with a view to maintaining the already existing distinction between the two classes of extraordinary ministers of confirmation, by special indult and by law.[33]

[28] Beste, *Introductio in Codicem* (3. ed., Collegeville, Minn.: St. John's Abbey Press, 1946), *super can.* 4, p. 57.

[29] *Normae Generales Iuris Canonici* (2. ed., Parisiis-Tornaci-Romae: Typis Societatis S. Joannis Evangelistae Desclée et Socii, 1949), I, p. 94, footnote 6.

[30] *Epitome Iuris Canonici* (7. ed., 3 vols., Vol. I, Mechliniae-Romae: H. Dessain, 1949), I, n. 74, p. 71.

[31] "Art. cit.," *ETL,* XXV (1949), 334.

[32] *AAS,* XXXVIII (1946), 352.

[33] Cf. canon 782, paragraphs 2 and 3.

There was an important effect of this distinction. Canon 782, § 4, places a restriction upon the faculty of the priests of the Latin rite who enjoy the power to confirm in virtue of an indult, namely, they can validly confirm only the faithful of their own rite. This limitation apparently does not affect the extraordinary ministers who in virtue of canon 782, § 3, enjoy this faculty by law. The Congregation thus expressed its intention that the new list of extraordinary ministers pertain to the former class. This conclusion is corroborated by the fact that the Sacred Congregation for the Oriental Church deemed it necessary to issue a year and half later a special decree which empowered the priests of the Latin rite who enjoyed an indult to validly confirm certain Orientals. In this decree specific mention was made of the increased danger of the invalid administration of confirmation to members of the Oriental rites, especially subsequent to the decree *Spiritus Sancti munera.*[34]

The second part of the decree *Spiritus Sancti munera,* which contains the discipline of the Code pertaining to confirmation, is entitled, *"Disciplina Codicis I.C. Servanda in Confirmatione Conferenda Vi Huius Apostolici Indulti."*[35] Accordingly the writer feels that the decree *Spiritus Sancti munera* can properly be considered as an extension of the second paragraph of canon 782, though nothing to that effect is anywhere expressly mentioned. The canon would read, if the *Code* were to be revised, "Extraordinarius minister est presbyter, cui vel iure communi vel peculiari Sedis Apostolicae indulto vel ex generali Apostolicae Sedis indulto ea facultas concessa est." That is why this concept must be taken into consideration in the final evaluation of the canonical nature of the decree under discussion.

What about the nature of the faculty itself? How should this power to confirm be regarded? First and foremost, whether conferred in the law or by means of an indult, it must be considered as a privilege.[36] A privilege can be considered objec-

[34] *AAS,* XL (1948), 422.

[35] *AAS,* XXXVIII (1946), 354.

[36] The canons on the extraordinary minister use both *"facultas"* and *"privilegium apostolicum": facultas,* canon 782, paragraphs 2, 3, 4 and 5; *privilegium,* canons 782, § 5, 784, 785, § 2. The faculty which cardinals en-

tively as a special and permanent faculty granted by a superior for acting contrary to or outside or beyond the limits set by the law.[37] In a strict sense, a privilege is a particular favorable rule given to determined persons or places or things, but not in the manner of a law. In a broad sense, it is generally established by a law through which some prerogative is granted to a certain category or kind of persons, places or things. A privilege in this sense is properly a law, and therefore it has a perpetual character and needs promulgation, not because it is a privilege, but because it partakes of the nature of a law.[38] Acceptance on the part of the beneficiary is not necessary, nor does the privilege cease by renunciation. This description fits in perfectly with the nature of the privilege of confirming which was granted by means of the decree *Spiritus Sancti munera.* As Roelker notes, it must be borne in mind that a *privilegium late sumptum* is not thereby an improper privilege or that the word privilege is employed merely in an accommodated sense. A real concession is made and the word privilege is properly used.[39]

A further analysis of the nature of this privilege reveals that it is a real privilege, for it attaches to an office. Hence it is a muneral privilege, although it is actually exercised by a person because of his relation to that office. It is a *privilegium gratiosum,* which finds its source in the pure liberality of the superior; it is a *privilegium conditionale,* since it has effect only under certain conditions; it is a *privilegium scriptum,* granted by direct concession of the lawmaker; it is a *privilegium perpetuum,* conceded without limit of time; it is a *privilegium commune,* granted for the common good, and accordingly cannot be renounced by the individual. Thus canon 72, § 4, rather than canon 69, has application.

Is this privilege one that is to be considered as *praeter ius* or

---

joy to administer confirmation is listed in the lengthy canon which enumerates their privileges, canon 239, § 1, n. 23.

[37] Beste, *op. cit.,* p. 57.

[38] Roelker, *Principles of Privilege According to the Code of Canon Law,* The Catholic University of America Canon Law Studies, no. 35 (Washington, D. C.: The Catholic University of America, 1926), p. 19.

[39] *Op. cit.,* p. 8.

contra ius? The answer to this question is of prime importance, for it will determine the rules of interpretation of the decree. After much deliberation and thought, the present writer chooses to call it a privilege *praeter ius* rather than *contra ius.* The first inclination was to classify it in the latter category, especially in consideration of Van Hove's description of a *privilegium contra ius,* wherein he declares that it is a privilege which induces a juridic condition by which something is permitted which is prohibited by law, or that some prerogative is conceded which the legislator by his law exclusively reserved to certain persons or classes of persons, or that there is involved the omission of something which is prescribed by law, e.g., subjection to the ordinary.[40]

The second phase of the description seemed aptly to indicate the juridic condition which the decree *Spiritus Sancti munera* effects. Yet upon closer examination one must admit that the faculty conceded in the decree does not empower a priest to confirm as an *ordinary* minister, and thus it is not constituted as a privilege contrary to canon 782, § 1, for that kind of privilege in any case could never be granted, since it would be contrary to the Tridentine definition. Rather, the decree constitutes the priest as an extraordinary minister for whom provisions are made in canon 782, § 2. Thus, one could more suitably say that this concession is a *privilegium praeter ius* in the sense that something is conceded which is neither forbidden nor granted by law, though nevertheless the concession of an authority is necessary if the priest is to enjoy this certain prerogative.[41] Privileges which by common or particular law regard certain persons or classes of persons can be granted to others apart from any determination of the right as being exclusive to those persons. Thus, in a proper sense, an extension to other persons or classes of persons is not against but outside the law. Concessions of this kind are exceptions in a certain measure from the common law, but such concessions do not militate against the common norm, but simply lie outside its orbit.

In summarizing the discussion on the juridical status of the

[40] *De Privilegiis—De Dispensationibus,* n. 33, p. 33.

[41] Van Hove, *op. cit., loc. cit.*

decree *Spiritus Sancti munera* one can consider it as a pontifical law which, so to speak, automatically confers upon the properly enumerated persons an indult whereby they receive a privilege which empowers them to confirm as long as they remain in the capacity envisaged by the law. Admittedly, this may seem to be a strange canonical concept, difficult to grasp at first sight, but the writer fails to see how any simpler solution can reconcile the various complicated dogmatic and canonical implications which one must consider when dealing with the question. Quinn calls the decree "a privilege granted by general indult of the Holy See, which has the force of law."[42] The present writer classifies it as a law granting an indult which confers a privilege, a law which grants pastors and certain other priests the power to confirm *ex indulto,* but not by ordinary power.

Article 2—Interpretation of the Decree

The analysis of the juridic nature of *Spiritus Sancti munera* has resulted in the declaration that this decree is to be considered primarily as a pontifical law which conceded an indult containing a privilege. Thus, in interpreting the provisions of the decree one must first apply the rules of the *Code* for the interpretation of laws and only subsidiarily those which relate to the interpretation of privileges.[43]

The purpose of the interpretation of a law is to ascertain its meaning according to the mind of the legislator. This can be attained through the application of various rules. The first of these is that ecclesiastical law must be understood according to the proper meaning of the words in their usual and juridical sense according to text and context. One should read integrally the words and phrases and compare the order and connection of the various provisions made. If the law's meaning remains

[42] *The Extraordinary Minister of Confirmation,* p. 76.

[43] Onclin, "art. cit.," *ETL,* XXV (1949), 334; Mostaza, *El Problema del Ministro Extraordinario de la Confirmación,* p. 347; Vermeersch-Creusen, *Epitome,* I, n. 183, pp. 169-170. Michiels (*Normae Generales,* II, 579-582) discusses the argumentations of the two different schools of thought on whether canons 67, 68, 49 and 50, or canons 18 and 19, are to be followed in the interpretation of privileges conceded in a law.

doubtful, obscure, or both, one may seek clarification by recourse to parallel texts, in the *Code*, if there are any, to the end (*finis*) of the law, to the circumstances of its enactment, and to the mind of the legislator.[44] Abbo-Hannan caution against the danger of confusing the end or motive of the law with the will of the legislator. The purpose of the law may not be called upon to include cases not clearly within its scope, unless the legislator would stand accused of imprudence, injustice or unreasonableness if the law were not to apply to those cases.[45]

Another reason for a broad interpretation of the provisions of the decree stems from the conclusion that the privilege is *praeter ius* and as such is usually to be interpreted widely.[46] The fact that the privilege to confirm is given, not for an individual or personal good, but for the common good of the faithful must also be considered as favoring a benign interpretation.[47]

Is it allowed to extend to others a privilege which is conceded by law? Cappello and Vermeersch-Creusen hold that in doubt one can do so. This is especially true if the legislator expressly states the reason for the privilege and if the person to whom it is to be extended has an equal or greater reason for possessing the privilege. This does not seem to be an extension of the privilege; it rather appears as a declaration of the mind of the legislator who remained tacit in this particular case. V. de Giudice even holds for an analogical application of such a privilege as being in accordance with canon 20 which supplies for the silence of the law.[48]

In any case, obviously, an extension is not allowed against the will of the legislator if he specifies that he intends to reserve the privilege to certain persons to whom it is conceded. In this instance it seems that the provision of canon 67 must exert its full force, namely that a privilege must neither be extended nor restricted. Hence a person with even a better reason for enjoy-

[44] Canon 18.

[45] *The Sacred Canons* (revised ed., 2 vols., St. Louis: B. Herder Co., 1957), I, 38.

[46] Van Hove, *op. cit.*, n. 183, p. 171.

[47] Vermeersch-Creusen, *op. cit.*, I, n. 179, p. 164.

[48] Cf. Van Hove, *op. cit.*, nn. 179-181, pp. 169-170.

ing the privilege would nevertheless not possess it without a specific concession.[49]

Such must be the principle which will govern one's interpretation with reference to the list of extraordinary ministers of confirmation as enumerated in the decree. The legislator, evidently influenced by historical considerations, and fully conscious of the dignity of the privilege and prerogative that would be conferred, expressly presented an exhaustive or exclusive list, commonly described as a *taxativa enumeratio.* In the words of the decree, "the faculty is granted in only the cases and exclusively under the conditions enumerated below, to the following priests and to them alone." [50]

To include any minister not specifically listed appears manifestly to be against the will of the legislator and to result in an improper extension. As will be noted, the exclusive enumeration creates a number of lacunae in the decree, i.e., situations where there would be no extraordinary minister available to administer confirmation to someone in danger of death. Some commentators, notably Regatillo, have tried to supply this lack by an appeal to the purpose of the decree and the intention of the legislator. Though such an extension may appear highly desirable, it seems much safer canonically to abide by the conclusion of Zerba that one must accept the will of the legislator in accordance with the axiom, *"Quod ipse voluit, expressit; quod noluit, tacuit."* [51]

Had the decree conferred this faculty in general terms upon pastors and their equivalents, or upon priests who have the care of souls, then an extension would have been perfectly permissible, especially since the terms could have been given a wide interpretation. However, the fact remains that the enumeration is restrictive and cannot be considered as simply illustrative; hence, it cannot be extended for any reason. Only by keeping

[49] Roelker, *Principles of Privilege According to the Code of Canon Law,* p. 73.

[50] "... sequentibus presbyteris, iisdemque dumtaxat ..."—*AAS,* XXXVIII (1946), 352.

[51] Zerba, *Commentarius,* p. 50. Cf. Bastnagel, "Parochial Vicars and the Faculty to Confer Confirmation," *The Jurist,* VII (1947), 178-179.

this principle in mind does the writer feel that he will arrive at the correct interpretation which is necessary to preserve the valid administration of the sacrament.[52]

Before entering upon the discussion of the different classes of extraordinary ministers of confirmation, one should note briefly that they automatically enjoy the faculty of confirming within their territory immediately upon taking canonical possession of their office.[53] The conferring of an ecclesiastical office consists in the designation of the appointee, in the granting of title to the office, and in the installation in office, that is, the formal act whereby possession of the office is gained. Either some form of corporal installation or an express dispensation from it is required, but the legitimate custom of the country as well as some specific local ruling can indicate the method for the corporal installation (*missio in possessionem*), the execution of which may either be concomitant with the appointment or achieve its effect at a later specified date.

The privilege is lost upon the cessation of the office[54] as a result either of the death of the incumbent, or of a fully free renunciation of the office when the acceptance of it has been duly intimated to the one who renounced it,[55] or of a lawful exchange of benefices between two pastors,[56] or of an administrative transferral to another parish,[57] or of an administrative removal in accordance with canons 2142 ff., or finally, of a deprivation of the office because of a delict which has deposition, or degradation, or both of these, as a consequence.[58] A malicious and deliberate transgression of the limits of the faculty will result in the automatic loss of the faculty in accordance with canon 2365.

[52] Cf. Pistoni, *De Confirmatione a Ministro Extraordinario,* p. 87.

[53] Concerning pastors, cf. canons 461, 1443-1445.

[54] Cf. canon 183, § 1.

[55] Canon 186.

[56] Canon 1487, § 1.

[57] Canons 193-194.

[58] Cf. canons 2298, 2303 and 1576.

CHAPTER IV

THE EXTRAORDINARY MINISTERS OF CONFIRMATION ACCORDING TO THE PROVISIONS OF *SPIRITUS SANCTI MUNERA*

Article 1—Pastors with Proper Territory

First and foremost among those upon whom was conferred the faculty to confirm are pastors of territorial parishes.[1] As a general rule, a diocese is divided into distinct territorial parts; and to each part there is assigned a church with a definite group of the faithful and a particular rector must be placed over it as its proper pastor for the requisite care of souls.[2] Each such territorial division is called a parish.[3] The pastor, therefore, according to canon law, is defined as a priest or a moral person upon whom a parish has been conferred in title, with the care of souls to be exercised under the authority of the local ordinary[4] with the right and duty of preaching and administering the sacraments to a specific body of the faithful who are obliged to be the passive subjects of his ministry.[5]

To settle various doubts and disputes concerning the nature of parishes in the United States and in general of those which had been subject to the Sacred Congregation for the Propagation of the Faith prior to the constitution of St. Pius X, *Sapienti Consilio,* issued June 29, 1908,[6] the Sacred Consistorial Congregation on August 1, 1919, promulgated a declaration[7] which affirmed that such parts of the diocese which had a particular

1 ". . . parochis proprio territorio gaudentibus"—*AAS,* XXXVIII (1946), n. 1 (a), p. 352.

2 Canon 216, § 1.

3 Canon 216, § 3.

4 Canon 451, § 1.

5 Abbo-Hannan, *op. cit.,* I, 445.

6 *Fontes,* n. 682.

7 *AAS,* XI (1919), 346.

rector assigned to them for the care of souls were thereafter to be considered and called parishes, whereas the name of quasi-parish or mission was to be reserved for those parts into which vicariates and prefectures apostolic were divided for the care of souls.[8] Mention was also made that, for the erecting of a parish, the decree of the ordinary had to define the boundaries of its territory, assign a parochial residence, and determine an endowment for the need of public worship and the support of the priest.

In the ensuing years the canonical nature of the parishes in the United States and the status of their pastors still remained uncertain. To resolve all doubt, the Apostolic Delegate to this country, Giovanni Bonzano (1911-1922), submitted to the Pontifical Commission for the Authentic Interpretation of the Canons of the Code the following question in a letter dated March 20, 1921:

> For the erection of a parish which does not have the character of a benefice (1) is it necessary that the Ordinary should issue a formal decree declaring explicitly that he erects a certain district into a parish; or (2) is it sufficient that, having divided a certain territory into several districts, the respective limits of which are definitely indicated, he assigns to each district a rector to take charge of the people and the church thereto pertaining, according to canon 216, numbers 1 and 3.[9]

Under the date of September 26, 1921, His Eminence, Cardinal Gasparri, the president of the commission, replied: "*Negative ad primam partem,*" i.e., a special decree of the Ordinary is not necessary for the erection of a parish; and "*affirmative ad secundam partem,*" i.e., it is sufficient for the erection of a parish that the ordinary define the territorial limits and assign a rector to the people and the church within said limits.[10] The Cardinal,

[8] Canon 216, § 3.

[9] Bouscaren, *The Canon Law Digest,* 3 Volumes and Supplements through 1956, Milwaukee: Bruce & Co., (1934-1957) Vol. I (1934), 150.

[10] *Canon Law Digest, loc. cit.* For a precise development of the canonical argumentation that a decree of erection, though it is the usual way of constituting a parish, does not seem necessary for its valid erection, cf. the resolution of the Sacred Congregation of the Council in a case submitted to it by the bishop of the diocese of Prince Albert and Saskatoon, Canada,

moreover, added that a parish is always an ecclesiastical benefice, according to canon 1411, no. 5,[11] not only when it has the proper endowment (resources or revenue) as described in canon 1410, but also when, though lacking such endowment (resources or revenue), it is erected according to the provisions of canon 1415, § 3.[12]

The Cardinal also declared, in answer to another question, that no formal decree of the ordinary was necessary to constitute as canonical parishes those which previous to the promulgation of the new *Code* had been established as described in the previous question. Such parishes automatically became canonical parishes upon the promulgation of the *Code.*

In a letter to the bishops of the United States, transmitted on the 10th of November, 1922, the Apostolic Delegate concluded with the following statement:

> It is evident from the official answer that all the parishes of the United States having the three necessary qualifications, viz., (1) a resident pastor; (2) endowment (resources or revenues according to the provisions of canons 1410 or 1415, § 3); and (3) boundaries, are not only parishes in the strict canonical sense, but also ecclesiastical benefices. Hence, pastors in the United States are real canonical pastors (*parochi*) having all the duties and obligations pertaining to such an office. . . .[13]

Therefore, there is no doubt that the pastors of the territorial parishes in our country are to be included in the first category of those who enjoy the faculty of confirming in danger of death. They are truly *"parochi proprio territorio gaudentes."* It makes no difference whether they enjoy the status of a removable or of an irremovable pastor.[14]

March 5, 1932. The resolution was approved and confirmed by Pope Pius XI in the audience of March 20, 1932.—*AAS,* XXV (1933), 436-438.

[11] Beneficia ecclesiastica dicuntur . . . curata vel non curata, prout curam animarum adnexam habent vel non.

[12] Non prohibetur tamen, ubi congrua dos constitui nequeat, paroecias aut quasi-paroecias erigere, si prudenter praevideat ea quae necessaria sunt aliunde non defutura.

[13] *Canon Law Digest,* I, 151.

[14] Cf. canon 454.

Article 2—Pastors with Cumulative Territory

The competence of a pastor may be determined not only by territory but by the quality of the subjects, or by a combination of quality and territory.[15] Thus, in addition to territorial parishes, where people are grouped by domicile or quasi-domicile,[16] the *Code* also considers other parishes, namely, such as are established in the same city or territory for the faithful of a different language or nationality,[17] as well as merely family or personal parishes. Without a special apostolic indult such parishes cannot be erected, nor can anything be changed in regard to such parishes when already established, without a consultation of the Holy See.[18] One should note in passing that canon 216 does not prohibit the erection of national parishes, should the need arise in the future. Nor does it abrogate or abolish the national parishes which existed before the *Code*. In fact, they are definitely designated as parishes.

Since family or personal parishes, which are constituted of persons belonging to a definite family, rank, or class, e.g., a royal family, are not known in the United States, there is no need to make them a subject of a canonical commentary. In any case, unless the pastors of these parishes enjoy cumulative territory, they do not possess the faculty to confirm.[19] However, language and national parishes are quite numerous in the United States;

[15] Vermeersch-Creusen, *Epitome,* I, n. 537, p. 401.

[16] Canon 92, § 1.—Domicilium acquiritur commoratione in aliqua paroecia aut quasi-paroecia, . . . ; quae commoratio vel coniuncta sit cum animo ibi perpetuo manendi, si nihil inde avocet, vel sit protracta ad decennium completum.

Canon 92, § 2.—Quasi-domicilium acquiritur commoratione uti supra, quae vel coniuncta sit cum animo ibi manendi saltem ad maiorem anni partem, si nihil inde avocet, vel sit reapse protracta ad maiorem anni partem.

[17] It appears from the context of the canon and from a subsequent response of the Pontifical Commission for the Authentic Interpretation of the Code that the words "*pro diversitate sermonis seu nationis*" are to be taken disjunctively. Cf. *AAS,* XVI (1924), 113.

[18] Canon 216, § 4.

[19] *AAS,* XXXVIII (1946), n. 1 (a), p. 352.

hence the pastors of these parishes, who constitute a species of the generic class of personal pastors, must be here considered.

Polish immigrants and their descendants number about six million today; they maintain approximately 900 parishes.[20] It is estimated that the Italian immigrants and their descendants also number six million.[21] The Czechs maintain over 120 parishes, while the Slovaks maintain over 200 parishes;[22] the Roman Catholic Croatians and Slovenes maintain 45 parishes, the Croatians 33, the Hungarians 58, and the Lithuanians 120.[23] The French-Canadian immigrants number between 2.5 and 3 million.[24]

Although it is difficult to give accurate statistics because of constantly changing situations throughout the various dioceses in the country, nevertheless one can conservatively estimate that there are nearly 2,000 language parishes. These parishes for the most part are what can be called mixed parishes, since in addition to a definite congregation determined by language or nationality they have a more or less determined territory.[25] There is no doubt that these are true canonical parishes.[26]

To say that the national parishes have no territory would not be absolutely correct. Besides the primary characteristic that they exist as personal parishes for a definite language group, their secondary characteristic is that the latter group is composed of a particular people in a certain locality within reasonable distance of the church which is erected for them. Therefore it must be concluded that the parish is also territorial. Though sometimes not outlined by clear and distinct boundaries, a certain

[20] *The Catholic Church, U.S.A.* (Chicago: Fides Publishers Association, 1956, edited by Louis J. Putz), chap. VIII, "Nationalities and American Catholicism," by John Thomas (pp. 155-176), p. 170.

[21] *Loc. cit.*

[22] *Ibid.*, p. 171.

[23] *Ibid.*, p. 172.

[24] *Ibid.*, p. 173.

[25] Cf. Ciesluk, *National Parishes in the United States,* The Catholic University of America Canon Law Studies, no. 190 (Washington, D. C.: The Catholic University of America Press, 1944), pp. 49-50.

[26] Ciesluk, *op. cit.*, p. 51.

district could be called the territory of the national parish, with the approval and understanding of the local ordinary.[27] Indeed one can safely say that the pastors of our national parishes enjoy territory cumulatively with the territorial or local pastors and thus enjoy the power to confirm. They are pastors in the true sense with all corresponding rights and duties.[28]

However, if it can be shown that a particular pastor of a national parish does not enjoy territorial limits, then it seems that he must be denied the power to confirm, since he must then be considered as a purely personal pastor; and this power was accorded to personal pastors and pastors of national parishes only when they have charge of all persons of a given class living in a definitely determined territory. On the other hand, by a strange anomaly of law, since the territory of a national pastor is very often coextensive with the territories of several local pastors,[29] the power of such a pastor to confirm is more extensive than that of the territorial pastor inasmuch as territory and not personal relationship is the basis for the valid and lawful use of this faculty.[30]

What is to be said of parishes established for the colored people? Abbo-Hannan in their commentary declare that a parish established for negroes within the confines of a territorial parish should be regarded as the equivalent of a national parish. Even though all the parishioners live entirely in a compact neighborhood inhabited solely by negroes, the parish is not to be considered territorial.[31]

Bastnagel differs on both points and holds that, since a territorial parish responds to the needs of the general population which in a well defined district speaks a uniform tongue and is

[27] Ciesluk, *op. cit.*, p. 50.

[28] Ciesluk, *op. cit.*, p. 111.

[29] Donovan in *Homiletic and Pastoral Review,* L (Oct. '49-March '50), 286: ". . . the proper territory is a regular parish, and this can be a national parish within the limits of a regular parish or overlapping two or more parishes, as well as the ordinary parish using the dominant language of the country . . ."

[30] Cf. articles 2 and 3 (a) of chapter VI, pp. 117; 120 ff.

[31] *The Sacred Canons,* I, 278.

of the same nationality, a church erected in a specific district which is solely inhabited by negroes is to be regarded as a territorial parochial church, which can be established without the intervention of a special apostolic indult.[32] If, however, the parish is established for the exclusive use of the negro people as distinguished from the general population, it is to be considered as a personal parish in the sense of canon 216, § 4. Since diversity of language or of nationality does not obtain in the case, the factor for the specification of parochial membership must correspondingly be sought in the diversity which exists between the white population and the negroes as specifically distinguished personal groups. Only if nationality is considered in its secondary meaning, as something characteristic of people of common origin rather than from the standpoint of political unity, could the parishes for the colored fall under the classification of a parish established *"pro diversitate nationis."* [33]

The latter argumentation seems perfectly reasonable and more acceptable. Whether one considers such parishes as national or personal parishes makes little difference in reference to the extraordinary minister of confirmation, inasmuch as the pastor, if he shares territory cumulatively with the local or territorial pastor, enjoys the power to confirm in virtue of the first category enumerated in the decree *Spiritus Sancti munera.*

It is the opinion of the present writer that quasi-pastors are not included under the listing of category (a). Zerba, Onclin and Quinn appeal to canon 451, § 2. Other commentators include them under category (c). The discussion of the entire question will be reserved for a subsequent article.[34]

Article 3—Vicars Who Are Included

In the second category (b) of extraordinary ministers of confirmation, the decree chooses two vicars from among the five types of vicars enumerated by the *Code.*[35] Only the vicar of

[35] Lib. II, cap. X, "De Vicariis Paroecialibus."

[32] "Is a Parish for Colored People a 'National' Parish?"—*The Ecclesiastical Review,* CVIII (1943), 383, 384.

[33] "Art. cit.," p. 383.

[34] Article 1, chapter V, pp. 107 ff.

canon 471 and the vicar econome are to enjoy the power to confirm.[36]

The rights and duties of a pastor may be enjoyed not only by a physical person but also by a moral personality, i.e., a juridical person such as a monastery, cathedral chapter, or seminary.[37] A parish may be united by the Apostolic See to a monastery or to a religious house only as to temporalities (*"quoad temporalia tantum"*), so that it remain a secular benefice and the religious house shares only in the income of the parish. The religious superior must present to the local ordinary a priest of the secular clergy who is to be installed as pastor, and a suitable portion of the parochial income must be allotted to him in compensation for his services.[38]

On the other hand, a parish may be joined to a moral entity, either collegiate or non-collegiate, *"pleno iure,"* that is, both as to temporalities and also with reference to the called for spiritual ministrations. This, of course, can be done only by way of an indult of the Holy See.[39] Under this arrangement, the title of pastor attaches to the moral personality.[40] However, a vicar, who must be a religious of the particular community if the moral entity is a religious house,[41] is to be appointed with full charge of the spiritual administrations.[42] The *Code* does not designate him with any particular term; it simply speaks of him as a parochial vicar who exercise the actual care of souls.[43] The decree retains this impersonal and innonimate designation and simply refers to these vicars as the *"vicarii de quibus in canone*

[36] *AAS,* XXXVIII (1946) n. 1 (b), p. 352.

[37] Cf. canon 451, § 1.—Parochus est sacerdos vel persona moralis. . . .

[38] Canon 1425, § 1.

[39] Canon 452, § 1.

[40] Canon 452, § 1.—Persona moralis, cui paroecia sit pleno iure unita, habitualem tantum curam animarum retinere potest. . . .

[41] Compare canon 1452, § 2, with canon 456. Cf. Golden, *Parochial Benefices in the New Code,* A Dissertation Submitted to the Faculty of Sacred Sciences of the Catholic University of America (1921), pp. 56-57. (No number or publisher given.)

[42] Canons 452, § 2, and 471, § 1.

[43] Canon 471, § 1.—. . . vicarius, qui actualem curam gerat animarum. . . .

471." Since the vicar enjoys the exclusive care of souls with all the rights and obligations of pastors according to the norms of the universal law, of the approved diocesan statutes, and of the entrenched praiseworthy customs,[44] it is only fitting and logical that the power to confirm should have been granted to him in the decree *Spiritus Sancti munera.*

In this country, however, it seems that most of the parishes which are placed under the care of the religious are not fully incorporated; rather, they are simply entrusted to the religious [45] without being juridically incorporated with the religious community. This type of relationship can derive its existence through an act of the Apostolic Delegate, who has the faculty to permit local ordinaries to entrust temporarily a parish to a religious group because of the insufficient number of the secular clergy in the diocese.[46] The religious who is appointed as pastor by the local ordinary is in reality a *"parochus"* in the sense of canon 630, § 1,[47] rather than the vicar who receives mention in canon 471.[48] Hence, he has the faculty to confirm in virtue of being included in category (a) rather than in category (b).[49]

The other vicar to whom the decree expressly gives the power to confirm is the vicar econome, who is often called the administrator. At this point a very important question must be resolved. Is the term to be limited to its strictest meaning to include only the vicar econome described in canon 472, n. 1, or is it to also include the administrators mentioned in canon 472, n. 2? The former can be considered as administrators appointed by the

[44] Canon 471, § 4.

[45] Canon 456.—. . . religiosis concredita. . . .

[46] Bouscaren, *The Canon Law Digest,* I, 184.

[47] Religiosus, qui paroeciam regit sive titulo parochi. . .

[48] Cf. Comyns, "The Relation of the Religious Pastor to the Local Ordinary," *The Jurist,* XV (1955), 187. Another excellent discussion of the canonical status of parishes held by religious in the United States was given by Dooley at the annual national meeting of the Canon Law Society of America, held Oct. 12-13, 1954, at Boston, Mass. The paper was printed in *The Jurist,* XV (1955), part I, pp. 225-251; part II, pp. 393-421.

[49] Smiddy, *A Manual for the Extraordinary Minister of Confirmation,* p. 35.

bishop, the latter, as administrators appointed by law. Authorities can be quoted for both sides. Zerba,[50] Pistoni,[51] Smiddy,[52] Connell,[53] Quinn,[54] Conway, (who states that there is little room for doubt on this point),[55] Bastnagel[56] and Coronata[57] include only the vicar econome, and exclude the senior curate or the neighboring pastor in the interim between the death of the pastor and the appointment of the new administrator. Cappello explains *"vicarii oeconomi"* as those who rule a vacant parish; he does not enumerate the neighboring pastor in the list of those who are excluded.[58] On the other hand, Onclin, who maintains that he is following the majority of the commentators,[59] Regatillo,[60] Mostaza, who also claims to follow the majority opinion,[61] Bergh[62] and Naz[63] favor the inclusion of the adminis-

[50] *Commentarius,* pp. 48, 49.

[51] *De Confirmatione a Ministro Extraordinario,* pp. 89, 93.

[52] *Op. cit.,* pp. 35, 36-37.

[53] "The Recent Decree Empowering Priests to Confirm," *The American Ecclesiastical Review,* CXVI (1947), 258 (hereafter listed as *AER*).

[54] *The Extraordinary Minister of Confirmation,* pp. 87, 90.

[55] *Problems in Canon Law,* p. 154.

[56] "Art cit.," *The Jurist,* VII (1947), 178, 179.

[57] *De Sacramentis,* I, n. 167 *bis,* pp. 126, 127.

[58] *De Sacramentis,* I, n. 201 *bis,* p. 183.

[59] "Art. cit.," *ETL,* XXV (1949), 339, 340. In footnote 24 of page 340 he also cites A. Bride, "Décret 'Spiritus Sancti Munera,' Commentaire Canonique," *L'Ami du Clergé,* LVII (1947), 408; W. Mulders, "Het H. Vormsel in Stervensgevaar," *Nederlandsche Katholieke Stemmen,* XLIII (1947), 117; H. DeMesmaecher, "De Ministro Extraordinario Confirmationis," *Collectanea Mechliniensia,* XVII (1947), 411. Bride, (*L'Ami du Clergé,* LXI [1951], p. 773, footnote 3) says that the question of the pre-vicar econome was not expressly treated in the cited commentary. He actually holds that the administrators mentioned in canon 472, n. 2, do not possess the faculty to confirm, unless a synodal statute establishes that without a specific designation of the bishop these administrators are to be constituted as vicars econome.

[60] *Ius Sacramentarium,* n. 4, p. 56.

[61] *El Problema del Ministro Extraordinario de la Confirmación,* p. 348.

[62] "Art. cit.," *NRT,* LXIX (1947), 85.

trators mentioned in canon 472, n. 2, under the term, vicar econome.

The chief contention of the first group is that canon 472, n. 1, uses the term *"vicarius oeconomus"* only in reference to one who is appointed as soon as possible by the local ordinary to take charge of a vacant parish until its canonical possession by the new pastor. Number 2 of the same canon provides that in the period preceding his appointment, unless other provisions have been made, the administration of the parish shall be assumed by the assistant, or by the first or senior of them, if there are more than one. If there are no assistants, the neighboring pastor who is closest, which determination shall be made by synodal or extra-synodal legislation, is to assume the administration. In the case of a parish entrusted to the religious, the superior of the religious house takes charge. These regulations are preceded by the expression *"ante oeconomi institutionem,"* which seems to indicate implicitly that those who are enumerated do not belong to that category. Further, since only the vicar econome, strictly so considered, enjoys all the rights and duties of a pastor in the care of souls,[64] he alone is the one to enjoy the power to confirm. Fernandez offers a further point of argumentation on the basis that the term of the administration of those who receive mention in n. 2 of canon 472 is of too temporary a nature to warrant their reception of the special faculty here in question.[65]

The opponents grant that as far as terminology is concerned the name of vicar econome has been applied by the *Code* solely to the administrator appointed by a bishop. In fact, however, the one who administers the parish in the interim is also a vicar econome. A number of commentators on the *Code* make no distinction between the two categories and list them both under

---

[63] *Traité de Droit Canonique* (4 vols. Paris: Letouzey et Ané, 1948-1949) v. II, *De Sacramentis,* n. 71, p. 67, ". . . il semble exclure . . mais non les quasi-curés ni, croyons-nous, celui qui *ipso facto* gouverne une paroisse avant la nomination du vicaire econome (can. 472, n. 2)."

[64] Canon 473, § 1. Onclin ("art. cit.," p. 340) denies this with the assertion that any priest charged with the administration of a parish fits within the ruling of canon 473, § 1.

[65] "Algunos Ministros Extraordinarios de la Confirmación," *Revista Española de Derecho Canonico,* II (1947), 650.

the general term *"vicarii oeconomi."*[66] Regatillo denies the validity of the objection of Fernandez for he asserts that the only difference in the temporary aspect and relative stability of the administration of the *ab homine* and the *a iure* designated vicar econome is one of degree, and not one of kind.[67]

In view of the *dubium iuris* created by reputable canonists[68] the present writer declares himself in favor of the school of thought which holds that every priest charged with the administration of a vacant parish, whether he is nominated by the local ordinary or designated by law, is to be considered a vicar econome and therefore invested with the power to confirm during the period of his administration. He does not regard this as an extension of the privilege, which extension is forbidden by the exclusiveness of the enumeration, but as a legitimate application, within the limits of the principles of interpretation set down in article 2 of chapter III, of the term *"vicarius oeconomus."* Such an application appears to be in perfect conformity with the mind of the legislator, since thereby the decree is encompassed with an aureola of logical perfection. Every conceivable situation is

[66] Both Mostaza (*op. cit.*, p. 349, footnote 109) and Onclin ("art. cit.," p. 340, footnote 23) list S. Sipos (*Enchiridion Iuris Canonici* [Pecs, 1936], p. 325), I. Chelodi-P. Ciprotti (*Ius Canonicum de Personis* [Vicenza, 1942], n. 229, pp. 361-362) and Vermeersch-Creusen (*Epitome Iuris Canonici,* I, n. 562-564, pp. 421-422) as authors who make no distinction in the terminology. Onclin adds the names of A. M. Koeniger (*Katholisches Kirchenrecht* [*Freiburg* i. B., 1926], p. 237) and F. Claeys Bouuaert-G. Simenon (*Manuale Juris Canonici,* Vol. I [4. ed., Gandae et Leodií, 1934], n. 582, p. 324).

[67] *Op. cit.*, n. 4, p. 56.

[68] Crosignani ("art. cit.," *Divus Thomas* XXIV [1947], 91) holds that the power of the administrators mentioned in n. 2 of canon 472 is doubtful. Mahoney in an article written in *The Clergy Review,* XXXVI (1951), p. 126, admitted that the difference of opinion on this question constitutes a *dubium iuris.* "It means, in practice, that on the death of the parish priest, his senior curate may administer confirmation to those dying within the parish, until an administrator is appointed by the Ordinary." He added a seemingly cryptic observation that a priest may accept this view "unless an instruction to the contrary has been given by local Ordinaries." The writer cannot grasp how an instruction of the bishop would affect the interpretation of a general law of the Church, since he is not its legislator (canon 17, § 1).

taken into consideration, so that at least *de iure* an extraordinary minister is always available to confirm one who is in danger of death. In other words, the decree thus provides an extraordinary minister of confirmation for parishes which do not have a pastoral incumbent either because the parish is united to a moral personality or because the parish has legally become vacant.

Article 4—Vicars Who Are Excluded

In the second category of extraordinary ministers only two types of parochial vicars are listed. Surely the legislator was aware of the existence of the others. The very fact that a general mention of parochial vicars was not employed, but rather a specific enumeration, seems a very strong indication that the lawmaker intended to confer this faculty on these two vicars and these two alone.[69] Therefore the vicar substitute, the vicar adjutant and the vicar assistant are not empowered to confirm in virtue of this decree.

The vicar substitute of canon 474 is understood as one who takes the place of a pastor in his absence for longer than the period of a week.[70] By the general law of the Church a pastor may be absent from his parish for two months a year at the maximum, whether counted continuously or in the aggregate, unless a serious reason, as judged by the local ordinary, would necessitate the extension or curtailment of this period.[71] Whenever his absence is to be prolonged beyond a continuous week, the pastor, in addition to a legitimate cause, needs the written permission of the local ordinary as well as his approval of the substitute who is to be engaged.[72] With the approbation of the

[69] Bergh, "art. cit.," *NRT*, LXIX (1947), 85, noted that by the exclusive enumeration the lawmaker derogated from the provision of canon 451, § 2, which makes parochial vicars endowed with full parochial powers equivalent to pastors.

[70] The discussion will also apply to the vicar substitute who, according to canon 1923, § 2, is to be appointed by the bishop as administering the care of souls in a parish when a pastor seeks redress from the Holy See against the judicial sentence of his removal from the parochial benefice.

[71] Canon 465, § 2.

[72] Canon 465, § 4.

bishop, the pastor may designate his assistant as the substitute.[73] If the pastor's departure is sudden, he must notify the local ordinary as soon as possible by means of a letter in which he will explain the reason for his going away and inform the bishop of the name of the substitute.[74] Although the vicar substitute enjoys complete ordinary power, unless a restriction is imposed by the bishop or the pastor,[75] he is not obliged to offer the official Mass for the people unless a special arrangement had been made by the absent pastor in accordance with canon 466, § 5.

Canon 475 makes provisions for spiritual ministrations in a parish where the pastor has been incapacitated for the duties of his office because of old age, mental infirmity, blindness or some other permanent affliction. The local ordinary is to appoint an auxiliary vicar, a vicar adjutant, who is to be given either complete or incomplete parochial authority. In the former contingency, he possesses all the rights and obligations of a pastor, with the exception of the offering of the official Mass for the people, which remains the pastor's obligation. In the latter contingency, the letter of his appointment will determine the extent of his rights and obligations.[76]

If a pastor, because of the great number of souls in his parish, or for other similar objective reasons, cannot, in the judgment of the local ordinary, provide by his own efforts for the needs of the parishioners, he is to be given one or more assistants (*vicarii cooperatores*).[77] The rights and obligations of the assistant are determined by the diocesan statutes, by the letter of his appointment, and by the assignments which the pastor commits to him. Unless other provision be made, he shall take the place of the pastor and assist him in the entire parochial ministry, with the exception of the official Mass for the people.[78] The assistant is to be subject to the pastor who shall in a fatherly manner in-

[73] Abbo-Hannan, *The Sacred Canons,* I, 462.

[74] Canon 465, § 5.

[75] Abbo-Hannan, *op. cit.,* I, 471.

[76] Canon 475, § 2.

[77] Canon 476, § 1.

[78] Canon 476, § 6.

struct him, direct his work of caring for souls, watch over him, and at least once a year render an account of his activities to the local ordinary.[79]

In reference to the power of confirming, the present writer has not found any author who holds that the faculty was conferred upon an assistant. Since the denial is unanimous, there is no need to cite the particular passages. In like manner, the present writer, to his knowledge, knows of only one commentator who attributes to vicars substitute and adjutant the faculty of confirming. Although Regatillo includes them under category (c) rather than category (b), his argumentations will be examined in this article rather than in article 6.

Before entering on a more detailed evaluation of the canonical reasoning upon which the inclusion of these two vicars is based, let it be stated at the outset that it seems hardly logical that the lawmaker, who set up a category for (a) pastors (b) vicars and (c) other priests, would have deviated to such an extent that he would enumerate certain vicars in category (b) and others in category (c), especially since he had clear and concise canonical terminology at his disposal by means of which to refer to vicars substitute and adjutant.[80]

In category (c) the faculty is conferred upon priests to whom the full care of souls with all the rights and duties of a pastor is exclusively and in a stabilized manner entrusted within a definite territory with a determined church.[81]

The first objection to the inclusion of the vicars substitute and adjutant is that they do not have *all* the duties of pastors, since neither is fundamentally (*per se*) obliged to offer the official Mass for the people. Canon 475, § 2, explicitly exempts the vicar adjutant even though he may be assigned to take the place of the pastor in all things; canon 466, § 5, presumes that the vicar substitute is not bound to say the Mass. Regatillo's answer

[79] Canon 476, § 7.

[80] Cf. Fernandez, "art. cit.," *Revista Española de Derecho Canonico,* II (1948), 646, 648; also, Alonso, "Commentario al Decreto de la S. Congregacion de Sacramentos sobre la Confirmacion de Moribundos," *Revista Española de Derecho Canonico,* I (1947), 158-170.

[81] *AAS,* XXXVIII (1946), n. 1 (c), p. 352.

that the phrase is to be understood in a moral sense is far from satisfactory.[82]

In a certain diocese there were four institutions exempted from all parochial jurisdiction—a large city hospital, a home for the aged poor, a provincial hospital for the insane, and a sanatorium for consumptives—which were commonly referred to as internal parishes. The priests assigned there had the complete care of souls: baptism, assistance at marriages, funerals, etc., except the obligation of the official Mass for the people. Accordingly the ordinary inquired of the Sacred Congregation whether these priests were empowered to confirm. The letter specified that the reason for doubting was that they do not have all the parochial obligations, e.g., that of applying the official Mass for the people.[83] In a private reply given on December 30, 1946, the Congregation for the Discipline of the Sacraments simply and tersely answered that, since the chaplains of the four institutions do not fulfill the conditions expressly and inclusively (*expresse* and *taxative*) laid down in section I, no. 1 (c), they do not have the power to confirm.[84] Granted that this answer binds only the persons to whom it is given and in the matters affected by it,[85] nevertheless it serves to reflect the mind of the Congregation that "all" is to be taken in the sense of entirety, not in a moral sense.

Category (c) further specifies that the priest is to exercise the care of souls *exclusively*. Can one speak of the vicar substitute as enjoying this prerogative? Surely, the pastor who departs from the parish does not completely relinquish his rights and obligations in the care of souls. The very fact that the *Code* insists that he provide a substitute is proof in itself of the continuance of this obligation. To argue, as Regatillo does, that in

[82] *Ius Sacramentarium*, p. 57.

[83] ". . . Ratio dubitandi est quod ipsi non omnes habent paroeciales obligationes, uti, e.g., applicandi Missam pro populo."

[84] The case is reported by Zerba in his *Commentarius*, pp. 54-56. At the conclusion Zerba commented that the chief reason for this negative answer seems to be that the four chaplains enjoy exempt territory, which is not proper territory.

[85] Canon 17, § 3.

his absence the pastor actually does not and cannot exercise his power and, therefore, does not possess it, appears a bit specious, and, one might be tempted to add, a bit too convenient.[86]

To grant that a pastor *de iure* preserves his jurisdiction, and then to assert that vicars substitute and adjutant *de facto* and *de iure* have exclusive care of souls involves a contradiction in terms. How could two people, e.g., the pastor and his vicar substitute both at the same time *de iure* have the exercise of souls, and one of them be said to enjoy *de iure* the exclusive care of souls? The very term "exclusive" connotes singleness. Actually here and now the substitute vicar is the only one who exercises the care of souls. But the pastor could return at any time and without permission or even knowledge of the substitute exercise any parochial function. In the light of this consideration, can one speak of the *stability* of the position of a vicar substitute? Even if it is granted that he possesses ordinary power and therefore must enjoy an office which has objective stability, the vicar substitute can be removed at any time not only at the will of the bishop but even at the will of the pastor.

The same, with all due adaptation made, both as to exclusiveness and stability, can be applied to the vicar adjutant, especially since, according to canon 475, § 3, if the pastor is not mentally enfeebled, the vicar adjutant in the exercise of his functions remains subject to the pastor's authority in accordance with the letter of the ordinary.

Finally, why describe the parish with which vicars substitute and adjutant are associated by means of such a special terminology as "within a definite territory with a determined church?" [87]

Since the vicars substitute and adjutant do not have *all* the rights and duties of pastors, and since they enjoy neither stability nor exclusiveness in the exercise of the care of souls, the present writer is compelled to disagree with Regatillo. In reply to an objection why the decree does not specifically enumerate the vicars substitute and adjutant as it does the vicar econome, Regatillo answers that it is indeed strange. In return, he then

[86] Regatillo, *op. cit.*, p. 57.

[87] *AAS*, XXXVIII (1946), n. 1 (c), p. 352.

asks why they should be excluded, if they can be adapted to category (c). With due reverence the writer responds that in view of the submitted refutation they cannot be made to fit in category (c), and therefore must be excluded. An appeal to the presumed will and benevolent humaneness of the legislator [88] cannot counteract the text and context of the law itself.[89] Besides, as has been shown,[90] the lawmaker has actually provided a *de iure* extraordinary minister for every situation. The fact that occasions will arise wherein actually, i.e., *de facto* such a minister will not be available is only accidental. It can happen, for example, that a pastor is ill when an emergency confirmation arises. Since he cannot delegate, on the presumption that the bishop is not available, that person would die without confirmation. Though the decree *Spiritus Sancti munera* has provided more ample opportunities for an unconfirmed person in danger of death to receive the sacrament, it neither intended nor was able to guarantee that every such person would be confirmed *in extremis*.[91]

To conclude the article on vicars who cannot confirm, one must mention the vicar capitular or the administrator of a vacant diocese, as mentioned in canon 432, § 1, and the vicar general, as mentioned in canon 366. Unless they possess episcopal orders or can be included in categories (a), (b) or (c), they do not possess the power to confirm solely in virtue of their ecclesiastical dignity.

Article 5—Other Priests Who Are Included

The third category of priests whom the decree enumerates has perhaps been the object of greatest discussion and commentary. Some have used it as a proverbial passkey with which they seek to allow as many priests as possible to enter the exclusive domain

[88] Regatillo, *op. cit.*, pp. 58, 59.

[89] McReavy in *The Clergy Review,* XLII (1957), 104-107, declared that one cannot accept Regatillo's view in respect to the vicar substitute as a safe one to follow, since it lacks both intrinsic and extrinsic probability.

[90] Article 3 of this chapter, pp. 87 ff.

[91] Cf. Zerba, *op. cit.*, pp. 51-52.

of those to whom the faculty has been granted by the Sacred Congregation. For the purpose of discussion the words of the decree are once more quoted:

> . . . sacerdotibus quibus exclusive et stabiliter commissa sit in certo territorio et cum determinata ecclesia plena animarum cura cum omnibus parochorum iuribus et officiis.[92]

The first striking feature is that the category is introduced with the word "sacerdotibus." By the law of progressive or, if one prefers, diminishing enumeration, it would seem logical that the ones in this category are neither pastors whom the *Code* discusses in book II, chap. IX, nor parochial vicars of whom the *Code* treats in the 10th chapter of the same book, for otherwise they should have been included in the first or second category. Hence it becomes necessary to search for a canonical concept which fits neither that of pastor nor that of parochial vicar. Chapter 11 of the second book deals with rectors, but, since the care of souls is only accidentally attached to this office and the rector may not perform parochial functions in his church,[93] the words of this category clearly do not find application.

Two principal possibilities remain. One is proposed by Fernandez, who concluded that the legislator in the third category has reference to a special type of territorial arrangement established by particular law.[94] Others invite us to consider an institute which is not familiar to American minds, namely that of the permanent or perpetual vicarage.[95] When canon 1427, § 1, provides for the authority of the local ordinary to divide any parish for a justifying canonical reason, it specifies that he may establish a permanent vicarage or a new parish. Paragraphs 3-5 of the same canon treat equally of the *"vicaria perpetua"* or *"nova paroecia."* A perpetual or permanent vicar-

[92] *AAS*, XXXVIII (1946), n. 1 (c), p. 352.

[93] Canon 481.

[94] "Algunos Ministros Extraordinarios de la Confirmación," Revista Española de Derecho Canonico, conclusion (e), p. 660.

[95] Zerba, *Commentarius*, pp. 50-54; Pistoni, *De Confirmatione a Ministro Extraordinario*, p. 90; Onclin, "art. cit.," *ETL*, XXV (1949), 341; Connell, "art. cit.," *AER*, CXVI (1947), 258, and others.

age differs from a parish principally in the fact that whereas the office of a pastor is well defined in the general law, the scope of the incumbent of a perpetual vicarage is left largely to the determination of the local ordinary. But the incumbent has a benefice, enjoys exclusively the care of souls attached to it and has, at least *de iure,* the obligation of saying the official Mass for the people on the specified days.[96] Under no condition can the ordinary reserve to the mother church the exclusive right to a baptismal font.[97]

A number of commentators include the quasi-pastor of mission territories. This will be discussed in a subsequent article.

Without attempting to particularize the various contingencies which might be included under this category, one can safely conclude that its primary purpose is to enable the lawmaker to provide for whatever special arrangements, other than parochial, might exist throughout the world. A priest in charge of such a territory who fully fulfills the specific requirements *"expresse et taxative"* enumerated in category (c) enjoys the power to confirm.

Article 6—Other Priests Who Are Excluded

By the canonical process of exclusion, it has been heretofore shown that purely personal pastors, i.e., such as are without specific territory, that vicars substitute and adjutant as well as parish assistants do not enjoy the faculty of confirming those who are in danger of death. Nor has this faculty been attached to the office of the vicar capitular or that of the vicar general. A brief consideration of other priests who are charged with the care of souls will complete the list of those who are excluded. Commentators are generally agreed on those who are mentioned as *"exclusi."*

The priest who supplies for the absence of the pastor who is gone for less than a period of seven days[98] does not enjoy the

[96] Abbo-Hannan, *op. cit.,* II, 660.

[97] Canon 1427, § 4.

[98] Canon 465, § 6.

power to confirm. Nor does the rector of a seminary, although, according to canon 1368, he enjoys the office of pastor for all who are in the seminary except in regard to marriage and without prejudice to the rule of canon 891. Clerical religious superiors, even in exempt communities, although they have the right and duty to administer in person, or through another, Holy Viaticum and extreme unction in case of illness to the professed, to the novices and to others who live day and night in the religious house by reason of services to be rendered, education to be received, hospitality to be engaged, or health to be regained,[99] cannot confer confirmation, if the need should ever arise. Chancellors and curial officials as well as all types of chaplains are excluded—chaplains or rectors of shrines, e.g., the director of the National Shrine of the Immaculate Conception in Washington, D. C., college chaplains, prison chaplains, chaplains of charitable institutions, military chaplains or hospital chaplains. The power of certain hospital chaplains to confirm infants in danger of death will be treated in article 2 of chapter V. A brief treatment of the status of military chaplains is contained in the supplement which follows.

SUPPLEMENT—MILITARY CHAPLAINS

On September 8, 1957, the Sacred Consistorial Congregation issued a decree whereby Pope Pius XII erected and established the Military Vicariate of the United States of America. In this document it was stated that "the military chaplains shall exercise the care of the souls entrusted to them with the duties and obligaions of pastors in accordance with the *Instruction on Military Vicars.*"[100] The military vicariate thus set up consists of a military vicar, both at present and in the future always to be the current archbishop of New York, who enjoys a double cumulative jurisdiction, of auxiliary bishops, appointed by the Holy See, of chaplain delegates or major chaplains, where they are necessary, to whom are assigned those functions which, with

[99] Canon 514, § 1.

[100] *AAS*, XLIX (1957), 972.

any required changes, the Code of Canon Law attaches to the office of vicar general,[101] and of military or minor chaplains.[102] The term "chaplains" includes secular and religious priests who are called on a habitual basis to the office of military chaplains for the armed forces of the United States, and also those who are called on a temporary basis during the time that they render their services, as also priests who are chaplains of hospitals commonly called Veterans' Administration Hospitals and Domiciliaries.[103]

Subject to their jurisdiction are all the faithful who actually serve in the armed forces of the land, air and sea; those who, organized in military fashion, pertain in any way whatsoever to these same armed forces; those who are bound by the laws made for these armed services along with their families, namely the wives, children, servants, relatives who habitually live with them in this country or who accompany them in any manner whatsoever outside their homeland; and likewise the Catholic family of a non-Catholic serviceman under the same circumstances.[104] Included also are those who serve under the banners of the forces commonly known as the Coast Guard, the National Guard, the Air National Guard or the Civil Air Patrol, as long as they are living in common in a military manner.[105]

All the faithful of both sexes, whether they are members of a religious institute or not, who are attached to hospitals, military schools, Veterans' Administration Hospitals and Domiciliaries, and reside there, along with all the faithful of both sexes who dwell on military bases or in homes reserved by the civil government for military personnel and their families, are subject to the military vicariate.[106] Finally, by a special provision, the military vicar also enjoys personal jurisdiction over non-military people who, living in distant places where military stations are

[101] *Loc. cit.*

[102] *AAS,* XLIX (1957), 970-971.

[103] *AAS,* XLIX (1957) nn. 1 and 2, p. 971.

[104] *AAS,* XLIX (1957), nn. 3 and 5, p. 971.

[105] *AAS,* XLIX (1957), n. 4, p. 971.

[106] *AAS,* XLIX (1957), nn. 6 and 7, pp. 971-972.

established, cannot be taken care of spiritually by the local ordinary through a pastor, missionary or some other priest.[107]

In all this arrangement it appears that the relation of the chaplain to the people is that of a personal pastor. As a matter of fact, in one instance the decree speaks of the *personal* jurisdiction of the military vicar, namely when it states that "the Military Vicar will enjoy a special personal jurisdiction, ordinary for both the internal and external forum, cumulative with the jurisdiction of local ordinaries. . . ." [108] However, inasmuch as in permanent military camps, and also in places reserved for the military personnel, jurisdiction is exercised primarily and principally by the military vicar, and only secondarily by the local ordinary and the pastor through their own proper authority, namely, whenever the military vicar and his chaplains are absent or not available,[109] it could seem that here there is an example of cumulative territory as mentioned in category (a) of the decree. Actually, though, after mature deliberation, it seems more proper to speak of a cumulative *personal* jurisdiction than of a cumulative *territorial* jurisdiction.[110] Zerba records an enquiry from a certain military vicar whether military chaplains who within the limits of a military hospital or permanent military camps exercise the functions of a pastor can be considered as personal pastors who enjoy proper though cumulative territory; if not, a request was made that the Sacred Congregation obtain this faculty for them from the Holy Father. On January 2,

[107] *AAS,* XLIX (1957), 972.

[108] *AAS,* XLIX (1957), 971, "Vicarius Castrensis iurisdictione pollebit personali. . . ."

[109] *AAS,* XLIX (1957), 971.

[110] In an unpublished doctoral thesis at the Gregorian University (1948), *De Cappellanis Militaribus,* its author, V. Bartuska, concluded that most military chaplains are personal pastors. One exception seems to have been the Polish Military, which by special concordat with the Holy See consisted of chaplains who were also territorial pastors. Cf. Quinn, *The Extraordinary Minister of Confirmation,* p. 94, footnote 127; also Mostaza, *El Problema del Ministro Extraordinario de la Confirmación,* p. 355, footnotes 122, 123. The latter concluded that in Spain, *per accidens,* the military chaplains in strictly military reservations are territorial as well as personal pastors.

1947, n. 7687, the answer given was: "*Non expedire.*" Zerba then concluded that one can implicitly deduce that chaplains do not have this faculty in virtue of the decree *Spiritus Sancti munera.* If the favor were desired, it had to be sought from the Pope.[111]

One could be tempted to apply no. (c) to military chaplains except for the fact that this category speaks of the exclusive care of souls. The expression "*semper vero iure proprio*" [112] indicates that the local pastor also enjoys the right to care for these souls with reference to the valid administration of the sacraments. This is substantiated by an instruction for military vicars, issued on April 23, 1951,[113] which stated that the jurisdiction of the military vicar is not exclusive, and that therefore the people, stations and places reserved for the military (i.e., military bases, naval dockyards, airports, military hospitals, etc.) are in no way withdrawn from the jurisdiction and power of the local ordinary. The granting of jurisdiction to military chaplains does not connote any exemption, nor does the service of military chaplains imply any excardination from the diocese.[114]

Another factor to be considered is that military chaplains are fundamentally (*per se*) not bound to apply the official Mass for the people:

> Cappellani militum sicut et Vicarius Castrensis minime tenentur obligatione applicandi Missam pro populo; si vero stipem vel notabile emolumentum ex officio percipiant, Vicarius Castrensis imponere eis valebit ut Sacrificium Missae applicent saltem diebus Canon. 306 C.I.C. statutis; quod et ipsi sit norma.[115]

However, faculty n. 13 for the chaplains of the U.S. armed forces reads as follows:

> You are not held to the *Missa pro populo* on the 86 days binding the Latin pastors in this country, but you are bound in justice to offer the *Missa pro populo* "*saltem*", at least,

111 *Commentarius,* p. 46.

112 *AAS,* XLIX (1957), 971.

113 *AAS,* XLIII (1951), 562-565.

114 *AAS,* XLIII (1951), 562.

115 *AAS,* XLIII (1951), 564.

on the following days: Christmas, Epiphany, Easter, Ascension, Pentecost, Corpus Christi, Assumption, Immaculate Conception, St. Joseph, Saints Peter and Paul, and All Saints.[116]

Mostaza in his treatise included the following rescript by which the Sacred Congregation for the Discipline of the Sacraments granted the faculty of confirming to military chaplains in reserved military stations to which access may be forbidden to a bishop or pastor:

BEATISSIME PATER,

Cum Episcopus aut parochus a stationibus vel locis militibus reservatis aliquoties prohibeantur et frequenter ad eos recursus impossibilis evadat, Emus Cardinalis Sacrae Congregationis Consistorialis Secretarius, S. Anulum humiliter deosculatus, postulat ut Sanctitas Vestra militum cappellanis Vicariatum Castrensium legitime constitutorum indultum concedere dignetur conferendi Sacramentum Confirmationis subditis a respectivo Vicario Castrensi ipsis concreditis, ad norman Decreti S. Congregationis de disciplina Sacramentorum *Spiritus Sancti munera* diei 14 septembris, anni 1946.

EX AUDIENTIA SANCTISSIMI DIEI 23 Iunii 1952

SSmus Dominus Noster Pius Papa XII, audita relatione infrascripti Cardinalis S. Congregationis de Sacramentis Pro-Praefecti, relatis precibus benigne annuere dignatus est, ea tamen lege ut Confirmationis Sacramentum, in adiunctis de quibus in praefato Decreto personaliter conferatur militibus ceterisque personis in precibus expositis a Cappellano militari ab Ordinario Castrensi *stabiliter* pro illis deputato, durante munere, aut si plures sint stabiliter constituti, ab eorum primo.

Cappellano autem hac facultate uti licebit tantum si Episcopus dioecesanus haberi nequeat aut legitime impediatur, quominus per seipsum Confirmationem conferat, nec alius praesto sit Episcopus communione gaudens cum Sede Apostolica, licet titularis

[116] *Vademecum for the Priests Serving the Military Vicariate of the United States of America,* issued by the Military Ordinariate in New York in November, 1957, p. 10.

dumtaxat, qui sine gravi incommodo ipsi suffici queat nec prohibeatur ad militaria loca accedere.

Itidemque si parochus loci, in iisdem adiunctis, haberi et ipse nequeat vel legitime impediatur quominus Sacramentum istud conferat.

In absentia autem Cappellani ut supra designati, aut in eius impossibilitate per seipsum confirmandi, nullus alius praeter Episcopum vel loci parochum idem Sacramentum valide conferre valeat.

Serventur in ceteris termini et clausulae memorati Decreti praesertim quod attinet ad *Relationem* quotannis mittendam huic S. Congregationi ab Ordinario Castrensi de numero confirmatorum et de ratione a Cappellanis militaribus suae dicionis in tam praeclaro munere perfungendo adhibita (cfr. I, n. 9).

Contrariis quibuslibet minime obstantibus.

Praesentibus valituris *ad biennium*, a data praefatae Audientiae computandum.

B. CARD. ALOISI MASELLA,
Episcopus Praenestinus, Pro-Praefectus.

L.S. F. BRACCI, *Secretarius.*[117]

Since the source in which this indult appeared was not given and the present writer was unsuccesful in his attempt to trace the indult through the *Acta Apostolicae Sedis* (1952-1956 issues) or through the Military Vicariate of the United States, he cannot state whether the indult had been renewed and is still in effect, inasmuch as it was to expire in 1954. In any case, the present writer must conclude that military chaplains of the United States, at least in virtue of the decree *Spiritus Sancti munera*, cannot confirm any of their subjects who are in danger of death.[118]

[117] *Op. cit.*, appendix iv, pp. 385-386.

[118] In a private reply to the present writer, dated December 19, 1957, the Very Rev. Joseph Marbach, J.C.D., chancellor of the vicariate, confirmed the conclusion. In the *Vademecum* no mention is made of the faculty of chaplains to confirm.

CHAPTER V

THE EXTRACTORDINARY MINISTERS OF CONFIRMATION ACCORDING TO THE PROVISIONS OF RELATED DOCUMENTS

Article 1—Priests in Mission Territories

After the decree *Spiritus Sancti munera* had been promulgated, the status of quasi-pastors with regard to the power of confirming was very much in doubt. Since they were nowhere explicitly mentioned in the exclusive list of extraordinary ministers, commentators sought to include them in the first or third category. Zerba and his followers appealed to canon 451, § 2, n. 1, which places quasi-pastors, i.e., priests in charge of the souls of persons in subdivisions of vicariates or prefectures, as constituted in line with the provision of canon 216, § 3, in the same category by law as pastors with all his rights and obligations.[1] A number of canonists, on the other hand, preferred to include them under category (c) rather than category (a).[2] Fernandez argued that quasi-pastors were not included at all, since the decree *Spiritus Sancti munera* did not refer to mission territories. It was issued by the Congregation for the Discipline of the Sacraments and no mention was made of an agreement with the Congregation for the Propagation of the Faith to have it apply to mission territory. Hence, there would be a question of jurisdictional competence. The conditions nn. 3, 6, 7 used terminology which denotes a diocesan set up, and condition n. 9 demanded that a report be sent to the Congregation for the Discipline of the Sacraments

[1] *Commentarius,* pp. 45-46. Quinn (*The Extraordinary Minister of Confirmation,* p. 86) states that they are a special class and have all the personal prerogatives of pastors and have a special name only because the law provides it. Cf. Onclin, "L'Administration de la Confirmation en Cas de Danger de Mort," *ETL,* XXV (1949), 338, and Coronata, *De Sacramentis,* I, n. 167 *bis,* p. 126, for a similar doctrine.

[2] Mahoney, "The Extraordinary Minister of Confirmation," *The Clergy Review,* XXVII (1947), 83; Bergh, "Administration de la Confirmation aux Fidèles dangereusement Malades," *NRT,* LXIX (1949), 85.

which actually does not govern the affairs of mission territories. Finally, the author contended that, even if the decree applied to mission territory, the references in category (a) and category (c) were too vague to warrant the inclusion of quasi-pastors.[3]

Delchard made mention[4] of a reply from the Congregation for the Propagation of the Faith on July 7, 1947, which was reported by the *Revue du Clergé Africain.*[5] In response to various inquiries by African Vicars Apostolic, this Congregation answered that the decree *Spiritus Sancti munera* intended to confer the indult upon quasi-pastors, not, however, upon superiors where quasi-parishes have not yet been erected.

In any case, on December 18, 1947, the Congregation for the Propagation of the Faith issued *in forma specifica*[6] a special decree, *Post latum.*[7] This decree resulted from the petitions of many missionary ordinaries that mission priests be granted the *same* or more extensive faculties.[8]

[3] "Algunos Ministros Extraordinarios de la Confirmación," *Revista Española de Derecho Canonico,* II (1947), 654.

[4] *Nouvelle Revue Théologique,* LXX (1948), 532.

[5] 1947, pp. 116-122.

[6] Cf. Cappello, *De Sacramentis,* I, n. 201 *bis,* p. 184. See also Quinn, *op. cit.,* pp. 121-122.

[7] *AAS,* XL (1948), 41.

[8] ". . . ad easdem amplioresve facultates obtinendas . . ."—Smiddy (*A Manual for the Extraordinary Minister of Confirmation,* p. 31) looked upon this as proof "beyond the shadow of a doubt" that the decree *Spiritus Sancti munera* did not apply to mission lands. Conway also seemed to imply this when he wrote: "It will be remembered, of course, that the decree of the Congregation of Propaganda last year—unlike the original decree of the Congregation of the Sacraments for non-mission countries, . . ." —*The Irish Ecclesiastical Record,* 5. series, LXXII (1949), 361. Onclin ("art. cit.," pp. 338-339) argued that the decree issued by the Congregation for the Discipline of the Sacraments applies in principle to the entire Latin Church, since it is a pontifical law of the Universal Church. The reason for the subsequent decree of the Congregation for the Propagation of the Faith was to include territorial establishments which do not have the status of a quasi-parish. He concluded that the quasi-pastors automatically enjoy the power conferred by the decree *Spiritus Sancti munera,* whereas the other missionary priests must receive this power through their local ordinary.

Certain canonical points should be observed with regard to the decree *Post latum.* The indult is not given directly and immediately to priests, as was done in the decree *Spiritus Sancti munera*, but to the ordinary, who can then grant it to certain priests.[9] Thus, one might say that the privilege of confirming was granted in the decree *Spiritus Sancti munera "in forma gratiosa"* whereas it was granted in the decree *Post latum "in forma commissoria,"* a procedure which enables the local ordinary to provide for all situations.[10]

The expression "local ordinary" in the present context includes not only a residential bishop, an apostolic administrator, a vicar general and vicar capitular, but also a vicar or a prefect apostolic, or a pro-vicar or pro-prefect apostolic after he has assumed the "*totum regimen*" of the vicariate or the prefecture,[11] and the ecclesiastical superior of a mission constituted with territorial independence (*sui iuris*). Conway doubts whether the term would include a vicar delegate, a prefect delegate, or a superior delegate.[12]

Quasi-pastors are not the only ones upon whom this power of confirming can be conferred. On the contrary, the decree mentions as the proper potential recipients of this indult all priests who have the care of souls.[13] The word "*plena*" is omitted in the expression "*cura animarum*"; hence, in accordance with the official reply of the Pontifical Commission for the Authentic Interpretation of the Canons of the Code, as given February 12, 1935, concerning the meaning of the expression "*religiosi curam animarum habentes*" in canon 131, § 3, wherein are listed the priests who have an obligation to attend clerical conferences,[14]

[9] "Omnibus itaque Ordinariis locorum . . . potestatem Sanctissimus fecit . . . ut Sedis Apostolicae indulto (canon 782, § 2) tribuere valeant . . . facultatem . . ."—*AAS*, XL (1948), 41.

[10] Cf. canon 38.

[11] Canon 309, § 2.

[12] *The Irish Ecclesiastical Record*, LXX (1948), 540. Cf. also Regatillo, *Ius Sacramentarium*, p. 59.

[13] ". . . omnibus sacerdotibus curamque animarum gerentibus,"—*AAS*, XL (1948), 41.

[14] *AAS*, XXVII (1935), 92.

any priest can be included who is actively engaged in the pastoral ministry. Pastors, in territories with parochial benefices, quasi-pastors, acting vicars (*vicarii actuales*), administrators (*vicarii oeconomi*), substitute vicars (*vicarii substituti*), auxiliary vicars (*vicarii adiutores*), assistants (*vicarii cooperatores*), and chaplains of hospitals and of other pious institutions when they have the care of souls by taking the place of the pastor and assisting him in the ministry [15] can therefore be empowered by the local ordinary to confirm those who are in danger of death.[16]

What is the significance of the phrase "*fidelibus infra fines missionalis circumscriptionis exstantibus*"? [17] Does it refer to only such of the faithful as are to be found within the boundaries of the territorial unit in which the priest in question exercises the care of souls? Paventi extends the priest's power to the territorial extent of the diocese or quasi-diocese of the ordinary who grants the indult.[18] Smiddy suggests that in view of the *dubium* the ordinary should be quite precise as to the extent of each grant which he makes.[19]

The decree *Post latum* limits the description of the proper recipients of confirmation as those who are "*in mortis periculo constituti.*" [20] Since the expression "*ex gravi morbo*" is not mentioned in the text proper of the decree, some commentators have included any person in danger of death, whether from an intrinsic or from an extrinsic cause.[21] However, the present writer,

[15] Cf. Hoffman, *Clergy Conferences ,Canon 131,* The Catholic University of America Canon Law Studies, no. 383 (Washington, D. C.: The Catholic University of America Press, 1957), pp. 77-78.

[16] Smiddy, *op. cit.,* p. 107; Regatillo, *op. cit.,* p. 59. Conway would exclude part-time chaplains to schools and hospitals, unless they have the full care of souls.—*The Irish Ecclesiastical Record,* LXXII (1949), 362.

[17] *AAS,* XL (1948), 41.

[18] "Adnotationes," *Monitor Ecclesiasticus,* II (1950), 58.

[19] *Op. cit.,* p. 107.

[20] *AAS,* XL (1948), 41.

[21] Cf., e.g., Damen, "Adnotationes," *Apollinaris,* XXII (1949), 75. The basis of his argumentation is the faculty already possessed by the local ordinaries of China to delegate to all their priests the faculty of lawfully and validly administering confirmation to adults and infants "*in articulo mortis*

along with others, feels that from the very inscription of the title of the decree, "De confirmatione administranda iis qui ex gravi morbo, in periculo mortis sunt constituti," the expression must be understood to imply "*ex gravi morbo*," since, according to the adage, "*a rubro ad nigrum valet illatio.*" [22]

ARTICLE 2—HOSPITAL CHAPLAINS IN THE UNITED STATES

On November 18, 1948, the Bishops of the United States received from the Sacred Congregation for the Discipline of the Sacraments a rescript, prot, n. 5869/48, which, in effect, was a favorable response to a petition of the American hierarchy requesting a derogation from the decree *Spiritus Sancti munera.* Because of the difficulty faced by local pastors, burdened with other duties of their ministry, to confirm in certain institutions where could be found a great number of infants in danger of death, a special indult was requested whereby chaplains of so called maternity homes, of hospitals for women about to give birth, and of foundling hospitals, could validly and lawfully confirm the infants therein.

In an audience, granted October 25, 1948, the Holy Father granted the faculty for one year [23] under the following conditions:

---

constituti." Paventi ("art. cit.," p. 58) states that it is the text, not the title of the decree, which received the approval of the Holy Father. Therefore, since the words "*ex gravi morbo*" are not in the text of the decree, any danger of death suffices for the exercise of this faculty. He concludes: "Unde si quis capite fuerit damnatus, valide recipere potest sacramentum confirmationis antequam necatus sit."

[22] Thus, also, Smiddy, *op. cit.*, p. 108; Mostaza, *El Problema del Ministro Extraordinario de la Confirmación,* p. 365.

[23] The rescript was renewed for one year on Feb. 6, 1950; cf. *The Jurist,* X (1950), 214. It was renewed again for three years by rescript N. 458/51; cf. *The Jurist,* XI (1951), 312-313. See appendix vii. It was renewed again for another period of three years on January 21, 1954; cf. *The Jurist,* XIV (1954), p. 208, footnote 26. The currently effective indult commenced to operate December 19, 1956. There are very strong indications that when the indult expires in 1959, no application will be made for its renewal. Already in their November, 1956 annual meeting in Washington, D. C., the Bishops of the United States were of the opinion that a petition for the renewal of the indult should not be made.

1) the proper subject must be an infant in danger of death at the institution, adult patients not being included; [24]

2) the chaplain must have a fixed appointment;

3) if there are several chaplains, the senior chaplain alone, to the exclusion of the other chaplains, enjoys the faculty;

4) lawfully the faculty can be used only if the local ordinary, or a titular bishop, or the local pastor is unavailable or lawfully impeded from conferring the sacrament, and

5) in the absence of the chaplain, only the bishop or the local pastor can confirm.[25]

In accordance with the provisions of this indult, the extraordinary minister of confirmation must be an established, regular chaplain. Though he need not be in residence at the institution and may hold other positions, nevertheless he must enjoy some form of official appointment to the chaplaincy. The present writer contends that the disposition of parochial activities by the pastor to the effect that assistant A will take charge of the hospital or orphanage within the territorial limits does not fulfill the demand inherent in the phrase *"stabiliter addicto"* of the indult.

How are the expressions, *"domibus sic nuncupatis maternitatis," "nosocomiis pro mulieribus parturientibus,"* and *"brephotropheis"* to be understood? So called maternity homes would include institutions for unwed mothers as well as homes where women are admitted with children for recuperation and convalescence after the birth. The expression, "hospitals for parturient women," has been the object of a strict interpretation, and consequently its application has been limited to hospitals which are exclusively maternity hospitals. The present writer fails to see how even a strict interpretation would exclude hospitals which have maternity wards, since such a hospital can lawfully be considered as one for parturient women, inasmuch

[24] The rescript uses the word *"puerulus,"* which can be considered equivalent to the *"parvulus"* or *"puer"* mentioned in canon 88, § 3. Therefore, it can be applied to anyone before the completion of the seventh year of age.

[25] For a copy of this rescript, cf. appendix vi.

as they are admitted therein. The expression "*pro mulieribus parturientibus,*" which follows the term "*nosocomiis,*" seems correctly interpreted as a distinctive specifier, i.e., as distinguishing this type of hospital from those which do not have accommodations for delivering babies, e.g., a convalescent or strictly surgical hospital. Hence, the writer would not hesitate to include chaplains of general hospitals with maternity wards as recipients of the faculty to confirm in virtue of this rescript.[26]

The other conditions seem quite clear and need no further elucidation. It should be noted that if two or more chaplains are attached to the same institution, only the senior chaplain enjoys the faculty, which he must exercise personally. He cannot subdelegate it to his assistants, and, in his absence, the bishop or the local pastor must be summoned.

Who are to be included under the expression "*loci parochus*"? It would not seem quite logical to interpret this strictly to mean the territorial pastor, and only him. Suppose that the parish is vacant. Could not the administrator be called? The present writer considers as included under this expression anyone who in virtue of the decree *Spiritus Sancti munera* could validly and lawfully confirm in those institutions, since the rescript cannot be said to deny what has been conferred by pontifical law.

Finally, it should be noted that the chaplain is bound to ob-

[26] Connell (*The American Ecclesiastical Review,* CXXXII [1955], 206) maintained that the reason for the privilege warrants the presence of at least a ward set aside for maternity cases. He concluded: "At any rate, even if a more lenient interpretation of the faculty were accepted, it should be remembered that this faculty can be granted only to a priest whose regular work is the care of the hospital. Moreover, this power to confirm is limited to infants in danger of death; furthermore, he may exercise this power only if neither a bishop nor the local pastor is available to confer the sacrament."

Delchard, in *Nouvelle Revue Théologique,* LXX (1948), 533, reports a similar indult, granted January 12, 1948, for the diocese of Nantes, which included chaplains of "les maternités," "cliniques d'accouchements," and "hôpitaux." A rescript was granted to the bishops of England and Wales on November 24, 1956, valid for three years. The petition reproduced in the rescript was a bit more specific and referred to chaplains of maternity homes, homes for infants, and hospitals containing a section exclusively reserved to infants. Cf. *The Clergy Review,* XLII (1957), 486-487.

serve the prescriptions of the decree *Spiritus Sancti munera* as to the notification of the bishop and of the proper pastor, the registration, the rubrical and gratuitous administration of the sacrament, etc.[27]

Article 3—Chaplains of Other Groups

Without canonical commentary, the present article simply presents the texts of faculties for confirming which have been granted to special categories of priests who exercise the care of souls.

The first one concerns the power of confirming as given to priests who operate under the provisions of the apostolic constitution, *Exsul Familia*, issued on August 1, 1952, under the title "*De Spirituali Emigrantium Cura.*"[28] On October 7, 1953, the Sacred Consistorial Congregation promulgated the following declaration:

> Missionariis emigrantium quibus, ad norman Constitutionis Apostolicae *Exsul Familia* nn. 34-40, curam animarum in propria dioecesi locorum Ordinarii commiserint, competat potestas administrandi subditis,[29] in articulo mortis constitutis, Sacramentum Confirmationis ad normam Decreti Sacrae Congregationis de disciplina Sacramentorum *Spiritus Sancti munera* diei 14 Septembris, 1946. SSm̃us Dominus noster Pius Divina Providentia Pp. XII hanc declarationem ratam habere dignatus est *in Audientia* diei 31 Augusti 1953.[30]

Another text concerns the faculty granted to ship chaplains and their directors.[31]

[27] "Servatis, in reliquis, terminis et clausulis memorati Decreti."

[28] The complete text of this document appears in *AAS*, XLIV (1952), 649-704. It consists of two parts; the English version of the second title can be consulted in Bouscaren, *The Canon Law Digest*, III (1954), 85-98.

[29] It should be noted that the power is expressly limited in favor of their subjects.

[30] *AAS*, XLV (1953), 758.

[31] Ferretto, "In normas et facultates pro sacerdotibus in spiritualem navigantium maritimorum et emigrantium curam incumbentibus adnotationes," *Apollinaris*, XXVIII (1955), 75-103 ("Confirmation," pp. 81-84),

This was issued by the Sacred Consistorial Congregation on the 19th of March, 1954.

> Normae et Facultates pro sacerdotibus in spiritualem navigantium curam incumbentibus nempe pro cappellanis navigantium et cappellanorum directoribus iussu Sanctissimi Domini Nostri Pii Divina Providentia Papae Duodecimi editae.
>
> II.
>
> 8. Cappellanis navigantium eorumque Directoribus, quae infra recensentur facultates seu privilegia, *durante munere* tribuuntur:
>
> 1° Facultas administrandi, ad norman Decreti Sacrae Congregationis de disciplina Sacramentorum *Spiritus Sancti Munera* (*AAS*, XXXVIII, p. 349ss.) sacramentum Confirmationis cuilibet christifideli in navi versanti ex gravi morbo in mortis periculo constituto.
>
> 2° Facultas administrandi sacramentum Confirmationis, itinere maritimo perdurante, cuilibet puero vel adulto, praesertim primum in ipsa navi sacra Synaxi refecto; dummodo adsit Episcopus communione gaudens cum Apostolica Sede, et praevideatur confirmandum vel aetate vel inscitia sermonis ad loci adiunctis nonnisi magna cum difficultate in regione immigrationis hoc Sacramentum recepturum, ceterisque servatis de iure servandis ac potissimum, quod attinet ad ritum, Instructione pro simplici sacerdote sacramentum Confirmationis ex Sedis Apostolicae delegatione administrante in *Appendice Ritualis Romani* inserta.[32]

An annual report of the number and circumstances of these confirmations was to be sent by the Director to the Sacred Consistorial Congregation as well as to the curia of the ordinary in whose diocese the office of the Director is located.[33]

The same faculties were granted on April 2, 1954, to the chaplains and the directors of the *Apostolatus Maris*.[34]

---

gives a very fine account of the historical evolution of these faculties and explains the meaning of the various provisions contained therein.

[32] *AAS*, XLVI (1954), 416-417.

[33] *AAS*, XLVI (1954), 416.

[34] *AAS*, XLVI (1954), 248-252, Confirmation, 250. The only difference is that the word *"praesertim"* (as used in 2°) is left out.

CHAPTER VI

CONDITIONS FOR THE VALID ADMINISTRATION OF CONFIRMATION BY THE EXTRAORDINARY MINISTER

To exercise the faculty of confirming properly, the extraordinary minister of confirmation must keep in mind certain conditions which are requisite for the valid and lawful administration of this sacrament. Since the decree specifically warns of invalidity after conditions enumerated in n. 2, these are to be considered as necessary for both validity and lawfulness. The other conditions, enumerated in nn. 3-9, are to be looked upon as affecting the lawful use of this power, without touching upon its validity.

Article 1—The Faculty Must Be Used Personally

The decree does not entertain any possibility of subdelegation of power on the part of the extraordinary minister of confirmation. It emphasizes this restriction when it states that for validity as well as for lawfulness the enumerated extraordinary ministers must "*per se*," "*personaliter*," administer the sacrament.[1] One might detect in this provision a very slight indication that the power conferred through this delegation seems more properly the power of orders than of jurisdiction, since this regulation so closely resembles the provisions of canon 210, which states that the power of orders, when attached to an office or committed to a person by a legitimate ecclesiastical superior, cannot be delegated to others, unless this is expressly permitted by law or by indult. Zerba, however, in explanation of this limitation, cites canon 199, § 2, which states that the power of jurisdiction delegated by the Holy See can be subdelegated, either for a single act or habitually, unless the delegated person was chosen because of his personal qualifications, or subdelegation is forbidden.[2]

[1] *AAS,* XXXVIII (1946), 352.

[2] *Commentarius,* n. 26, p. 58.

Actually, since the decree did not wish to express adherence to either school of thought or opinion in this intricate problem of whether it is the power of orders or the power of jurisdiction which is conceded, one can safely attribute this restriction with reference to any potential subdelegation simply to the expressed will of the Sacred Congregation.[3]

Therefore, a pastor who is ill or unable or unwilling to go out to confer confirmation cannot subdelegate the task to his assistant, to the neighboring pastor, to a visiting priest, etc. Such a subdelegation would possess no juridic force, and the confirmation administered in consequence of it would be *invalid.*

Article 2—The Faculty Must Be Used within the Territorial Limits

The valid exercise of this power is limited not only to a personal use but also to specific territorial confines. The extraordinary minister can confirm only within the physical boundaries of his parish.[4] Thus, if one of his subjects were in a hospital which is geographically located beyond the territory over which he governs, the pastor could not enter the hospital to confirm, but would have to rely upon the pastor in whose parish the hospital is situated, since a pastor cannot confirm one of his parishioners outside the parish limits.[5] Admittedly this can create a rather difficult situation at times and imposes a great responsibility upon the pastor, for example, of a parish within whose boundaries one or more hospitals are located. Only he can validly confirm, so that he cannot subdelegate this power to the pastor whose subject is in danger of death at the hospital.

Another factor to be considered is the necessity of every pastor to discover precisely the boundaries of his parish as established by the local ordinary. If a pastor were to exercise

[3] Cf. Pistoni, *De Confirmatione a Ministro Extraordinario,* n. 100, p. 94.

[4] "Fines paroeciales physice sumendi sunt, et non moraliter, ita ut distantia unius passus a territorio reddat sacramentum invalidum."—Pistoni, *op. cit.,* n. 101, p. 96.

[5] "Praefati ministri Confirmationem valide et licite conferre valent per se ipsi, personaliter, fidelibus tantummodo in proprio territorio degentibus . . ."—*AAS,* XXXVIII (1946), 352.

this prerogative of administering confirmation in a home or in a hospital which he thought to be within the boundaries of his parish, but which actually was outside his proper territory, the sacrament would not be conferred either lawfully or even validly. Whether canon 209 would supply in such a case will be discussed later in another article. Pastors of national parishes in particular should assiduously ascertain the extent of the cumulative territory which they enjoy since often the territorial sphere of their jurisdiction is indicated only vaguely and obscurely. Pistoni offers the helpful suggestion that, since this is a question of a person in danger of death, in a case of doubt about the boundaries of the parish, the confirmation should be conferred conditionally, *"si possum."* [6]

On these two particular points, namely the prohibition of any subdelegation of power by the extraordinary minister and the limitation of his power within specified territorial boundaries, since the decree is so clear in its statements of these provisions, all commentators are in agreement.

Article 3—The Recipient Must Be a Member of the Church

The subject to whom the extraordinary minister can administer confirmation is any member of the faithful, residing or more properly at the time sojourning in his territory and constituted in a true danger of death, which latter condition shall be explained at greater length in a subsequent article.[7] The recipient can therefore be any baptized infant [that is, one below the age of reason, or one who, though physically matured, has never reached the use of reason] [8] or a baptized adult, who for some reason has never been confirmed.

Twice in paragraph n. 2 the decree uses the word *"fideles"* to describe the proper recipient. One might ask who are to be included in this term. Canon 1325, § 1, uses the words *"fideles Christi"* when it speaks of the necessity of outwardly professing

[6] *Op cit.*, n. 101, p. 96.

[7] *AAS*, XXXVIII (1946), 352.

[8] Canon 88, § 3; also canon 745, § 2, n. 1.

the faith, and then in paragraph 2 defines a heretic as one who, after the reception of baptism, though he retains the name of Christian, pertinaciously denies or doubts about any of the truths which must be believed by divine and Catholic faith; an apostate, as one who gives up the Christian faith entirely; a schismatic, as one who refuses submission to the Supreme Pontiff or rejects communion with the members of the Church subject to him. Therefore, excluded as proper recipients would be infidels, properly so called, that is, those who are not yet validly baptized, and infidels, improperly so called, that is, those who indeed have received a valid baptism but now are heretics, apostates or schismatics.[9]

Cappello notes that it would certainly be gravely unlawful to administer the sacraments to formal heretics or schismatics. Likewise the sacraments are not to be administered to material heretics or schismatics until they have renounced their errors and become reconciled with the Church. The reason for this is that the administration of the sacraments has been entrusted by Christ to the Church, and only those are able to receive the sacraments who are members of the body of the Church of Christ.[10]

Pistoni adds that, from the very tenor of the decree, the administration of confirmation by an extraordinary minister to anyone who is not classified among the faithful would not only be unlawful but invalid as well.[11] Mahoney, on the other hand, with some hesitancy, offered it as a probable opinion that the sacrament of confirmation could be validly administered to dying heretics for the reason that they are not expressly excluded. He held that its administration would certainly be unlawful, since confirmation is not absolutely necessary for salvation and, inasmuch as the decree excludes the presence of heretics during the administration of confirmation,[12] *a fortiori* the very adminis-

[9] Pistoni, *op. cit.*, p. 95.

[10] *De Sacramentis*, I, n. 62, pp. 54-55.

[11] *Op. cit.*, p. 95.

[12] *AAS*, XXXVIII (1946), 356.

tration of the sacrament to them would be excluded.[13] Connell suggests that *per se* there is no reason why a priest could not (*validly*) confirm a baptized infant of Protestant parents, when there is no danger of scandal or detriment to the Church. He advised, however, that this be done only in exceptional circumstances and then only when there seems to be no possibility that the child will survive.[14]

a—THE RECIPIENT NEED NOT BE A PROPER SUBJECT

The decree, in wishing to emphasize the territorial aspect of the concession, does not mention proper subjects; hence, the question of parochial domicile or quasi-domicile [15] does not enter the discussion. A resident with a domicile in the parish (*incola*), a tenant who has a quasi-domicile (*advena*), as well as a visitor who is actually outside the place where he has a domicile or a quasi-domicile (*peregrinus*) and a wanderer who has neither a domicile nor a quasi-domicile (*vagus*) [16] are proper recipients of confirmation as long as they are at the time within the territorial confines of the jurisdiction of the extraordinary minister. This is the consensus among the commentators.[17] The reason for their presence does not affect the use of this faculty. They may be there of their own free choice, be forcibly detained there, or they even may have been brought there for the specific purpose

[13] *The Clergy Review,* XXXI (1949), 338-341; cf. also Umberg, "Sacramenta Acatholicis Nonnisi Condiocionate Conferenda," *Periodica,* XXXVII (1948), 97-102.

[14] "Art. cit.," *AER,* CXVI (1947), 260. See also Donovan, "Questions Answered—Practical Cases Arising from the Recent Indult Empowering Priests to Confirm," *The Homiletic and Pastoral Review,* XLIX (1949), 248-249.

[15] Cf. canon 92, §§ 1 and 3.

[16] Cf. canon 91.

[17] Quinn (*The Extraordinary Minister of Confirmation,* p. 98) stated that if the Latin words used by the decree, "*degentibus*" and "*commorantibus,*" were held to their strict canonical interpretation, then the decree would have to be understood to demand a title of domicile or quasi-domicile for the person. He concluded, however, that the only condition for validity is that the person be actually present in the territory of the minister.

of receiving the sacrament, inasmuch as their own pastor was unavailable or unable to administer it.[18]

A practical question may arise in a particular situation wherein two or more pastors cumulatively enjoy jurisdiction within certain territorial confines proper to each of them, for instance, in a certain city wherein there is but one "territorial" parish, but also a so called Polish parish and a so called French parish. Is there any limitation on the respective rights of each pastor to confirm? Following the lead of Zerba, Undersecretary of the Sacred Congregation for the Discipline of the Sacraments, the commentators who treat of the problem[19] concluded that each pastor can *validly* confirm anyone in the territory, not only his own subjects but even outsiders living in the common territory. *Validly and lawfully* each pastor can confirm only his proper subjects, provided, of course, that they are in the territory at the time. A territorial pastor validly and lawfully confirms also other subjects, not of the national pastor, who for any reason are actually in his territory. A national pastor would require a just cause to lawfully confirm such an outsider or the subject of a territorial pastor. Likewise a territorial pastor would require a just cause to confirm the subject of a national pastor.[20] Smiddy added that, if one remembers that each of these pastors has power only in the case of the dying, it appears that instances of outright unlawfulness would be very rare.[21]

With proper reverence to the eminent authority of Zerba and the other commentators, it appears to this writer that, though such a distinction may be perfectly applicable to the parochial reserved functions listed in canon 462,[22] the nature of the faculty

18 Pistoni, *De Confirmatione a Ministro Extraordinario,* n. 101, p. 96.

19 Quinn, *op. cit.,* p. 86; Smiddy, *A Manual for the Extraordinary Minister of Confirmation,* p. 52; Coronata, *De Sacramentis,* I, n. 126 *bis* under (c), p. 126.

20 Zerba, *Commentarius,* pp. 44-45.

21 *Op. cit.,* p. 52.

22 Kelly, *The Functions Reserved to Pastors,* The Catholic University of America Canon Law Studies, no. 250 (Washington, D. C.: The Catholic University of America Press, 1947), p. 88, includes the administration of confirmation as a reserved function, although he adds (p. 89), "No other

to confirm does not warrant the introduction of a distinction between the valid and the valid and lawful exercise of the power. Zerba himself insists that the indult is territorial, not personal, and that a priest with the delegated faculty could validly and lawfully confirm the faithful, even though not his subjects, who here and now are in his territory, by reason either of domicile, or of quasi-domicile, or of simple sojourn (*simplex commoratio*).[23] Nowhere does the decree speak of a pastor-parishioner relationship as necessary for validity, or even for lawfulness. Quinn himself admitted this, at least indirectly, when he commented that the decree did not want to create additional difficulty for the extraordinary minister by obliging him to determine whether the person who is in danger of death is a permanent or a quasi-permanent resident, a visitor, or a mere transient without any fixed abode.[24] As a matter of fact, the basis for the use of the faculty is a territorial relationship:

> Praefati ministri [with no exception] confirmationem valide et licite [with no distinction] conferre valent per se ipsi, personaliter, fidelibus [with no limitation, "*Subditis*" is not used] tantummodo in proprio territorio degentibus [the only requirement].[25]

An example may perhaps serve to clarify the writer's position. In regard to baptism, the law specifies that, though the ordinary minister of baptism is a priest, the conferring of it is reserved to the pastor or some other priest who possesses the permission of the pastor or of the local ordinary, which permission is lawfully presumed in case of necessity.[26] Even the one absent from his domicile or quasi-domicile is at a later time to receive solemn baptism from his own pastor in his own parish, if this can be done readily and without delay.[27] Similarly, the rule for the

---

priest could validly confirm within the parish limits, unless it be the pastor of a national parish, who has cumulative jurisdiction over the same territory."

[23] *Op. cit.*, p. 59.

[24] *Op. cit.*, n. 2, p. 98.

[25] *AAS*, XXXVIII (1946), 352.

[26] Canon 738, § 1.

[27] Canon 738, § 2.

contracting of matrimony is that a marriage shall be lawfully celebrated in the presence of the pastor of the bride,[28] and a pastor who assists at a marriage without the permission required by law is not entitled to the stole fee, but must return it to the proper pastor of the contracting parties.[29] The *Code* considers the pastor of the place in which the sick person is found, i.e., the local pastor, as the ordinary minister of extreme unction. His reasonably presumed permission suffices for the lawful use of the power by any other priest.[30]

Though this may be an analogical basis for the distinction made by Zerba, the decree *Spiritus Sancti munera* does not contain such an indication. Clerical courtesy might demand that the "prior" [31] right of the territorial pastor over his subjects and the *peregrini* and the *vagi* sojourning in his territory, on the one hand, and that of a national pastor over his personal subjects, on the other hand, be recognized and respected in common and cumulative territory. The writer, however, hesitates, in the light of the provisions of the decree, to brand as unlawful the action of either in confirming the subject of the other, even without what Zerba refers to as a *"iusta causa."* The legal adage, *"ubi legislator non distinguit, neque nos distinguere debemus,"* can readily be applied to this discussion, especially since this particular distinction results in the creation of an unlawful act. Though the writer doubts that there will be many occasions for pastors to quarrel over their right to confirm a particular recipient, he feels that a bishop would be perfectly justified in establishing the policy whereby a hospital, in a city where a number of pastors hold cumulative rights over the same territory in which the hospital is located, would follow a rotating sequence in calling upon them to confirm patients found to be in danger of death. This would be one way of relieving the burden

[28] Canon 1097, § 2.

[29] Canon 1097, § 3.

[30] Canon 938, § 2.

[31] Such is the term used by Quinn, who states: "The territorial pastor has prior right to use his faculty for outsiders (not the subjects of the personal pastor) who are residing in the territory."—*Op. cit.,* p. 86.

of the "territorial" pastor in whose parish a large hospital or maternity home is situated, since he cannot subdelegate the power to anyone else.

Another point to be noted in respect to the subject of confirmation by the extraordinary minister is that in these cases the principle of exemption has no application. As Connell observes, even an exempt religious—in the rare instance that he has never been confirmed—can receive this sacrament from the parish priest of the territory wherein the monastery or convent is situated.[32] To this statement one can add "can and must receive," since only the parish priest possesses the faculty, not the local superior or the chaplain.

Exemption by which religious, religious communities and pious houses within the territorial confines of the parish are removed from parochial authority may be granted by law, or also by the local ordinary for a grave and justifying reason in accordance with the authority given to him by the second paragraph of canon 464. Regulars, both men and women, including novices, except nuns who are not subject to regular superiors, are exempt along with their religious houses and churches, from the jurisdiction of the local ordinary, hence *a fortiori* from the jurisdiction of the pastor, except in cases expressly specified in law.[33] Also exempted from parochial jurisdiction is the seminary, where the rector performs all parochial functions except assistance at marriage and without prejudice to the rule of canon 891, wherein the rector is forbidden to hear the confession of a seminarian unless a serious emergency requires it in a particular case and the seminarian approaches the rector of his own accord.[34]

Thus, the decree clearly states that the power of the extraordinary minister extends even to persons who are staying in places which ordinarily are outside his parochial jurisdiction, including seminaries, lodging houses, hospitals, and other institutions of all kinds, even though religious, no matter how they are exempt.[35] This would even include a papal cloister.[36] The

[32] "Art. cit.," *AER,* CXVI (1947), n. 2, p. 259.

[33] Cf. canons 615 and 464, § 1.

[34] Canon 1368.

right of the extraordinary minister is thus similar to that of the bishop who can administer confirmation even in exempt places.[37]

The question arises whether the extraordinary minister of confirmation is able to confirm in a place which exclusively belongs to another rite, *"locus exclusivae iurisdictionis alius ritus."* For example, in Washington, D. C., St. Josaphat's seminary is established for the training of seminarians of the Ukranian rite. Could the Latin pastor, in whose territory the institution is located, enter the building to administer the sacrament of confirmation to a person who therein is in danger of death, or is the place to be considered as withdrawn from the boundaries of his territory? The solution of this problem must be sought in the official reply issued *"de speciali mandato Sanctissimi"* by the Pontifical Commission for the Redaction of the Code of Oriental Canon Law on July 8, 1952. An extensive interpretation was given to canon 86 of the motu proprio, *Crebrae allatae,* promulgated on February 22, 1949 with the provision that the canons were to have the force of law from the 2nd of May of the same year, whereby in virtue of canon 86, § 1, n. 2 [38] the pastor and the local hierarch within the confines of their territory could validly and lawfully assist at the marriage of the faithful of their rite, even in places which are exclusively of another rite (*"in locis quae sunt exclusive alius ritus"*) provided (*"dummodo"*) there be the express consent of the ordinary, or pastor or rector of the aforesaid places.[39]

[35] *AAS,* XXXVIII (1946), n. 2, p. 352.

[36] Zerba, *op. cit.,* p. 60. Cf. canon 600 for a listing of those who may enter an enclosure for nuns. The latest legislation on the rules governing the papal cloister of nuns is the "Instruction Regarding the Cloister of Nuns," issued by the Sacred Congregation for the Religious, March 25, 1956, a little more than five years after the famous Apostolic Constitution *Sponsa Christi* of November 21, 1950. The Latin text of the Instruction can be found in *AAS,* XLVIII (1956), 512-526.

[37] Canon 792.

[38] Parochus et loci Hierarcha valide matrimonio assistunt: . . . Intra fines dumtaxat sui territorii sive contrahentes sunt subditi, sive non subditi, modo sint sui ritus.

[39] *AAS,* XLIV (1952), 552.

This response clearly and definitely admits the existence of places which exclusively belong to one rite. At the same time, indirectly and implicitly it assumes that a priest or hierarch of another rite does not have the faculty to assist at a marriage within the confines of such a place.[40]

The church, the bishop's residence, the parish house, a hospital, a seminary established by the authority of the bishop for the faithful of his particular rite, are, thus, carved out, so to speak, from the territory in which they are located with the result that the pastor who would attempt to administer the sacrament of confirmation would not do so validly since the recipient was not within his territory.[41]

As a final consideration one may ask whether the provision of canon 784, similar to the rule for bishops in canon 783, § 1, has a binding and restricting effect on the use of the power by an extraordinary minister. Herein it is stated that a priest, fortified with a local apostolic privilege, can lawfully confirm even outsiders in his designated territory, unless their local ordinary has expressly forbidden it. Since the decree makes no mention of such a limitation, the writer concludes that it has no application. Smiddy adds that it is inconceivable that a bishop would want to include even the dying in his ruling which prohibits the reception of confirmation by his subjects outside the diocese.[42] The writer questions whether the bishop would have any right at all to bar his subjects from receiving confirmation outside his diocese when they are in danger of death.

b—THE RECIPIENT MAY BE THE MEMBER OF AN ORIENTAL RITE

Another point to be considered in the question of the proper recipient of confirmation from the hands of an extraordinary minister concerns members of the Oriental or Eastern rites.

40 Herman, "Pontificia Commissio ad Redigendum Codicem Iuris Canonici Orientalis—Adnotationes," *Monitor Ecclesiasticus,* IV (1952), 423. "Aliis verbis, in locis quae sunt exclusive alius ritus, Hierarcha loci vel parochus, vel alii qui iurisdictionem habent in suo ritu hanc exercere valide non possunt."—*loc. cit.*

41 *AAS,* XXXVIII (1946), n. 2, p. 352.

42 *Op. cit.,* p. 52.

Though there are 5 basic or fundamental rites from which the others are derived,[43] the Oriental Church officially includes seventeen rites: the Greek or Hellenic, the Italo-Albanian, the Melchite, the Ruthenian, the Serbian, the Russian, the Georgian, the Rumanian and the Bulgarian Church of the Byzantine rite; the Coptic and the Ethiopian Church of the Alexandrian rite; the Chaldean and Malabar Church of the Chaldean rite; the Syrian, Maronite and Malankarese Church of the Antiochean rite; and the Armenian Church of the Armenian rite.

Canon 782, § 4, states that a priest of the Latin rite to whom, in virtue of an indult, the power to confirm has been granted, can *validly* confer confirmation *only* on the faithful of his own rite, unless contrary provision has been expressly made in the indult. Since the decree *Spiritus Sancti munera* expressly states that the faculty to confirm on the part of extraordinary ministers is granted *"ex generali Apostolicae Sedis indulto,"*[44] it seems clear that these aforesaid ministers have only a limited power in their administration. Commentators are generally agreed that this restriction does not apply to those who enjoy the faculty by the law itself.[45] Thus Regatillo, who holds that pastors now confirm with ordinary power by law,[46] seems compelled to hold the opposite of the writer's view. If such be the case, there would not have been the pressing need for the Sacred Congregation for the Oriental Church to issue on the 1st of May, 1948, a special decree to protect the sacrament of confirmation against nullity when it was administered to a member of the Oriental rite by priests of the Latin rite in virtue of an indult.[47]

[43] "Ritus orientales de quibus canones decernunt sunt alexandrinus, antiochenus, constantinopolitanus, chaldaeus et armenus, aliique ritus quos uti sui iuris expresse vel tacite agnoscit Ecclesia."—Canon 303, §1, no. 1, *De Verborum Significatione,* in the Oriental Code.

[44] *AAS,* XXXVIII (1946), n. 1, p. 352.

[45] Canon 782, § 3.

[46] *Ius Sacramentarium,* p. 58.

[47] *AAS,* XL (1948), 422-423. For the Latin text and translation of this decree, cf. Appendix iii. Mostaza (*op. cit.,* p. 361) declares that the Sacred Congregation presumes that the restriction of canon 782, § 4 affects the priests who confirm in virtue of the power authorized for them through

This decree, which juridically is also to be considered as a pontifical law because of its relation to the decree *Spiritus Sancti munera* and its own specific approbation,[48] thus extends to all Latin priests, if by indult, either general or particular, they are empowered to confirm, the power to administer the sacrament to certain members of the Eastern rites. Two conditions must be ascertained: (1) that the person was not confirmed in infancy, and (2) that the member of the Oriental rite comes under the classification of the ones enumerated in the Apostolic Constitution, *Orientalium dignitas*.

The sacraments of baptism and confirmation are conferred together in the Oriental rites which in this country come under the jurisdiction of the Latin ordinaries, with the exception of the Maronite rite.[49] Thus, for practical purposes, unless one has proof to the contrary, the extraordinary minister of confirmation in taking care of a member of the Oriental rite in danger of death, provided he is not a Maronite, and provided that he has been under the ministrations of the Oriental clergy, can presume that he has already received confirmation. However, it may happen rather often, as the decree points out, that many of these Eastern rite Catholics have been cared for by priests of the Latin rite for such a long time that they believe they belong to it or do not know to which rite they belong. They may have

---

the decree *Spiritus Sancti munera,* which presumption cannot be admitted by those who hold that the new extraordinary ministers enjoy the faculty by common law, not by indult.

[48] ". . . Sanctitas Sua benigne dignatus est adprobare, simulque iussit id publici iuris fieri praesenti Decreto . . ."—*AAS,* XL (1948), 422. Cf. also Quinn (*op. cit.,* p. 120) who, though he holds for a specific approbation in that the decree stands in juxtaposition to and in extension of the first decree, contends that it does not have sufficient juridical qualifications in itself to signalize an approbation *in forma specifica.* Bastnagel ("Confirmation of Orientals by Latin Priests," *The Jurist,* IX [1949], 87) states: "From the wording of the decree it is evident that one must consider it a general decree. Accordingly, it is vested with the nature of a newly promulgated law."

[49] Diederichs, *The Jurisdiction of the Latin Ordinaries over Their Oriental Subjects,* The Catholic University of America Canon Law Studies, no. 229 (Washington, D. C.: The Catholic University of America Press, 1946), p. 86.

been baptized by a priest of the Latin rite, and accordingly they would not have been confirmed at the time of baptism. A Latin pastor may be called out for the emergency baptism of a child of an Oriental rite father. Ordinarily a person belongs to the rite by the ceremonies of which he was baptized, unless baptism was administered by a minister of another rite through fraud, or because of necessity inasmuch as a priest of the proper rite could not be approached, or in virtue of an apostolic dispensation.[50] In the case visualized, the child, though baptized by a Latin priest according to the Roman rite, would nevertheless belong to the Oriental rite of its father.[51] Previous to the decree of 1948, the child could not have been validly confirmed by the extraordinary minister of confirmation. This difficulty has now been removed, so that a Latin priest need never question his power to confirm a child which he has just baptized because of proximate danger of death.

There seems to be one exception to this general rule. Are members of the Ruthenian Byzantine rite included? The Ruthenians of Podcarpathia, those of Hungarian and Croation nationalities, and especially the Ruthenians from Galicia, the Ukrainians, who by far constitute the greatest number of Oriental Catholics in this country, actually have their own ordinary to whom they are subject. The head of the Byzantine Rite Apostolic exarchate in Pittsburgh is the Most Rev. Nicholas T. Elko; the Most Rev. Constantine Bohachevsky heads the exarchate of Philadelphia, while the Most Rev. Ambrose Senyshyn has charge of the newly created exarchate of Stamford, established in 1956. The decree of the Sacred Congregation for the Oriental Church applied to priests to whom the spiritual care of Oriental Catholics remains entrusted in virtue of the ninth article of the Apostolic Constitution, *Orientalium dignitas*, dated November 30, 1894, which states: "Every Oriental Catholic

[50] Canon 98, § 1. The parallel canon in the Oriental Code ("De Ritibus Orientalibus," canon 6, § 2), which was promulgated by the Motu proprio *Cleri sanctitati* on June 2, 1957 and acquired the force of law on March 25, 1958, gives to the proper Hierarch the faculty to grant the permission for the baptism to be conferred by the minister of another rite.

[51] Canon 756, § 1.

living outside his patriarchical territory shall be under the administration of the Latin clergy."[52] The decree *Cum data fuerit*[53] placed the Ruthenians in this country under the jurisdiction of their own ordinaries. They are obliged, in accordance with article 28, to receive the sacraments from their own pastors in communities where such are found. In other distant localities they are to be served by the local clergy.

Since they are not subject to the Latin ordinaries, they seem to be excluded from the category of those *"extra proprium territorium sub iurisdictione Ordinarii Latini ritus degentes."*[54] Therefore, it seems that a Latin priest who in an emergency baptized an infant of a Ruthenian father could not validly follow this up with confirmation. The same would be true of an adult Ruthenian Catholic who had never been confirmed and is in danger of death. There seems to be no doubt about this in places where a priest of that rite is available.

What is to be said of the circumstances wherein the Ruthenian has been under the ministrations of the Latin clergy for years because there is no parish conducted by a priest of his rite? In this case Smiddy ventures the opinion that, since the document actually gives the faculty to confirm those of the Oriental rite whose spiritual care has been permanently entrusted to Latin rite priests,[55] the administration of the sacrament would be valid. The same opinion, based on the same reasoning, is held by Wojnar, professor of Oriental Canon Law at the Catholic University of America. He adds, as an argument "ex conveni-

[52] *AAS,* XL (1948), 422.

[53] This decree was issued by the Sacred Congregation for the Oriental Church on May 1, 1929 (*AAS,* XXI [1929], 152-159) for a period of ten years; it was renewed on November 23, 1940 (*AAS,* XXXIII [1941], 27 ff.) for another ten years. On November 23, 1950, in virtue of a special mandate from this Sacred Congregation, the Apostolic Delegate of the United States confirmed and prorogued the decree with a few added provisions for another ten years. (*Temporary Diocesan Statutes of the Byzantine Apostolic Exarchy of Philadelphia, Pa., U.S.A.* [Paterson, N. J.: St. Anthony's Guild Press, 1955], 23-24.)

[54] *AAS,* XL (1948), 423.

[55] ". . . quorum spiritualis cura ipsis commissa permaneat . . ."—*AAS,* XL (1948), 423.

entia," that, otherwise, the child of the Ruthenian rite in danger of death where there is no priest of his own rite available for confirming, would be in a distinctly disadvantageous position to suffer spiritual losses. Smiddy, however, cautions that it would be unwise to act on the affirmative opinion until the point is settled officially.[56] Damen, on the other hand, held that the Ruthenians in the United States are not subjects for valid confirmation by priests of the Latin rite. He suggested that a special indult be obtained from the Holy See to cover these circumstances.[57]

Article 4—The Recipient Must Be in Danger of Death

The presence of the recipient in the territory of the extraordinary minister is not the only condition postulated for the valid use of the faculty of confirming. Another one of equal importance, to the extent that the words were italicized in the decree, is that the recipient must be in true danger of death from a serious illness from which it is foreseen that the recipient will die.[58]

In the early days following the issuance of the decree some commentators inclined to a rigorous interpretation of the terms involved. At first Hannan excluded accident from the notion of *morbus* [59] although he later changed his opinion,[60] so that in his two volume canonical commentary he states: "The faculty can

[56] *Op. cit.*, p. 114. In the *Temporary Diocesan Statutes,* cited above, mention is made (n. 9, pp. 37-38) of the decree of the Sacred Congregation for the Oriental Church by which a priest of the Latin rite is empowered to confirm Eastern rite Catholics without the introducing of any distinction by which Ukrainian Catholics would be excluded.

[57] "Attamen, si in tali territorio ob penuriam Sacerdotum proprii ritus, fidelibus orientalibus non satis provisum foret, Ordinarii orientales facile indultum huc spectans a SS. implorare atque obtinere posse videntur."—"Annotationes," *Apollinaris,* XXII (1949), 79.

[58] " . ex gravi morbo in vero mortis periculo sint constituti, ex quo decessuri praevideantur."—*AAS,* XXXVIII (1946), n. 2, p. 352.

[59] *Denver Register,* January 24, 1947, p. 1.

[60] "Decretum de Confirmatione—Commentary," *The Jurist,* VII (1947), 228.

be used in behalf of a person in danger from a wound as well as from a disease."[61] Connell, however, from the very beginning held that any bodily ailment likely to cause death, whether its source be a disease or an accident, would justify the use of the faculty.[62] This was the general opinion of most of the commentators and is practically unanimously adopted today.[63] Death which is imminent from an extrinsic source does not, however, suffice for the administration of the sacrament. Thus, confirmation could not be conferred by the extraordinary minister upon a criminal who faces execution for a capital crime, a soldier who is about to enter into active combat, a civilian in danger of death from air raids, etc.[64] Basically this is the fundamental teaching of canonists and moralists on the nature of *"morbus"* in a subject capable of receiving extreme unction.[65] Following is a typical definition of a serious illness as given by Noldin-Schmitt:

> Gravis morbus censetur qui ex se et natura sua letalem exitum habere potest et ad illum terminum processit, in quo probabiliter iudicari possit mortem allaturus.[66]

What about old age? Cappello notes that all theologians agree on equating old age with *"infirmitas"* or *"gravis morbus."* This

[61] *The Sacred Canons,* I, 780.

[62] "The Recent Decree Empowering Pastors to Confirm," *AER,* CXVI (1947), 260.

[63] Regatillo, *Ius Sacramentarium,* p. 60; Onclin, "L'Administration du Sacrement de la Confirmation en Cas de Danger de Mort," *ETL,* XXV (1949), 344; Smiddy, *A Manual for the Extraordinary Minister of Confirmation,* p. 53; Quinn, *The Extraordinary Minister of Confirmation,* p. 101; Pistoni, *De Confirmatione a Ministro Extraordinario,* p. 98.

[64] Onclin, "art. cit.," 344; Connell, "art. cit.," 260; Hannan, "art. cit.," 228; Mahoney, "The Extraordinary Minister of Confirmation," *The Clergy Review,* XXVII (1947), 83; Smiddy, *op. cit.,* p. 53; Quinn, *op. cit.,* p. 101; Zerba, *Commentarius,* p. 61; Regatillo, *op. cit.,* p. 59.

[65] Cappello, *De Sacramentis* (v. III, *De Extrema Unctione,* 3. ed., Taurini-Romae: Marietti, 1949) III, n. 232, p. 158.

[66] *Summa Theologiae Moralis iuxta Codicem Iuris Canonici,* H. Noldin accommodavit ab editione XVII A. Schmitt (Oeniponte, Lipsiae: ex typis Feliciani Rauch, 1940), III, n. 444, p. 457.

consensus was approved by the Church and incorporated in canon 940, § 1, wherein it is stated that extreme unction can be administered only to one of the faithful who, after attaining the use of reason, is in danger of death through sickness or old age. Thus old age would be sufficient for the valid conferring of confirmation by an extraordinary minister.[67] Mahoney, however, made one distinction. If the person is in danger of death from old age or from some lingering sickness, he may receive extreme unction and other rites validly and lawfully; but quite probably the administration of confirmation, though valid, might, in such circumstances, be unlawful since in the case of a lingering sickness it might be more easily possible to secure the services of a bishop as required in n. 3 of the decree.[68]

The expressions *"in* VERO *mortis periculo"* and *"ex quo decessuri praevideantur"* also caused some hesitation. As an example, Mahoney considered that the prospect of recovery must be more remote than is required for the administration of extreme unction, so that the phrase might be translated, "those in real danger of death from an incurable disease." [69] Cappello said that the danger of death must be certain, and not doubtful or merely probable.[70] At present he explains *"verum periculum mortis"* as one which is truly and solidly probable.[71]

Various subsequent documents, both private and official in nature, have served as a practical norm for the interpretation of these terms. The first is a reply by the Congregation for the Discipline of the Sacraments, issued March 6, 1947, to the

[67] Conway, "Notes and Queries—New Decree on Confirmation in Danger of Death," *The Irish Ecclesiastical Record,* 5. series, LXIX (1947), 229.

[68] "Confirmation: Grave Sickness," *The Clergy Review,* XXVII (1947), 345.

[69] "The Extraordinary Minister of Confirmation," *The Clergy Review,* XXVII (1947), 83-84. In the same article, however, he concluded that a sickness which warrants the reception of extreme unction also warrants the reception of confirmation. He then added: ". . . doubts will be covered by canon 209."

[70] "Decretum de Confirmatione," *Periodica,* XXXV (1946), 387.

[71] *De Sacramentis,* I, n. 201 bis, p. 184. Thus Pistoni (*op. cit.*, n. 104, p. 100) stated that "verum" is opposed to false, not to probable; and that "verum" is not to be understood as the equivalent of "certum."

Cardinal of Palermo.[72] Smiddy in his *A Manual for the Extraordinary Minister of Confirmation* gives an English translation of the pertinent texts:

> . . . Your Eminence asks precisely why in the Decree it is said *in vero mortis periculo* and not, as would seem sufficient, *in mortis periculo*. . . . Apropos of this it may be observed that the words of the first clause are to be interpreted in a moral sense: namely either when the doctor may have judged that the sick person is actually in real danger of death; or when, even in the absence of a doctor, the extraordinary minister from his own prudence and experience, considering all the circumstances, the gravity and duration of the sickness, the age and general conditions of the sick person . . . may convince himself that actually the sick person is not in a doubtful or even merely in a probable but in a certain and real danger of death.
>
> . . . Furthermore Your Eminence asks what is the minimum necessary to consider as verified the other clause: *ex quo decessuri praevideantur*. . . . The other words, *ex quo, etc.* should be considered in practice as equivalent to those used by the Code in analogous circumstances, *urgente mortis periculo* (cc. 1043, 1044, 1046). It will be useful to consult what his Eminence Card. Gasparri has written in his Tract. *can. de mat.* (*ed. nova ad mentem Codicis*, Vol. I, n. 393) as well as other authors who have commented on these canons. . . .[73]

In this private reply there is a twofold suggestion. On the one hand, it is stated that the person must be in a certain and real danger of death, whereas on the other hand the danger of death is to be estimated by means of a moral judgment and can be presumed to exist when there is a true and serious probability that death will follow.[74] Thus, the sufficiency of a probable danger of death is not ruled out; the very certainty of the danger of death is subject to the fallibility of a human judgment. When the decree from the Sacred Congregation for the Propagation of

[72] *Il Monitore Ecclesiastico* (1948), 24-25. Citation is taken from Smiddy's *Manual*, p. 55, footnote 13.

[73] Pp. 54-55.

[74] "Periculum autem mortis est moraliter aestimandum et adest si sit vera et gravis probabilitas secuturae mortis."—Gasparri, *Tractatus Canonicus De Matrimonio*, ed. nova ad mentem Codicis I. C. (Typis Polyglottis Vaticanis, 1932), n. 393, p. 231.

the Faith was issued on December 18, 1947, the words *"vero etc."* were omitted. It simply stated that the recipient must be in danger of death, "*. . . in mortis periculo. . . .*" [75]

In light of these developments, commentators have concluded that, if the sickness permits the administration of extreme unction,[76] then it also warrants the giving of confirmation.[77]

The priest should not wait until the patient is *in articulo mortis,* that is, when he is nearly unconscious and at the brink of death, since in an adult both his intention to receive it and due instruction regarding this sacrament are called for.[78] However, Smiddy suggests a "wait and see" policy if the subject's illness is serious but death is not imminent. A distinction made by Noldin-Schmitt in regard to extreme unction has application in the present discussion. They observe that as soon as it is judged that the first probable danger of death is present, extreme unction can be administered (*"conferri potest"*) because the subject is capable; but it should not be administered at once (*"nondum dari debet"*). It should be administered when there is at least moral certainty that death is impending.[79] It does not seem probable that one could administer confirmation conditionally, as canon 941 allows the administration of extreme unction, when there is a doubt whether the sick person really and truly is in danger of death.[80] The present writer suggests this "wait and see" policy especially in relation to the confirmation of infants. Though one would readily baptize a newly born baby at the first signs of danger of death because this sacrament is

[75] *AAS,* XL (1948), 41.

[76] Canon 940, § 1.

[77] Mahoney, "The Extraordinary Minister of Confirmation," *The Clergy Review,* XXVII (1947), 84; "Confirmation: Grave Sickness," *ibid.,* 344-347; Bergh, "Administration de la Confirmation aux Fidèles dangereusement Malades," *NRT,* LXIX (1949), 86; Conway, *Problems in Canon Law,* p. 150; Pistoni, *op. cit.,* n. 105, p. 102; *Ephemerides Iuris Canonici,* II (1946), 341, " . . quotiescumque parochus rationabiliter, seu non inepte, mortem secuturam praevidit, adeo ut et extremam unctionem—si expedisset—ministrandam duxerit, confirmatio valida erit et haberi debebit. . . "

[78] *AAS,* XXXVIII (1946), n. 5, p. 353; Pistoni, *op. cit.,* n. 103, p. 99; Zerba, *op, cit.,* p. 62.

[79] *Summa Theologiae Moralis,* III, n. 444, p. 457.

[80] Smiddy, *op. cit.,* p. 56.

absolutely necessary for salvation, discretion should govern the immediate administration of confirmation. This attitude is necessary not only to avoid the danger of failing to verify a condition necessary for the valid administration of confirmation, but also to give consideration to the importance parents and children attach to the reception of the sacrament from a bishop, which is usually the occasion of a solemn ceremony in the parish. Since confirmation can be received only once, such a child could not join his class. This policy, however, should not be an occasion for the extraordinary minister to refrain absolutely from the confirmation of infants.

Knowledge regarding the presence of the danger of death basically results from the prudent judgment of the priest who is to administer the sacrament of confirmation. Alvarez offers three practical factors which one can consider in making a prudent moral estimate of the condition of the patient. First is the decision of the doctor, whose medical opinion as a professional expert must be respected; then, the presence of certain signs, which usually indicate that the end is near; and, finally the nature of the illness. Above all, the actual condition of the patient *must* influence the judgment, for there are more ill people than there are types of illnesses.[81] Suppose that the patient recovers. The confirmation remains valid, since in the case one had to deal with a moral judgment.[82] As a matter of fact, rule number 5 of the decree precisely provides for further instruction of the patient, if he should recover.[83]

Various possibilities proposed by Cappello in his discussion of the valid administration of extreme unction could profitably be applied to the administration of confirmation. If the illness is light, but it is found that it will develop into a dangerous condition, the sacrament *cannot* be validly and lawfully administered until the fear actually materializes.[84] If there is a prudent doubt as to the nature of the illness when it is at least probably

[81] "De Extraordinario Confirmationis Ministro iuxta recentiora praesertim S. Sedis Documenta," *Angelicum,* XXIV (1947), 192.

[82] Cf. Zerba, *op. cit.,* p. 62.

[83] *AAS,* XXXVIII (1946), 353.

[84] *De Sacramentis,* III, n. 233, p. 159.

serious and dangerous, the sacrament can be conferred.[85] If the doctor considers the illness serious and the patient looks upon it as slight, the opinion of the doctor can be followed.[86] On the contrary, the doctor might lightly consider the illness but the patient considers himself in danger of death. In this case, the opinion of the patient, provided that it is prudently reasonable in the estimate of the priest, can be followed.[87] If in fraud the patient feigns a serious sickness, the administration of the sacrament is invalid.[88] However, if the illness seems to be serious and dangerous, but actually there does not exist objectively any danger of death, the administration of the sacrament is valid and lawful as long as there actually existed an illness, and a prudent moral judgment was made in estimating its gravity. Its administration is not to be repeated even conditionally.[89]

The priest-minister of confirmation in the ultimate analysis should strive to avoid two extremes in his attitude towards the condition postulated by the decree for the valid administration of the sacrament, namely that the patient be in real danger of death. On the one hand, he should avoid overeagerness and too great haste in administering confirmation, lest the sacrament be exposed to nullity. On the other hand, he should not so delay or neglect the administration of this sacrament that as a result of this do-nothing policy the faithful depart from this world without having received the wonderful supernatural effects of confirmation.[90]

On the supposition that the requisite conditions are present, a person can be confirmed in accordance with the decree *Spiritus Sancti munera* even after he has lost consciousness. It is true, if he is an adult, that he must have at least the habitual intention of receiving confirmation. In the case of one who has lived a truly Catholic life, such an intention is reasonably presumed to

[85] *Ibid.*, n. 240, p. 161.

[86] *Ibid.*, n. 235, p. 159; Pistoni, *op. cit.*, n. 104, p. 100.

[87] *Ibid.*, n. 234, p. 159; Pistoni, *op. cit.*, n. 104, p. 100.

[88] *Ibid.*, n. 238, p. 160.

[89] *Ibid.*, n. 237, p. 159; Zerba, *op. cit.*, p. 62; Pistoni, *op. cit.*, p. 101.

[90] Zerba, *op. cit.*, p. 62; Smiddy, *op. cit.*, p. 57.

be present from the very fact that he was always devoted to his religious practices. Even one who has been careless in the practice of religion can usually be presumed to have the intention of accepting whatever spiritual aid the Church will offer him in the last crisis.[91] If there is reason to doubt the intention of a Catholic when he is deprived of consciousness at the approach of death, then the priest could administer the sacrament conditionally, *"si vis confirmationem recipere."* [92]

In regard to those who are apparently dead, Pistoni suggests that the extraordinary minister can and should administer confirmation as long as there is a possibility, even though slight, of some life remaining, and provided that there would be no scandal.[93] The principles governing the administration of extreme unction to this category of recipients also have application here.[94]

SUPPLEMENT—THE EXISTENCE AND USE OF A SHORT FORM IN EMERGENCY CASES

Inasmuch as occasions will arise when the recipient is in such imminent danger that time will not allow for the complete ceremony of confirmation, an interesting question comes to the fore. Is there any short form which can be used in the administration of confirmation in urgent necessity as there is for baptism, Viaticum, absolution, extreme unction and the apostolic blessing *in articulo mortis?* Smiddy referred to three commentators who adverted to this possibility. Noirot and Mahoney ventured that one's act of anointing with chrism while saying the complete

[91] "Pro confirmatione, viatico et extrema unctione sufficit intentio habitualis implicita (quae minus proprie a nonnullis interpretativa dicitur), iuxta communem doctrinam."—Cappello, *De Sacramentis,* I, n. 74, p. 65.

[92] Connell, "Confirmation Administered by a Pastor," *AER,* CIX (1948), 148-149.

[93] *De Confirmatione a Ministro Extraordinario,* n. 106, p. 103. Madden ("Confirmation in Danger of Death," *The Australasian Catholic Record,* XXXII [1955], 36) comments: "We believe that confirmation could be given conditionally to a person who was apparently dead, in the same circumstances as some other sacraments are thus administered."

[94] Cf. Cappello, *De Sacramentis,* III, nn. 243-247, pp. 162-164 inclusive, "An et quando extrema unctio ministrari possit ac debeat recenter mortuis."

form inclusive of the triple blessing would suffice, if one fears that the patient will die before the conclusion of the ceremonies, or if confirmation is being administered in a case of apparent death. Verhamme simply stated that the regular rite is to be used, and that there is no short form in urgent cases.[95]

Madden examined the question in *The Australasian Catholic Record* and concluded that the omission of all the ceremonies at confirmation except the anointing of the forehead and the pronouncing of the words of the form would not make the sacrament invalid, but that such a procedure would be unlawful.[96] He based his argumentation on the premise stated in canon 733, § 1, that in confecting, administering and receiving the sacraments there shall be an exact observance of the rites and ceremonies prescribed in the ritual books approved by the Church. *Atqui*—no provision is made either in the *Roman Pontifical* or in the *Roman Ritual* for a short form to be used in cases of emergency. Therefore, any abbreviation would be contrary to what is prescribed in the approved liturgical books.

The proponents of the "short form theory" argued that in accordance with the axiom, *"Sacramenta sunt propter homines,"* the priest is allowed to do whatever can rightfully assist the dying person in his last moments. The opponents logically counter-argued that, if the Congregation had wanted to provide a short form it would have done so, especially since the faculty was granted in favor of those who are in danger of death. Surely the possibility of emergency situations would not have escaped the diligent deliberations of the consultors.

In an attempt to arrive at a possible official declaration on this point, the present writer, with the kind permission of the Most Rev. Bernard J. Flanagan, Bishop of Norwich, had the following question submitted to the Sacred Congregation for the Discipline of the Sacraments:

> Quaeritur a Reverendissimo Episcopo Norvicensi:
> Utrum in causa urgentissima seu in casu verae necessitatis in confirmatione administranda a simplici sacerdote iis qui ex gravi morbo in mortis periculo sunt constituti ("Spiritus

[95] *Op. cit.*, p. 100. Smiddy favored the former view.

[96] "Art. cit., p. 36.

Sancti munera," *AAS*, XXXVIII, p. 349 ss.) licite et valide adhiberi possit, tamquam formula brevissima, sequentia verba cum rubricis, scilicet: "N., signo te signo cru ✠ cis (quod dum dicit, imposita manu dextera super caput confirmandi, producit pollice dexterae manus chrismate intacta signum crucis in fronte illius, deinde prosequitur) et confirmo te chrismate salutis. In nomine Pa ✠ tris et Fi ✠ lii et Spiritus ✠ Sancti. ℟. Amen."

Reportedly, this *dubium*, which was submitted in early January of 1958, passed from the Sacred Congregation for the Discipline of the Sacraments to the Sacred Congregation of Rites and finally to the Supreme Congregation of the Holy Office which on April 10th issued the following favorable reply:

Ex Aedibus S.Officii, die 10 Aprilis 1958

SUPREMA S. CONGREGATIO
SANCTI OFFICII

PROT. N. 71/58
(In responsione fiat mentio huius numeri)

Exc. me ac Rev.me Domine,

Huic Supremae S. Congregationi propositum fuit ab Excellentia Tua Rev.ma sequens DUBIUM:

"Utrum in casu vera necessitatis in Confirmatione administranda a simplici Sacerdote iis qui ex gravi morbo in mortis periculo constituti sunt, licite et valide adhiberi possit formula brevissima:

"N. Signo te signo Cru ✠ cis (quod dum dicit, imposita manu dextera super caput confirmandi, producit pollice signum crucis in fronte illius, deinde prosequitur) et confirmo te chrismate salutis. In Nomine Pa ✠ tris et Fi ✠ lii et Spiritus ✠ Sancti. Amen."

Ad praecedens DUBIUM Sanctum Officium respondet: AFFIRMATIVE.

Quae dum Tecum communico, quo par est obsequio, me profiteor

Excellentiae Tuae Rev.mae
Addictissimum
(Signed) G. CARD. PIZZARDO

Exc.mo ac Rev.mo Domino
D.no BERNARDO JOSEPHO FLANAGAN
Episcopo NORVICEN.

The importance of this reply is all the more striking with the realization that its canonical and rubrical effect is the definite establishment of a short form for emergency confirmation which can readily be listed under the "*formulae brevissimae adhibendae in casu verae necessitatis.*"

In summarizing the multiple findings of this chapter, it can be stated that the extraordinary minister of confirmation who is empowered to administer this sacrament by the decree *Spiritus Sancti munera* and related documents along with the subsequent decree of the Sacred Congregation for the Oriental Church can validly and lawfully confer confirmation, personally and anywhere within the limits of his territory, upon all persons, not necessarily his parishioners, but members of the Church, actually within the territorial limits of his parish, who have not yet been confirmed and are truly in danger of death from a serious illness. These may be infants or adults, lay or religious, even exempt, members of the Latin rite or even of the Oriental rites, if they are under the jurisdiction of the Latin clergy.

CHAPTER VII

CONDITIONS FOR THE LAWFUL ADMINISTRATION OF CONFIRMATION BY THE EXTRAORDINARY MINISTER

ARTICLE 1—THE NON-AVAILABILITY OF A BISHOP MUST BE DETERMINED

> They can use this faculty both in the episcopal city as well as beyond it, whether the see is occupied or vacant, as long as the bishop of the diocese is unavailable or is lawfully prevented from administering confirmation himself; and there is not present any other bishop who is in communion with the Apostolic See, even though he be only a titular bishop, and who, without great inconvenience, could substitute for the bishop of the diocese.[1]

To protect the prior right of a bishop to confirm, the decree insists that the extraordinary minister can exercise his faculty only if a bishop, either the ordinary or a titular bishop, cannot be obtained. Whether this condition affects the valid or only lawful use of the faculty has been a moot question among commentators. Since the condition is introduced with the word "*dummodo*," which according to canon 39 postulates the fulfillment of the appended condition for the validity of the grant bestowed in the rescript, the commentators interpreted this condition to bind under the pain of invalidity. This was the opinion of Zerba, one of the earliest commentators. In his "Marginal Notes" he said that the condition was binding for validity.[2] In his *Commentarius* he tempered his position slightly by declaring

[1] *AAS*, XXXVIII (1946), n. 3, p. 352.

[2] "In Margine al Recente decreto della S. C. Dei Sacramenti circa il Conferimento della Cresima ai Moribundi," printed in the *Osservatore Romano*, October 31, 1946, reproduced in *The Irish Ecclesiastical Record*, 5. ser., LXIX (1947), 160-166; English translation, pp. 257-264. ". . . e ai ministri straordinari . . è vietato in tal caso valersi, pena la nullità, del loro mandato."—p. 164.

that there is a serious prohibition against the use of the faculty if a bishop is available.[3] Connell, writing in the April, 1947, issue of *The American Ecclesiastical Review*, stated that a priest who would perform the rite of confirmation on a dying person, if a bishop can be procured without great inconvenience, would not validly confer the sacrament.[4] In June of 1952, however, he changed his stand from validity to lawfulness and considered it a "fully safe" opinion.[5] Alonso held that because of the "*dummodo*" the inavailability of the bishop is essential for the validity of the priest's act of confirming.[6]

Mahoney did not consider it an invalidating clause, notwithstanding the use of the word "*dummodo*," for the faculty of confirming which had long been enjoyed by priests on the foreign missions carried a similarly expressed restriction, and yet the commentators were agreed that this affected the lawfulness, and not the validity, of the act. Moreover, continued the author, in the present document it is explicitly stated that the restrictions set in number 2 must be observed for validity, which warning is not repeated after number 3, in which this prohibition is mentioned.[7]

Conway cautiously stated that it is possible, though by no means certain, that the condition affects merely the lawful use of the faculty, and therefore does bind under pain of invalidity. A comparison of the actual wording of nn. 2 and 3 of the decree shows a much stronger emphasis on validity in number 2. The former denies the existence of the faculty if the conditions are not present; the latter presumes the existence of the faculty and

[3] P. 41. However, on p. 66 he stated: "Ministris igitur extraordinariis erit prorsus sub gravi abstinendum ab usu facultatis sibi factae, quae in casu tamquam suspensa haberi debet."

[4] "The Recent Decree Empowering Priests to Confirm," *AER*, CXVI (1947), 261.

[5] *The American Ecclesiastical Review*, CXXVI (1952), 467.

[6] "Commentario al Decreto de la S. Congregacion de Sacramentos sobre la confirmación de Moribundos," *Revista Española de Derecho Canonico*, I (1947), 169.

[7] "The Extraordinary Minister of Confirmation," *The Clergy Review*, XXVII (1947), 84.

governs its use, since it begins, "*haec facultate uti possunt.*"[8] Pistoni taught that the condition was required for lawfulness, "*minime ad valorem.*"[9] His reasoning, based on Wernz-Vidal, was that if the law had stated, "*illud fieri nequit,*" that would have been equivalent to an invalidating expression. However, when it is said of a person, "*aliquid facere non posse,*" the law is merely a prohibiting, not an invalidating, law.[10] As a result, today one finds the vast majority of commentators favoring the opinion which considers the condition as one which affects lawfulness and not validity. Coronata still holds for validity,[11] while Regatillo,[12] Onclin[13] Bergh,[14] Smiddy,[15] Hannan,[16] Mostaza,[17] Quinn,[18] Cappello,[19] Vermeersch-Creusen,[20] as well as the ones already cited above, hold for lawfulness.

The present writer naturally shares what might now be considered the common opinion in view of the weight of the eminent authority attaching to it. It seems that one can canonically argue with justification that, since the decree is a law, canon 11 and not canon 39 is to be applied in the interpretation of condition number 3. There is neither an express nor an equivalent expression of invalidity like that which attaches to condition number 2. Secondly, the determination of the objective un-

[8] "Confirmation Decree—One of the Conditions," *The Irish Ecclesiastical Record,* 5. series, LXIX (1947), 432.

[9] *De Confirmatione a Ministro Extraordinario,* n. 110, p. 106.

[10] *Op. cit.,* 109.

[11] *De Sacramentis,* I, n. 167 *bis,* p. 128.

[12] *Ius Sacramentarium,* p. 62.

[13] "L'Administration du Sacrement de la Confirmation en Cas de Danger de Mort," *ETL,* XXV (1949), 349.

[14] "Administration de la Confirmation aux Fidèles dangereusement Malades," *NRT,* LXIX (1949), 86.

[15] *A Manual for the Extraordinary Minister of Confirmation,* p. 62.

[16] *The Sacred Canons,* I, 780.

[17] *El Problema del Ministro Extraordinario de la Confirmación,* p. 361.

[18] *The Extraordinary Minister of Confirmation,* p. 106.

[19] *De Sacramentis,* I, n. 201 *bis,* p. 184.

[20] *Epitome Iuris Canonici,* II, n. 62, p. 35.

availability of a bishop is too intangible and imponderable to serve as a norm for regarding the administration of a sacrament as invalid. Here, as in a previous case of interpretation, subsequent documents issued by the Congregations for the Propagation of the Faith and for the Discipline of the Sacraments can serve as a quasi-official interpretation of this clause as looking simply to the element of lawfulness.[21]

At the time when the question still remained doubtful, Conway suggested that the local ordinary can use his discretion and, if he desires, can make it clear to his priests that he is unable to administer confirmation outside the regular occasion for general confirmation, and that, therefore, they may regard this condition as always being fulfilled outside the regular occasions.[22] Smiddy reported that *L'Ami du Clergé,* May 8, 1947, contained a pastoral letter, issued by the Bishop of Moulins in France, which declared:

> Pastors and parish administrators may exercise their power without need of prior recourse to the ordinary minister, the Most Reverend Bishop. For the issuance of the decree necessitates no modification in the habitual practice in this matter, even as regards the administration of the sacrament in the episcopal city.[23]

Onclin denied the validity of such legislation on the basis that a local ordinary does not have the competence to dispense from a general law of the Church.[24] Therefore he could not exempt

21 ". . . necnon *licite* in ipso loco residentiae Episcopi, absente quolibet Episcopo vel legitimo impedito. . . ," *AAS,* XL (1948), 41. ". . . cappellano autem hac facultate uti *licet* tantum si Episcopus dioecesanus haberi nequeat . . ."; a little further on it is stated in this same document, " . . nullus alius praeter Episcopum vel loci parochum, idem sacramentum valide conferre valet." In this indult granted October 25, 1948, for hospital chaplains in the United States, protocol number 5869/48, one can clearly perceive two different modes of expression, one touching the matter of unlawfulness, the other that of invalidity.

22 "Art. cit.," *The Irish Ecclesiastical Record,* 5. series, LXIX (1947), 432.

23 *Op. cit.,* p. 63.

24 Cf. canon 81.

his priests from the observance of a clause prescribed by a decree-law.[25]

Granted that the choice of expression in the above cited pastoral is not the happiest, the present writer feels that a bishop could justifiably by synodal law or pastoral legislation determine that the normal duties of his office will impede him from administering confirmation personally to those who are in danger of death.[26] The "*grave incommodum*" would thus be interpreted to apply to the general practice rather than to each individual case.[27] Actually the bishop is not dispensing from the general law, but rather he is declaring what constitutes for him a lawful impediment which prevents his administration of the sacrament. Such a declaration would prove a great help in giving the extraordinary minister moral certitude that he is acting lawfully.

In a private reply to the Cardinal of Palermo, the Sacred Congregation for the Discipline of the Sacraments declared that for the administration of confirmation outside the episcopal city itself, it may be considered that this constitutes a permanent legitimate impediment for the cardinal and a "*grave incommodum*" for his auxiliary bishops, unless they find themselves accidentally in the locality where the sick person lives or at a convenient distance from the same.[28]

Some bishops of the United States have notified their clergy that in the episcopal city itself they wish to be called out in all emergencies. Others require particular inquiry concerning the

[25] "Art cit.," *ETL,* XXV (1949), 351.

[26] Cf. Regatillo, *op. cit.*, p. 62; Mahoney, *The Priest as Minister of Confirmation* (London: Burns Oates & Washbourne Ltd., 1952), pp. 55-56.

[27] "It should be remembered, however, that even if a bishop (particularly one in charge of a large diocese) could confer the sacrament without much inconvenience *in a particular case,* he could reasonably look on it as a grave inconvenience to attend to *all* cases of dying persons, and for that reason regard it as justifiable to attend none, since he might encounter serious hostility if he confirmed some dying persons and refused others. For such a reason, a priest might be justified in confirming a person living next door to the bishop."—Connell, "art. cit.," *AER,* CXVI (1947), 261; cf. also Connell, "The Pastor's Right to Confirm," *AER,* CXXII (1950), 61.

[28] *Il Monitore Ecclesiastico* (1948), pp. 24-25, as reported by Smiddy, *op. cit.*, p. 55.

availability of the bishop in each case. This, of course, must be done, unless legislation similar to that discussed above exists. Obviously this inquiry is not necessary if the see is vacant, unless it is known that a titular bishop is easily available.[29]

It should be noted that the inquiry regarding the availability of the bishop does not constitute the seeking of permission from the local ordinary to administer confirmation. This is not within the scope of his competence to grant or to refuse, since the Holy See has already made the concession to certain categories of priests. The bishop could neither allow other priests, e.g., assistants, to exercise this faculty, nor could he forbid a certain pastor from exercising this prerogative. Connell has aptly expressed this sentiment in the following paragraph:

> Since the Sovereign Pontiff directly deputes pastors to administer confirmation in certain circumstances, the pastor does not need the permission of the bishop to confirm validly and licitly when the requisite conditions are realized. However, if there is even a probability that the bishop will be able to come and give confirmation to a dying person, the pastor must take measures to find out whether his services can be procured, and he himself may administer the sacrament only when he discovers that the Ordinary or another bishop is not available.[30]

In conclusion, it may be added that a priest who would deliberately violate the prescription of number 3 and administer

[29] Mahoney (*op. cit.*, n. 95, p. 56) makes the following appropriate observation: "Failing a declaration of this or of any other kind on the bishop's part, a priest must decide, without necessarily having recourse to the telephone, which is always frowned upon canonically, but by any suitable means, that a bishop is unobtainable without grave inconvenience. Thus, if a retired bishop is living in an institution, he should first be asked to confirm the sick therein; if the sick person is living at a long distance from the episcopal residence, it would be useless to ask for his ministration, because unreasonable to expect it. On the other hand, if the bishop has issued some guidance on the point, priests must act in accordance with it, including even the use of the telephone if that is the bishop's ruling. Finally, grave inconvenience may exist not at the bishop's end but at the other end; with the sick person, whose death is imminent, or with the priest who cannot get in touch with the bishop."

[30] "The Pastor's Right to Confirm," *The American Ecclesiastical Review*, CXXII (1950), 60.

confirmation without any moral assurance or apart from all search into the unavailability of the bishop, and/or contrary to the expressed assurance of the bishop that he is prepared to confirm the person, would be guilty of serious sin.

Article 2—The Recipient Must Be Properly Disposed

If the recipient has reached the use of reason, the state of grace is necessary for the fruitful reception of the sacrament, since confirmation is a sacrament of the living. Instruction on the rudiments of the faith and especially on those the knowledge of which is absolutely necessary must be given. The teaching on the nature and the effect of confirmation should also be imparted to the person in danger of death.[31] If the patient should recover, more detailed instruction should be given according to the mental capacity of the recipient.[32]

Article 3—The Sacrament Must Be Administered Rubrically and Without Charge

Two other conditions which affect the lawful administration of confirmation are fidelity to the canonical and rubrical prescriptions and compliance with the regulation that prohibits seeking any manner of remuneration for the use of this faculty.[33] Appendix iv contains a translation of the canons which govern the discipline of the Code of Canon Law which must be observed by the priest who confirms in virtue of an apostolic indult. Included are practical observations of a pastoral nature. Appendix v contains the entire rite of confirmation with the rubrics and practical liturgical comments in English.

One point requires more elaborate elucidation. It is considered here with a view to avoiding as much complication as possible in the presentation of the ceremony itself. It is the requirement that the sacrament is not to be administered in the presence of heretics or schismatics. Much less are they to be

[31] Canon 786. Cf. article 1 of Chapter I in the first section of this dissertation, pp. 3-6.

[32] *AAS*, XXXVIII (1946), n. 5, p. 353.

[33] *AAS*, XXXVIII (1946), n. 4, p. 352.

allowed to assist in the ceremony.[34] Without attempting to examine the motives of the Holy See in promulgating this prohibition, one must nevertheless seek for a proper understanding of its meaning. Connell feels that the word *"coram"* is to be understood in the sense of "before heretics or schismatics who are aware of the particular rite which is being administered." These, especially if they were Presbyterians or Oriental schismatics, might think that there has been a change of doctrine on the part of the Church regarding the superiority of the episcopal office over the presbyterate.[35]

Thus, it would usually be permitted to give confirmation in a hospital ward, even without a screen around the bed, although Protestant patients and nurses were in the same room, since they would scarcely be aware of what sacrament is being administered. If the presence of a guard were necessary to forestall violence on the part of an insane person, or the doctor or a nurse could not leave the bedside of a patient for a minute, *epikeia* would justify the minister's not requiring that they leave the room, if they are not Catholic, especially in a state or sectarian institution.[36] In any case, it seems that, if serious repercussions would ensue from a stringent insistence that heretics and schismatics leave the room, confirmation can lawfully be administered for the good of the recipient.[37] There should, however, be no exception to the rule that non-Catholics be not used as servers or assistants in any manner whatsoever.

As regards the prohibition of remuneration, the decree makes it quite clear and emphatic that confirmation conferred by virtue of its grant is to be given completely free of charge, no matter what title could be alleged for recompense. Herein is reflected the teaching of canon 736, which states that for the administration of the sacraments the minister shall not for any reason or pretext demand or request, directly or indirectly, any compensation beyond the offerings spoken of in canon 1507, § 1, i.e., offer-

[34] *AAS,* XXXVIII (1946), 356.

[35] "Art. cit.," *AER,* CXVI (1947), 262-263.

[36] Cf. Hannan, "Decretum de Confirmatione—Commentary," *The Jurist,* VII (1947), 230; Smiddy, *op. cit.*, p. 86.

[37] Cf. canon 2259, § 2.

ings on the occasion of the ministration of the sacraments as determined by a provincial council, or by the meeting of the bishops of a province, and officially approved by the Holy See.[38]

In his commentary on canon 736, Cappello notes that the words "*exigat aut petat*" do not preclude the acceptance of voluntary offerings.[39] However, the wording of the present decree seems to prohibit even such remuneration.[40] Thus it would be unlawful to accept anything, even though there be a just title for recompense, e.g., the expense of transportation, or a free-will offering of gratitude by the family of the sick person.[41] Both in the wording and italicization the Church reveals its will in this matter. The sacrament is to be conferred gratuitously, "*gratis vero quovis titulo est conferenda.*"[42]

The violation of this prohibition could well imply a serious sin, especially if the minister would demand or seek compensation. This is evident both from the matter and the purpose of the law.[43] Whether this is a matter of simony as offending against the divine or simply the ecclesiastical law, or whether it is purely the violation of an ecclesiastical prohibitory law, involves a question which is disputed among the authors. In line with their arguments one would look to canon 727, §§ 1-2 or canon 736 for the relevant answer.

Article 4—Proper Notification and Registration Must Be Made

Another condition for the lawful use of the faculty is the notification of the proper diocesan ordinary who must immediately (*statim*) be informed by the extraordinary minister each time (*singulis vicibus*) he has conferred confirmation. The re-

[38] Quinn (*op. cit.*, p. 114) doubts that the Sacred Congregation of the Council would ever approve the specification of a fee for the administration of confirmation by an extraordinary minister.

[39] *De Sacramentis,* I, n. 81, p. 72.

[40] Smiddy, *op. cit.*, p. 95.

[41] Quinn, *op. cit.*, p. 114.

[42] *AAS,* XXXVIII (1946), n. 4, p. 352.

[43] Cappello, *De Sacramentis,* I, n. 82, p. 73.

port must also include a brief description of the circumstances.[44] This report is to be made whether the person is still alive at the time or has already passed away since the time the sacrament had been administered.

It was the purpose of this regulation to enable the bishop so to supervise the administration of this sacrament as to make sure that its dignity and reverence would be properly preserved, and to obtain a record of what he was annually to report to the Holy See. This report by the local ordinary, as will be pointed out in a subsequent article, is no longer required.

What should the report include? The following is a sample formulary which may serve as a practical guide for the priests who must render an acount of their ministrations:

Date

The undersigned, pastor of ____________ (or whatever position is held), in virtue of the decree, *Spiritus Sancti munera* (or an indult, if he be a hospital chaplain), administered the sacrament of confirmation, the bishop being lawfully impeded, to (an adult or infant) on (date) at (a private home or hospital), within the territorial confines of the parish, (a parishioner or visitor), who was in danger of death because of a serious illness.

The following provisions of the decree were faithfully observed (explain exceptions in detail):

a) the *Ritus Servandus* was carried out to the letter; or the *Formula brevissima* had to be used;
b) no heretics or schismatics were present;
c) no remuneration was sought or received;
d) all necessary steps were taken to dispose the patient properly;
e) the proper entries were made in the baptismal and confirmation registers;
f) notification was sent to the church of baptism;
g) notification was sent to the proper pastor;
h) add whatever particular information the local ordinary demands by special legislation.

Seal Signed ____________________

[44] *AAS*, XXXVIII (1946), n. 7, p. 353.

Naturally, f-h will be used only when the particular circumstances warrant it.[45]

A report such as this will give the bishop a clear and concise account which will assure him that the extraordinary ministers under his jurisdiction are truly conscientious "in the discharge of so distinguished a duty." [46]

Commentators have discussed the question as to who is meant by the "*ordinarius dioecesanus proprius*." Does this refer to the ordinary of the extraordinary minister or to the ordinary of the place where the sacrament was administered? If one rules out the possibility of confirmation being administered by a vicar substitute, it seems rather rare when the two will not coincide, since the power is enjoyed only within territorial limits. The question might arise if a bishop of diocese A would appoint a priest, either on vacation or on sick leave, from diocese B as an administrator of a vacant parish. In any case, it seems most logical to conclude that the local ordinary would be the proper one to receive the report on confirmation conferred anywhere within his diocese.[47]

In addition to notifying the bishop, the extraordinary minister must record the fact of confirmation in the register of confirmation. It seems that this can lawfully be done in one of two ways. The first, which the present writer prefers, is to record the names on a separate sheet in the confirmation register with the title, "*Confirmatio collata est ex apostolico indulto, urgente mortis periculo, ob gravem confirmati morbem*," *sequentibus:*

[45] Cf. Smiddy, *op. cit.*, pp. 74-75; Connell, "art. cit." *AER*, CXVI (1947), 264. If printed copies of the formulary were distributed among the clergy, the priest would simply have to check the conditions which had application in each individual case.

[46] *AAS*, XXXVIII (1946), 353.

[47] Hannan ("art. cit.," *The Jurist*, VII (1947), 233) at first held that the specific language of the decree suffers no other interpretation than that the information should be sent to the ordinary of the priest rather than to the ordinary of the place in which the sacrament was conferred. However, in his *The Sacred Canons*, I, 781, he professes adherence to the view which favors the latter ordinary. Cf. Mahoney, "art. cit.," *The Clergy Review*, XXVII (1947), 87.

Name of person con-firmed	Parish and diocese	Name given at confirm.	Date and of place bap-tism	Name of father; maiden name of mother	Sponsor	Date and place of confirm.	Minister

The other possibility is to record the name along with the list of those confirmed by the bishop. There the necessary adaptations will have to be made and the notation "*confirmatio collata est*, etc." added after the name of the minister.[48]

In accordance with the norm of canon 470, § 2, the simple fact of the date of confirmation must be annotated in the baptismal register. The word "emergency" might be added to indicate to succeeding pastors the condition under which the confirmation was conferred. This would be especially helpful in the case of infant confirmation. The child may recover, move out to another city, and later seek a baptismal record in preparation for confirmation. The "emergency" notation would assure the pastor that the confirmation record was not an error or a slip of the pen, and would enable him to explain why the child cannot be reconfirmed.

If the person who was confirmed belongs to another parish, the minister must notify the person's proper pastor as soon as possible by means of an authentic document which contains the necessary information to be recorded in the confirmation register.[49]

Date

I, the undersigned pastor (chaplain) of ______________ in the diocese of ___________, hereby certify that (N.N.)

[48] Cf. *AAS*, XXXVIII (1946), n. 6, p. 353.

[49] *AAS*, XXXVIII (1946), n. 6, p. 353.

(son, daughter) of __(father's name)__ and __(mother's maiden name)__, residents at __(home address *)__ in the parish of __________ baptized at __(place and date)__, received on __(date)__ the sacrament of confirmation, administered by the undersigned in virtue of an apostolic indult, the recipient being at the time in danger of death from a serious illness. _______ acted as sponsor. __________ is the name given at confirmation.

Seal Signed ________________

* The domicile of the person is to be given, if it differs from that of the parent.

An additional notification must be sent out by the extraordinary minister to the place of baptism, if it differs from the place of parochial residence. The decree implies this in its wording, "*adnotatio facienda est etiam in libro baptizatorum ad normam can. 470, § 2.*" [50]
This notification can be brief:

Date

____________ (son, daughter) of __________ and _______, baptized at the church of ____________ in ____________, on __(date)__, received confirmation from ___________ (pastor or chaplain) of ____________ on __(date of confirmation)__ in virtue of an apostolic indult, the recipient being in danger of death from a serious illness.

Seal Signed ______________

Since the decree makes no mention of transmitting the information through the chancery office if the person was baptized in or belongs to a parish in another diocese, the present writer does not see that it is necessary or more proper to do so. There does not seem to be room, *a pari*, for an application of the norms related to the transmision of marriage documents according to the Instruction *Sacrosanctum*, issued by the Sacred Congregation for the Discipline of the Sacraments on June 29, 1941,[51] nor does

[50] *AAS*, XXXVIII (1946), n. 6, p. 353.

[51] As against Quinn, *op. cit.*, p. 109.

the document need any further authentication since the parish seal and signature of the pastor are sufficient to authenticate the document.[52] It should be noted, however, that the obligation to make the necessary annotations and report is fundamentally *per se* a grave obligation.[53]

[52] As against Pistoni, *op. cit.*, p. 115.

[53] Cappello, *De Sacramentis*, I, n. 217, p. 197.

CHAPTER VIII

RELATED QUESTIONS

Article 1—Duties of the Local Ordinary

The local ordinary was charged with the responsibility of providing adequate information so that the extraordinary ministers will be thoroughly instructed and fully apprised of the multiple canonical and liturgical provisions for the valid and lawful administration of confirmation to those in danger of death.[1] Various methods were employed by the bishops of this country. Some made the decree a subject of discussion at one of the clergy conferences, others sent out copies of the decree with appropriate explanations, while still others arranged to have the topic treated at a special session during the annual retreat. At any rate, the bishop is the one person who is in the most advantageous position to judge whether or not the instructions have been fruitful.

If the sum total of confirmations administered by the extraordinary ministers during the course of the year is negligible, even in a small diocese, the local ordinary has grounds for suspicion that the ultimate good anticipated by the decree has not been realized in his territory. Therefore, he should repeatedly remind his pastors of the apostolic privilege which they enjoy, and encourage them to exercise their power of confirming, especially infants who otherwise would pass from this world without the added graces and character which are imparted through this august sacrament. The present writer suggests that the rite of confirmation, as it is to be performed by the extraordinary as well as the ordinary minister, be henceforth made part of the standard curriculum in the seminary in connection with the liturgical course on the administration of the sacraments.

The decree also placed upon the local ordinary the obligation of sending a report at the beginning of each year to the Sacred Congregation for the Discipline of the Sacraments. The report

[1] Cf. *AAS*, XXXVIII (1946), n. 8, p. 353.

was to include a mention not only of the number of the confirmed but also a brief descriptive summary of the manner in which the extraordinary ministers under the bishop's jurisdiction exercised this precious prerogative.[2] No doubt, the purpose of this regulation was to keep the Congregation informed on the frequency of the use of this privilege, and also to enable the consultors and those concerned to scrutinize and evaluate the response and reaction of both the clergy and the laity. Had there been too much wonderment or scandal on the part of the faithful, or too frequent indications of abuses on the part of the minister, then, without a doubt, necessary preventive or restrictive measures would have been taken.

On the contrary, the Congregation has been quite satisfied with the diligence and reverence exercised in the fulfillment of the prescriptions of the decree during the past ten years. Therefore, after consultation with the Holy Father, a decree was issued, on July 1, 1957, by the Sacred Congregation.[3] By virtue of this decree, the bishops are released from the obligation of making an annual report:

> Porro exacto iam decennio a prodito Decreto, huic S. Dicasterio visum est, facto verbo cum Sanctissimo, eosdem Ordinarios, inde a labente anno 1957 et iugiter deinceps, liberare obligatione praefatam Relationem mittendi, quum ex relationibus infra decursum decennium heic receptis satis compertum fuerit sacramentum Confirmationis fuisse rite collatum, diligenter servatis eiusdem Decreti praescriptionibus.[4]

The local Ordinary is urged, however, to continue his vigilance lest through carelessness and indifference the administration of confirmation be exposed to the danger of nullity and the sacrament itself be the victim of irreverence and disrespect. He must immediately correct any abuses, and, if need be, report the flagrant violators to the Holy See.[5]

Thus, it would seem that only prescription number 9 of the

[2] *AAS*, XXXVIII (1946), n. 9, p. 353.

[3] This decree was published in the *AAS*, XLIX (1957), 943-944.

[4] *AAS*, XLIX (1957), 943-944.

[5] *AAS*, XLIX (1957), 944. Cf. canons 78 and 336, § 2.

Spiritus Sancti munera has been abrogated. Consequently, pastors are still obliged to inform the local ordinary immediately after each occasion upon which the faculty of confirming was exercised.[6] Only in this manner will the ordinary be able to fulfill his obligation of watchful supervision.

ARTICLE 2—OBLIGATION OF THE EXTRAORDINARY MINISTER TO USE THE FACULTY

A specific determination of the obligation of the priest-minister to confirm the dying is one of the most difficult points which has arisen from the issuance of the decree *Spiritus Sancti munera.* The commentators are still striving to reach a satisfactory solution, although most of them are agreed that the obligation basically is a serious obligation.

All those who have the care of souls are bound by justice, i.e., by an obligation arising from a quasi-contract, to administer the sacraments to those who are under their charge.[7] Hence, in virtue of their office, pastors and other priests, when the faculty of confirming has been conceded to them through an indult promulgated by law, must administer the sacrament when it is reasonably requested by a person in danger of death.

> . . . It follows that those priests who have the new faculties are bound *sub gravi* to exercise them when reasonably requested to do so—that is in those circumstances in which a priest with the care of souls would be gravely bound to administer the Sacrament of Extreme Unction.[8]

Cappello observes that it is certain that those who are constituted in a pastoral office, are *per se* held *sub gravi*, and that, *ex iustitia*, to administer the sacraments to their subjects who make either an express or tacit reasonable request.[9]

The *Code* specifies that priests who have the apostolic faculty

[6] *AAS,* XXXVIII (1946), n. 7, p. 353.

[7] Canon 467, § 1: Debet parochus officia divina celebrare, administrare Sacramenta fidelibus, quoties legitime petant. . . .

[8] Conway, "Obligation to Avail of New Confirmation Faculties," *The Irish Ecclesiastical Record,* 5. series, LXIX (1947), 348.

[9] *De Sacramentis,* I, n. 53, p. 49.

of confirming are bound by the same obligation to administer the sacrament as are bishops.[10] Since the obligation of bishops to confer confirmation on those who request it *"rite et rationabiliter"* is generally accepted by canonists, e.g., by Merkelbach, Vermeersch, Noldin, Cappello, Conte a Coronata, as being intrinsically (*per se*) grave, it follows that those priests who have the new faculties also have the same obligation to exercise them when reasonably requested to do so.[11]

Of course, since confirmation is not required as an absolutely necessary means of salvation, such as baptism and penance, and at times extreme unction, the obligation is correspondingly less serious. Conway likewise admits of slightness of matter, so that an occasional refusal would constitute a venial sin, unless grave scandal would result.[12] The parish priest may also be excused from the obligation in consequence of a disproportionate inexpedience or discommodity (*incommodum*).[13] Therefore, various circumstances must be taken under consideration: the distance to be travelled, the hour of the day or night, the state of health on the part of the parish priest, the degree of the danger of death, etc. As a matter of fact, Conway suggested that a parish priest who has retired for the night would not be gravely bound to heed the call to administer confirmation.[14]

McCarthy, on the other hand, did not feel that the fact that a priest would have to arise at night constitutes a disproportionately grave inconvenience. Consequently, he does not offer any excuse from the obligation on that score.[15] In view of canon 468, § 1,[16] and the evident solicitude of the Church to fortify her children with the sacrament of confirmation, the writer is

[10] Canon 785, § 2.

[11] Conway, *Problems in Canon Law,* p. 146.

[12] *Op. cit.,* pp. 147-148.

[13] Cf. Zerba, *Commentarius,* p. 73.

[14] *Op. cit.,* p. 149.

[15] *Problems in Theology: I, The Sacraments,* p. 84.

[16] Sedula cura et effusa caritate debet parochus aegrotos in sua paroecia, maxime vero morti proximos, adiuvare, eos sollicite Sacramentis reficiendo eorumque animas Deo commendando.

inclined to agree with McCarthy. Unless other factors such as ill-health, etc., are involved, a priest would be seriously negligent if he habitually refused to confer confirmation during the night, especially if it were of paramount importance that the administration be not delayed.

Another obligation rests upon the extraordinary ministers of confirmation, namely, the instruction of the faithful, i.e., to make known the main terms of the new decree in their catechetical instructions on confirmation.[17] A parish priest might be tempted to justify his lax attitude concerning his serious obligation to administer confirmation by the claim that no one has sought the sacrament from him. The reason for this, however, lies not in the fact that the laity does not want this sacrament, but rather in the fact that they are not, and indeed are not expected to be, fully informed of the latest decrees and regulations of the Church. They had been taught that the bishop alone is the ordinary minister of confirmation, with very little mention ever having been made of an extraordinary minister. Hence, there is need for instruction that in danger of death the sacrament can be administered by the pastor.

It is not to be admitted that the failure of the dying person to actually and specifically request the sacrament can serve as a legitimate excuse from the obligation. As was noted above, the priest is obliged even by a tacit request, and it is perfectly reasonable to presume that the person at this critical moment desires that the Church equip him with every means of acquiring a greater increase of sanctifying grace. It may well be that his greatest struggle is with temptations against faith, so that the roborant strength of confirmation would mean the difference between victory or defeat. That is why the present writer would suggest, not as a matter of obligation in justice but at least from the motives of charity, that the priest who has been summoned to a death-bed inquire whether or not the party had been confirmed especially if he himself could act as an extraordinary minister of confirmation, or if one were readily available. If such enquiries were faithfully made, the number of adults who

[17] Cf. canon 1332.

have not been confirmed might loom large to the amazement of many a parish priest. This was forcibly brought home to the present writer in his review of the statistical data of a census taken in a parish in which an attempt was made to discover how many parishioners were not confirmed.

In reviewing the findings of this article, one can safely conclude:

1) that the extraordinary minister has a general obligation to inform the laity of the present discipline of the Church as regards the administration of confirmation;

2) that his obligation to confer the sacrament to those who reasonably request it is fundamentally (*per se*) a grave one;

3) that it is a serious sin to completely disregard the provisions of the decree and habitually to refuse or neglect to use the faculty, and

4) that it is a venial sin to fail to administer the sacrament upon occasions without a proportionately serious cause, provided that the refusal does not cause scandal or create antagonistic enmities against the Church.[18]

[18] Commentators are divided on conclusion n. 4. Connell ("The Recent Decree Empowering Priests to Confirm," *AER*, CXVI [1947], 259) states: "It would seem that, apart from scandal . . . , the sin would be venial, if the refusal referred to an individual case." Regatillo, (*Ius Sacramentarium*, p. 65) teaches: "Si solum in aliquo casu, culpam gravem non putarem ex supra dictis a S. Alfonso. Ipse Cappello ait: presbiter facultate praeditus tenetur *sub levi* confirmare rationabiliter petentes, si commode possit, et nequeat confirmatio in proximum differri." Mahoney ("Obligation of Confirming the Dying," *The Clergy Review*, XXXV [1951], 328) contends: "Nevertheless, it is not certain that the obligation to confirm each individual applicant is grave, and we agree with those writers who think it be only binding *sub levi*." On the other hand, Onclin ("L'Administration du Sacrement de la Confirmation en Cas de Danger de Mort," *ETL*, XXV [1949], 355) teaches: ". . . nous n'oserions pas *per se* excuser de manquement grave à ses obligations le curé qui refuserait la confirmation à un fidèle en état de danger de mort, du moins si celui-ci demandait d'être confirmé." McCarthy also holds: "The more common, and, we think, the better view is that *per se* he is under a grave obligation to accede to every reasonable request for this sacrament."—"The Obligation of a Priest to Administer Confirmation," *The Irish Ecclesiastical Record*, LXXXI (1954), 206.

Article 3—Penalties for the Misuse of the Faculty

Though a priest should readily and willingly make use of the generous concession granted by the Holy See, he must ever be mindful of the penalties which follow the misuse of this faculty. The decree warns that the provisions of canon 2365 can be invoked against those who exceed the limits of this mandate.[19] According to this canon, a priest incurs a *ferendae sententiae* suspension if he dares to perform the rite of confirmation without having the faculty to confer this sacrament. He is automatically, i.e., *ipso facto*, deprived of the faculty, if he presumes to transgress its limits.

Inasmuch as the more benign interpretation is to be adopted in the evaluation of penalties, one should keep in mind that the canon uses the expressions "*ausus fuerit*," and "*praesumpserit*," which are to be strictly interpreted.[20] Hence, only if the extraordinary minister would deliberately and with full malice transgress the limits of the decree, would he suffer the automatic loss of his faculty.[21] The same would hold true for the suspension which is to be imposed upon a priest who deliberately exercises a faculty which he does not possess.

Does the penalty of automatic deprivation of the faculty apply to the transgression of the conditions which affect the valid AND lawful use of the faculty? Wernz-Vidal taught that any limitation, whether it regards the valid or the lawful use of the faculty, is included.[22] Connell, implicitly at least, subscribed to

[19] *AAS,* XXXVIII (1946), 352.

[20] Canon 2229, § 2: Si lex habeat verba: *praesumpserit, ausus fuerit, scienter, studiose, temerarie, consulto egerit* aliave similia quae plenam cognitionem ac deliberationem exigunt, quaelibet imputabilitatis imminutio sive ex parte intellectus sive ex parte voluntatis eximit a poenis latae sententiae.

[21] Connell states: ". . . if a priest has some doubt when he administers confirmation as to whether or not he is acting validly, he would not incur the penalties mentioned in canon 2365."—"Confirmation Administered by a Pastor," *AER,* CXIX (1948), 149.

[22] *Ius Canonicum ad Codicis Normam Exactum* (7 vols. in 8, Vol. VII, Romae: Apud Aedes Universitatis Gregorianae, 1937), VII, n. 501b, p. 559. His opinion is generally followed by those who comment on this canon.

the same opinion when he observed that a priest should not attempt to give confirmation until he is morally sure that all the requirements for its valid and lawful use are present.[23]

Quinn cited Wernz-Vidal as well as canon 78, which states that whoever abuses the power permitted by privilege deserves to be deprived of the faculty, and therefrom concludes that any abuse merits the penalty.[24] Mahoney, on the other hand, appealed to canon 2219, § 1, and submitted a more benign interpretation. He limits the incurring of the penalty to those abuses which affect validity.[25] The writer prefers to follow Mahoney, especially since in the very make-up of the decree the admonition concerning the penalties follows n. 2, which lists the conditions necessary for the VALID administration of confirmation. No. 3 and ff. list the conditions requisite for lawfulness. Had the lawmaker intended to apply the penalty to the violation of all conditions, logically it should have been given at the beginning or at the completion of the series.

In the case of the first penalty, a *ferendae sententiae* suspension, the local ordinary, his successor or his competent superior, can remove it since he is the one who imposed it.[26] However, in the case of the *latae sententiae* deprivation of the faculty, only the Holy See can remove the penalty in the external forum, since it involves the privation of a privilege given by the Holy See, and therefore the ordinary is not competent.[27]

It seems, however, that canon 2290 in conjunction with the provisions of canon 2254 leaves room for a removal of the faculty in the internal forum. If a priest would betray himself and injure his good name or cause scandal, then, in very urgent cases, the confessor could suspend the obligation of observing the penalty. The confessor, of course, should advise immediate re-

[23] "The Recent Decree Empowering Priests to Confirm," *AER*, CXVI (1947), 265.

[24] *The Extraordinary Minister of Confirmation,* p. 116.

[25] "Confirmation—Privation of the Faculty," *The Clergy Review,* XXVIII (1947), 408.

[26] Canon 2236, § 1.

[27] Canon 2237, § 1, no. 3.

course to the Holy See, which recourse must be made at least within a month, namely to the Sacred Penitentiary. Quinn suggests that should a case requiring confirmation arise before a response is had from the Sacred Penitentiary, the confessor can advise the pastor that he may use the faculty during this time.[28]

ARTICLE 4—THE NATURE OF THE POWER CONCEDED BY THE HOLY SEE

The faculty of confirming which was granted in the decree *Spiritus Sancti munera* recalls a difficult problem with which distinguished theologians and canonists have grappled through the centuries. In what precisely does the commission of the Holy See consist? Is it a power of orders, of jurisdiction, a combination of both, or some other kind of power?

Through the teaching and practice of the Church as manifested by the various grants throughout the course of history, it is quite clear that a simple priest can be empowered for confirming. However, the Church has been silent on the precise nature of this power which has been delegated. The decree *Spiritus Sancti munera* itself gives no practical solution; therefore a penetrating analysis of the multifarious schools of thought would be beyond the scope of this dissertation, the primary purpose of which is to comment on the provisions of the decree. However, a summary survey should sufficiently show the complexity of the problem involved.

If the priest possesses the power to confirm by ordination, why is a special delegation necessary for the valid administration of confirmation when conferred by a priest? If this power belongs strictly to episcopal consecration, how can this be transmitted to a simple priest? If it is a power of orders which is supplied, why is not a ceremony of ordination or consecration necessary, since this is the manner in which orders are transmitted? If it is a power of jurisdiction which is supplied, why could not any cleric be constituted an extraordinary minister, since a cleric is capable of exercising jurisdiction?

The Council of Trent has defined that it is wrong to hold that the power of confirming which bishops have is common to them

[28] *Op. cit.*, p. 117.

and to priests.[29] What exactly constitutes the difference? It is a defined dogma that consecrated bishops are superior to ordained priests. In what does this superiority consist? What is the exact nature of the relationship of priestly powers to episcopal powers, and episcopal powers to papal powers? These are only a few of the intricacies which are basic to the present problem. The ultimate solution of these questions in turn depends upon the solution of the fundamental question of the extent of the power of the Church over the sacraments, *"salva illorum substantia."* [30]

Cappello, for practical purposes, gives us a suitable division of the different opinions on this difficult problem.[31]

1) The priest who confirms as extraordinary minister does so validly from the power of orders alone. The delegation of the Pontiff adds nothing.—This opinion is erroneous, especially in the light of the words of the letter *Ex Quo* of St. Pius X: ". . . *cui haud minus absonum est, validam habendam esse confirmationem a quovis presbytero collatam.*" [32]

2) In the early centuries of the Church a simple priest administered the sacrament of confirmation validly by the power of orders alone. Delegation was necessary only for lawfulness. Today, because of the will of the Church, both orders and delegation are necessary for validity.—It seems that St. John Chrysostom and St. Jerome can be cited in support of this theory. Its adherents are Mendive, Dölger (1879-1941) and DeSmet, (1868-1927), who offered the most convincing explanation. Its chief value lies in the fact that it seems to best agree with the tenor of various statutes and regulations from early times.[33]

3) The delegation of the Pontiff gives a particular power of orders, a peculiar augmentation of the power of orders, to the priest by which he is constituted an extraordinary minister.—The main objection is that the power of orders *iuris divini* cannot be

[29] Denzinger-Rahner, *Enchiridion,* n. 967.

[30] Denzinger-Rahner, *Enchiridion,* n. 931.

[31] *De Sacramentis,* I, n. 197, pp. 177-179.

[32] *AAS,* III (1911), 119.

[33] Wassmer, "The Power to Confirm," *The American Ecclesiastical Review,* CXXXVI (1957), 251-254.

conferred by the mere delegation or commission of the Pontiff; it can be conferred by sacred ordination alone.

4) The delegation of the Pontiff gives to the priest a peculiar power of jurisdiction, which when conjoined with the power of orders renders him an extraordinary minister. The proponents compare this with the sacrament of penance and assistance at marriage.—In refutation one can ask whether the administration of confirmation is a judicial act which truly requires jurisdiction. If so, would not then a bishop who has taken possession of his diocese, though not yet consecrated, have the power to confirm in his diocese in the same manner as he would have the power to hear confessions and assist at matrimony? How explain the power of confirming which a titular bishop enjoys, though he posseses no jurisdiction? Wassmer in his article states that most authors now hold that the delegation of the Pontiff confers a power of jurisdiction and nothing else.[34] Unless the present writer receives a satisfactory solution of the above enquiries, he cannot accept this thesis.

5) The simple priest has a power which is absolute, perfect and independent with regard to the sacraments of baptism and the Eucharist. However, this power is inchoative, imperfect, conditioned and dependent upon the delegation of the Holy Father with regard to the administration of confirmation. Once the commission of the Pope has perfected this power, the priest confirms "*ex ipsa sua potestate presbyterali.*"—Fundamentally this is the opinion of Suarez, which is adopted by Bellarmine and a large number of canonists and theologians.[35] What is the nature of this accretion? Lehmkuhl teaches that it is a "*dignitas*" which is not the power of jurisdiction, nor the power of orders, but something akin to it, since it is conferred extrinsically by means of the exercise of a power of jurisdiction on the part of the Holy Father. Others use expressions such as "extrinsic amplification of the power of orders" (Otten), "extrinsic augmentation to the dignity of the simple priest" (Van Noort).

[34] *Ibid.*, p. 255.

[35] Cf. Wassmer, "art. cit.," *AER*, CXXXVI (1957), 256, for an extensive listing of these men.

Generally they are agreed that, though the Holy Father exercises jurisdiction in conferring the delegation, the delegate himself receives some extrinsic deputation.[36]

6) The simple priest has the full and perfect power to confirm, but the power is always conditioned and dependent upon the will of the legitimate superior for its exercise. This is the opinion of Billot, which is considered by Cappello as the more probable opinion.[37] Others who subscribe to this opinion are Lepicier, D'Ales, Diekamp, McCarthy, Canon Smith, Canon George.[38]

McCarthy thus sums up the defense of the theory that the priest's power of confirming is not absolute but conditioned:

> It seems to us, then, that priests who confer Confirmation act in virtue of a twofold power—a power of orders and a power of jurisdiction. Primarily and fundamentally—as in the case of Penance—the conferring of Confirmation is the exercise of a power of orders—a power contained in the sacerdotal character. The actual valid exercise of this power, however, is restricted in the case of priests. When the Holy See empowers a priest to confirm, it removes, within prescribed limits, that restriction. The limited removal of the restriction can most satisfactorily be understood as a grant of jurisdiction in relation to certain defined classes of confirmands.[39]

[36] Cf. *ibid.*, pp. 255-260.

[37] *De Sacramentis,* I, n. 197, p. 179. If one is to presume that this is the opinion adopted by Cappello, it will be difficult to reconcile his acceptance of this theory, which contends that the simple priest has the full and perfect power of confirming though it be conditioned, with the following statement in refutation of the objection that the episcopacy is not an order distinct from the priesthood, since no peculiar or distinct power is acquired through consecration. Cappello answers: "Nedum falsum, sed falsissimum est, in episcopatu peculiarem potestatem distinctam a potestate ordinis presbyteralis, non conferri. Traditur sane potestas *confirmandi* et *ordinandi presbyteros* seu ministros qui possint *valide* conficere sacramentum Eucharistiae. Nonne potestas *confirmandi* et *ordinandi presbyteros* est vera potestas eaque distincta a potestate ordinis presbyteralis, qua presbyteri carent omnino?"—*De Sacramentis,* IV (1951), n. 53, p. 35.

[38] Cf. Wassmer, "art. cit.," *AER,* CXXXVI (1957), 261.

[39] *Problems in Theology,* I: *The Sacraments,* p. 71.

In the midst of these eminent opinions, the present writer with some hesitation proposes as his own a theory which more closely resembles n. 5 than any other. Its terminology is based on statements of St. Bonaventure and St. Thomas Aquinas. The Seraphic Doctor held that the reason why only bishops can confirm rests neither in jurisdiction nor in the sacerdotal power but in authority and episcopal dignity—"*. . . nec a iurisdictione, nec ab ordine sacerdotali, sed auctoritate et dignitate episcopali.*"[40] This statement, combined with the explanation of the Angelic Doctor that the bishop has a power superior to that of the priest in relation to the *corpus mysticum*, whereas the Pope has the supreme power *in corpus mysticum*,[41] can offer a probable solution, especially since the speculation still remains an open question. Thus, since confirmation pertains to the *corpus mysticum*, the Pope can delegate this "*auctoritas*" which bishops enjoy in virtue of their episcopal character, or the extension of their sacerdotal character, which was received through consecration.

Just as a priest, and only a priest, in virtue of his sacerdotal ordination can absolve sins but needs jurisdiction, so a priest, and only a priest, is capable of receiving this authority which can be granted under certain conditions by an act of jurisdiction on the part of the Supreme Pontiff. It does not seem correct or necessary to insist that all power in the Church be reducible to one of two species, either of orders or of jurisdiction. What is to be said of the power of the priests to assist at matrimony?

The writer submits that to speak of the mere removal of a limitation as proposed by theory no. 6 is not sufficiently satisfactory. As noted in the historical section of this treatise,[42] the wording of the text of Gregory the Great, which serves as the basis for the doctrine of the extraordinary minister of confirmation, indicates more than a permission. The term "*concedimus*" implies the giving of something positive. In like manner, to say

40 *S. Bonaventurae Opera Omnia* (9 vols., Vol. IV, ad Claras Aquas prope Florentiam, 1889) Dist. VII, art. 1, q. 3 ad 4*um* in *Sententiarum lib. IV.*

41 *In IV Sent.*, dist. VII, q. 3, a. 1. Cf. pages 28-29 of this dissertation.

42 Article 3b of section A, chap. II, p. 19.

that the only difference between the episcopal and sacerdotal power of confirming is a "conditioning" does not seem to fully fulfill the demands of the Council of Trent.[43]

Nor can the writer clearly understand the meaning of a perfected incomplete power, the reducing of a potency to act, as proposed by theory n. 5. Indeed, once the perfection has been accomplished, how can it be removed so that a priest deprived of this delegation would no longer be able to confirm validly, unless one were to hold for a separate and individual reduction of a general potency for each individual act of confirmation? However, it does seem perfectly reasonable to speak of the radical power to confirm, which, when accompanied with this "*auctoritas in corpus mysticum*," enables a priest to administer confirmation. Here it is not a question of an incomplete radical power perfected by "*auctoritas*" but rather of a radical power, while though perfect in itself, needs the accompanying, or concomitant "*auctoritas*" to function with respect to the valid administration of confirmation.[44] Remove the faculty, and you have removed the "*auctoritas*," and thus the radical power has been rendered helpless, so to speak. A theory such as this would also be in keeping with the definitions of ordinary and extraordinary minister as these are commonly given by the canonists and theologians. Particularly appropriate is the following distinction made by Zubizarreta y Unamunsaga (1862-1948):

> Minister confirmationis potest esse ordinarius, qui vi sui ordinis sine ulla alterius delegatione valide illam confert; et

[43] Mahoney remarks that one cannot readily understand how the restriction on the use of a power received at ordination can do more than make its use gravely unlawful—*The Priest as Minister of Confirmation,* n. 59, p. 41.

[44] Bidagor evaluated an opinion similar to that proposed by the writer as "singularis."—"Casus cum canone 209 Codicis I.C. connexi seu de Iurisdictione ab Ecclesia suppleta," *Periodica,* XLV (1956), 263. What the writer calls "auctoritas," is referred to as "superioritas." Bidagor concluded his discussion of this theory as follows: "Ita presbyter confirmat potestate ordinis, in ordinatione presbyterali accepta. Cum ergo potestas collata a Summo Pontifici sit alterius ordinis, nempe iurisdictionis, suppleri censenda est ad normam canonis 209."—*loc. cit.* The present writer agrees with the first statement but cannot subscribe to the second.

extraordinarius, qui ex vi ordinationis habet auctoritatem incompletam et indiget delegatione superius.[45]

Article 5—The Application of Canon 209

A problem which is intimately associated with the debated question concerning the exact nature of the priestly power obtained by the act of delegation of the Holy See is the application of canon 209 to the doubts concerning some of the provisions of the decree *Spiritus Sancti munera.* Canon 209 declares that, in common error or in positive and probable doubt of law or of fact, the Church supplies jurisdiction for both the internal and external forum. Commentators have been divided as to the valid use of this liberality of the lawmaker with respect to confirmation administered by an extraordinary minister.[46] If, of course, it could clearly be shown that the delegation of the Pontiff confers jurisdiction, then canon 209 would be definitely applicable. However, if it is the power of orders, then the contrary is true, though Regatillo seems to consider canon 209 applicable even with reference to the power of orders.[47]

[45] *Theologia Dogmatico-Scholastica ad Mentem S. Thomae Aquinatis,* Vol. IV, *De Sacramentis in Communi et in Particulari ac De Novissimis* (4. ed., El Carmen: Vitoria, 1949), n. 289, p. 160.

[46] Smiddy (*op. cit.,* pp. 43-45) concluded that, since it is at least probable that the power of orders is involved, canon 209 cannot be said to apply. Zerba (*op. cit.,* pp. 61-71) stated that canon 209 has no application for the reason that without the granted faculty the power of priestly orders would be of no avail for the conferring of confirmation. Bride ("Erreur Commune et Suppléance de Juridiction," *Revue de Droit Canonique,* IV [1954], 39) feels that the argumentation of those who hold for the supplying of the power of confirming is convincing. Mahoney (*The Priest as Minister of Confirmation,* n. 58, p. 48) taught that there is good canonical reason for adopting the favorable view. Bidagor ("art. cit.," *Periodica,* XLV [1956], 265) concluded that the sacrament of confirmation administered under such circumstances would at least be doubtfully valid. Quinn (*op. cit.,* p. 82) ventured the opinion that the papal faculty granted in the decree falls under the provisions of canon 209. He further added that, since there is a doubt of law here, in virtue of canon 15, an extraordinary minister who would look to canon 209 in his administration would confer a valid sacrament.

[47] *Ius Sacramentarium,* p. 64.

Onclin, one of the most outstanding proponents of the applicability of canon 209, based his reasoning on the principle that the act whereby the Roman Pontiff confers the delegation is an act of jurisdiction; therefore, the power of confirming, as granted by means of a law or an indult, is a power of jurisdictional nature.[48]

It seems that one may reasonably ask whether this argumentation is fully satisfactory. It is generally agreed by the canonists that the granting of delegation is an act of jurisdiction on the part of the Pontiff.[49] But that is not the issue at stake. The question looks rather to the EFFECT which this act of the Pontiff produces.[50] By an act of jurisdiction the Pope appoints a priest as a titular bishop. That act does not of necessity produce either orders or jurisdiction in the subject. The power by which a bishop dispenses from fast and abstinence is certainly an exer-

[48] "Nous concluons: relativement au sacrement de la confirmation, *le pouvoir* d'ordre est conféré au prêtre par l'ordination sacerdotale; toutefois, l'*exercice* valide de ce pouvoir est soumis à un mandat qui doit être donné par le pouvoir de juridiction. Dès lors, ce mandat, cette *deputatio a Summo Pontifice,* nécessaire aux simple prêtres pour qu'ils puissent administrer validement la confirmation, est une acte qui émane, non du pouvoir d'ordre, mais du pouvoir de juridiction. En conséquence, le pouvoir de confirmer, en tant qu'il est attribué par une loi ou un indult, est un pouvoir de nature juridictionelle. Il pourra donc être suppléé par l'Église et il sera de fait suppléé, conformément au canon 209, au cas de doute de fait au sujet des conditions auxquelles le même pouvoir de juridiction soumet son octroi."—"L'Administration du Sacrement de la Confirmation en Cas de Danger de Mort," *Ephemerides Theologiae Lovanienses,* XXV (1949), 348. See also McCarthy, "The Nature of a Priest's Power to Confirm," *The Irish Ecclesiastical Record,* LXX (1948), 349.

[49] ". . . Quamvis confirmare sit actus ordinis episcopalis, cuius firmitas et validitas a Pontificis nutu non pendet, delegare tamen simplici presbytero potestatem exercendi eiusdem actus, potius ad iurisdictionem quam ad ordinem pertinet."—Benedictus XIV, *De Synodo Dioecesana,* Tom. I, lib. 7, c. 8, n. 7.

[50] This thought is well expressed by Bidagor: "In hac re bene distinguendum est duplex assertum: primum, Romanum Pontificem actum iurisdictionis exercere dum simplici sacerdoti potestatem confirmandi confert; alterum qua potestate praeditus minister extraordinarius confirmet."—"art. cit.," *Periodica,* XLV (1956), 261. "Cum agitur de eo quod Ecclesia ad normam canonis 209 supplere deberet, nempe de iurisdictione supplenda, haec manifeste non ad iurisdictionem Romani Pontificis se refert, sed ad potestatem qua utitur simplex sacerdos in confirmando."—*ibid.,* 262.

cise of jurisdiction, but surely jurisdiction is not communicated to the recipient. In other words, it seems that the basic point which calls for proof has still to be proved. The problem, as it appears to the writer, revolves around the nature of the power *non ex parte concedentis, sed ex parte recipientis*. That both must necessarily be of the same nature is not a valid conclusion. At best, the thesis as proposed by Onclin eliminates the theory that the power of orders is conferred, since, as was noted previously, the power of orders of divine right distinct from the priestly power can be transmitted only by ordination.[51]

Regatillo favors the thesis that the Church supplies the otherwise lacking power for the reason that what the Church gives to the priest-ministers pertains to the jurisdictional or administrative power. The priest at ordination receives the power of confirming. However, in order to validly exercise this power, the priest needs the commission of the Pope, which adds nothing of the power of orders, but adds solely to the power of jurisdiction.[52]

If the effect of the mandate is simply to remove a hindrance which stands in the way of the valid use of a power, the present writer fails to see how anything at all is supplied. Actually, something is taken away. The question would then resolve itself into whether or not the Church chooses to remove the obstacle in doubtful circumstances. If, on the other hand, jurisdiction is supplied, then Regatillo, to prove his thesis, must show how jurisdiction is a necessary component in the administration of confirmation.

The other explanation which Regatillo proposes is the application of canon 209, even if the question were regarded as involving the conferring of the power of orders through the pontifical delegation.[53] To say that it is evident that canons 197-208 apply to the power both of orders and of jurisdiction and that therefore the power of orders like that of jurisdiction can be supplied through the suppletory principle enunciated in canon 209, cer-

[51] Cappello teaches that, if there be question simply of a power of orders of ecclesiastical origin, then the problem resolves itself into a question of jurisdiction.—*De Sacramentis,* I, n. 197, p. 178.

[52] *Op. cit.,* n. 89, p. 63.

[53] *Op. cit.,* p. 64.

tainly goes contrary to the common teaching of cannonical commentators.[54]

The present writer holds that a requisite "*auctoritas*" is conceded through the delegation of the Holy See whereby a simple priest can then validly exercise the power of confirming which radically derives from his possessed power of orders. Inasmuch as this "*auctoritas*" is closely allied to jurisdiction, it could seem that under the circumstances contemplated in canon 209 the Church would be ready to supply the otherwise lacking power, especially to safeguard the spiritual welfare of the recipient of confirmation. Moreover, on March 26, 1952, the Pontifical Commission for the Authentic Interpretation of the Canons of the Code affirmatively approved of the application of the prescription of canon 209 to assistance at marriage in the absence of any delegation, and to the dominative power which superiors and chapters have in religious institutes and in societies of men or women living in common without public vows.[55] But despite this analogy, the writer feels that canon 209 will not operate until the time when an equivalent official declaration has emanated from the Church with regard to the delegated power of confirming, for although the suppletory principle enunciated in canon 209 has been declared applicable in relation to the power of official notarization, as in the act of assistance at marriage, and also with reference to the domestic and familial authority, as exercised by lay superiors in religious institutes, the same suppletory principle seems inapplicable with reference to the "*auctoritas*" that must accrue to the power of priestly orders before the power of confirming is established for the extraordinary minister of confirmation.

[54] Cf. Onclin, "art. cit.," *ETL,* XXV (1949), p. 348, footnote 49.

[55] *AAS,* XLIV (1952), 497.

CONCLUSIONS

1. The preamble to the canonical provisions of the decree *Spiritus Sancti munera* reemphasizes the preeminent excellence of the sacrament of confirmation. Because of its nature and the spiritual effects it produces, the sacrament is both a moral necessity and an invaluable asset in the spiritual development of the follower of Christ. Consequently, its administration to those in danger of death is not to be regarded lightly by the extraordinary minister.

2. During the first thirteen centuries the rôle of the simple priest in the administration of confirmation varied in degree from an acceptance, or at least a toleration, to a relatively complete suppression in the time of Gratian and the early Scholastic theologians.

3. Among the texts of the first five centuries on the question of the minister of confirmation, the most important document is that of Pope Innocent I, issued by him on March 19, 416, inasmuch as it enshrines the first papal resistance to the "presumed" administration of confirmation by any priest.

4. The first lengthy reference to the minister of confirmation in the treatise of Gratian does not occur as an *ex professo* undertaken treatment of the subject. Rather, it can be found in Distinction 95, where the "Father of the Science of Canon Law" discussed the famous concession of Gregory the Great. This letter, frequently designated with its opening word *"Pervenit,"* was issued in May, 594.

5. Of all documents, this letter of Gregory the Great exerted the greatest influence toward the preservation of the doctrine on the extraordinary minister of confirmation.

6. The distinction between the *ordinary* and *extraordinary* minister of confirmation implicitly received its first impulse in the letter *Super quibusdam* of Pope Clement VI, September 23, 1351, gained momentum through the *Decretum pro Armenis* of the Council of Florence (1431-1439), and reached its full formal

fruition with the solemn definition of the seventh session of the Council of Trent (March 3, 1547) that only the bishop is the *ordinary* minister of confirmation.

7. Subsequent documents issued by the Pontiffs and Sacred Congregations, notably by the Sacred Congregation for the Propagation of the Faith, sanctioned the development of the practice of the Church to commission simple priests as extraordinary ministers of confirmation.

8. One of the earliest applications of the terminology "extraordinary minister" occurs in the Instruction *Eo quamvis tempore,* issued on May 4, 1745, by Pope Benedict XIV, a strong advocate of this privilege.

9. The difference between the Latin Church and the Oriental Church with regard to the ordinary and extraordinary minister of confirmation lies not in the doctrine but in the practice. A delegation of the Holy See, at least tacit, is absolutely necessary for the valid administration of confirmation by a simple priest, whether he be of the Latin or the Eastern rite. The preliminary discussions of the Vatican Council indicate that this might have become a defined doctrine if the Council had been able to complete its sessions.

10. The document *Spiritus Sancti munera,* issued by the Sacred Congregation for the Discipline of the Sacraments with the specific approbation of Pope Pius XII, historically must be considered as the most extensive application of the principles of the doctrine and practice of the Latin Church with regard to the extraordinary minister of confirmation.

11. Juridically the decree *Spiritus Sancti munera* appears as a universal pontifical law, with no limitations of time or place, which empowers pastors and certain other priests to administer in virtue of a papal indult the sacrament of confirmation to the unconfirmed in danger of death. Though this granted concession does not connote ordinary power, the incumbent possesses it as long as he remains in the status and capacity envisaged by the law.

12. Though the provisions of the privilege for confirming can receive a broad interpretation since they are contained within a law, the exclusive enumeration of the extraordinary ministers

cannot be extended to supply *de facto* or *de iure* any lacunae of the law.

13. Pastors of most national and colored parishes in this country can be canonically included under the term of the decree, "personal pastors with cumulative territory."

14. Sufficient extrinsic authority exists to warrant the inclusion of administrators of vacant parishes who function by law (canon 472, 2°) as well as those who function by appointment of the bishop (canon 472, 1°) under the term *"vicarii oeconomi"* of the decree. Hence, they possess the faculty of confirming.

15. Neither the intrinsic nor the extrinsic evidence is sufficiently satisfactory to justify the use of the faculty by vicars substitute or adjutant (*vicarii substituti/adiutores*).

16. The presence of a maternity ward in a general hospital adequately meets the requirement for the use of the special indult granted to the hospital chaplains in the United States.

17. The fundamental basis for the valid and lawful exercise of the privilege granted in the decree *Spiritus Sancti munera* rests in territorial jurisdiction and also finds its limits therein. Hence, the pastors of proper territory and the pastors of cumulative territory both have equal rights to administer the sacrament to any validly baptized but unconfirmed infant or adult who is neither an apostate, nor a heretic, nor a schismatic, as long as he is in danger of death in territory which is common to both pastors.

18. Conditions which suffice for the valid administration of extreme unction justify the administration of confirmation by the extraordinary minister. Special caution, however, may dissuade the immediate administration of confirmation after an emergency baptism, lest the infant on later recovery be deprived of the solemn reception of the sacrament from a bishop. This policy, however, should not be the occasion for the extraordinary minister to refrain absolutely from confirming infants in danger of death.

19. In view of an official reply from the Holy See to an enquiry submitted by the writer through his ordinary, a short form can validly and lawfully be used in the emergency administration of confirmation.

20. That the determination of the non-availability of a bishop binds only for the lawful use of the faculty can now be considered a common doctrine.

21. The obligation of the extraordinary minister to use the faculty is intrinsically (*per se*) a grave one. Habitual negligence would constitute a serious sin and dereliction of duty. An occasional refusal, provided that no scandal ensues therefrom, seems in all likelihood to involve a venial sin.

22. The transgression of the limits of the faculty with the result of incurring the penalties listed in canon 2365, as far as the provisions of the decree *Spiritus Sancti munera* are concerned, seems associable only with those conditions which look necessarily to the element of validity.

23. The nature of the power conceded by the Holy See has not been clarified in this decree and in consequence still remains a moot question. The theory proposed by the present writer is that the Pope, in virtue of his supreme power, by an act of jurisdiction, delegates to the simple priest an *"auctoritas in corpus mysticum,"* an added eminence, in virtue of which he can exercise the power of confirming as radically deriving from his possessed power of orders.

24. Though some reputable canonists advocate the application of canon 209 in cases of doubt, the proposition seems to lack adequate sanction without an official declaration of the Church.

25. In the light of subsequent decrees and special indults, the spiritually fruitful application of the privilege conferred in the decree *Spiritus Sancti munera* leads to the fervent hope and prayerful expectation that the Holy See in the near future will grant to the Church Universal a faculty similar to the one that was granted in the decree which was issued in favor of the priests of mission territories. Without any diminution of the distinctive reverence which has enshrined the administration of confirmation, and without any infringement on the prerogatives of the episcopacy, every priest who is engaged in the pastoral ministry and who participates in the care of souls could profitably be empowered to confer as an extraordinary minister the sacrament of confirmation upon the unconfirmed who are in danger of death within, e.g., the confines of the diocese.

APPENDIX I

Acta Apostolicae Sedis, XXXVIII (1946), 349-354

SACRA CONGREGATIO DE DISCIPLINA SACRAMENTORUM

I

DECRETUM

DE CONFIRMATIONE ADMINISTRANDA IIS, QUI EX GRAVI MORBO IN MORTIS PERICULO SUNT CONSTITUTI

Spiritus Sancti munera sacramento Confirmationis conferri catholica doctrina proclamat. Hinc impensa Ecclesiae cura ut pueri, aquis baptismi abluti, tali reficiantur sacramento, quo superni Paraclyti charismata adipiscantur ad robur susceptae baptismo fidei adiiciendum, ut gratiae amplitudine perfusi Christique militis charactere insigniti ad omne opus bonum instructi evadant ac renuntientur.

Licet explorati iuris sit Confirmationem ad animarum salutem de necessitate medii haud requiri (can. 787 Codicis I.C.), ob ejus tamen praecellentiam et ampla quae secumfert praeclara dona, omni ope est adnitendum parochis ceterisque pastoribus ut christianorum nemo, data occasione, tam excellens salutiferae Redemptionis mysterium negligat; quum admirabili sit adiumento ad acriter decertandum contra diaboli nequitiam, mundi et carnis illecebras; ad gratiae virtutumque omnium in terris, gloriaeque maius incrementum assequendum in coelis.[1]

Quamquam nihil intentatum relinquunt vigiles animarum rectores ut, quantum fieri potest, baptizati omnes hoc sacramento rite muniantur et quidem vix cum ad aetatem rationis participem pervenerint, scilicet circa septennium: quod profecto septennium antevertere licet, prout expresse cavetur canone 788, "*si infans in mortis periculo sit constitutus, vel ministro id expedire ob iustas et graves causas videatur*"; permultos nihilominus ex habitis hac de re rationariis constat pueros, utpote morti magis obnoxios, etiam multo antequam aetatem ratione utentem attigerint, ex hac vita sacro chrismate non delibutos decedere, praesertim hisce nostris temporibus post dirissimum belli flagitium; quod et de adultis non paucis, qui in puerili aetate variis de causis confirmari non potuerunt, cotidiana experientia testatur.

[1] S. Thomas, p. III, quaest. 72, art. 8, ad 4.

APPENDIX I

Acta Apostolicae Sedis, XXXVIII (1946), 349-354
[Translation of the decrees by the writer]
THE SACRED CONGREGATION FOR THE DISCIPLINE OF THE SACRAMENTS

I

DECREE

ON THE ADMINISTRATION OF CONFIRMATION TO PERSONS WHO ARE IN DANGER OF DEATH FROM A GRAVE ILLNESS

The gifts of the Holy Spirit are bestowed, according to Catholic doctrine, by the sacrament of confirmation. That is why the Church is so solicitous that children, cleansed by the waters of baptism, be strengthened by this sacrament; for in it the special spiritual gifts of the heavenly Paraclete are acquired for a strengthening of the faith received in baptism, so that, saturated with an abundance of grace and adorned with the insignia of a soldier of Christ, the recipients are made ready for and become acclaimed in the performance of every good work.

Although it is established in law that confirmation is not absolutely necessary for salvation (canon 787 of the Code of Canon Law), nevertheless, in view of its outstanding excellence and the remarkable gifts it confers in great abundance, pastors and other shepherds of souls must exert every effort that no Christian neglect the opportunity of receiving this marvellous mystery of sanctifying redemption. This is especially true since it is an admirable aid in the bitter and fierce struggle against the wickedness of the devil and the allurements of the world and the flesh as well as a means of augmenting grace and all virtues on earth and of acquiring a greater increase of glory in heaven. (St. Thomas, *Summa Theologiae,* part III, q. 72, a. 8 in answer to the 4th objection.)

Although alertly watchful directors of souls leave nothing undone in order that, as far as possible, all baptized persons be properly fortified by this sacrament as soon as they have reached the age of the use of reason, i.e., about the age of seven, which seventh year may certainly be lawfully anticipated, as is expressly noted in canon 788, "if the infant is in danger of death, or if it seems advisable to the minister because of just and serious reasons," nevertheless, from many reports received, it is evident that very many children, among whom the mortality rate is higher, depart from this life without being anointed with holy chrism long before they reach the age of the use of reason, particularly in these times following upon the most frightful affliction of war. Daily experience shows that the same is true of not a few adults who, for various reasons, were unable to receive confirmation in childhood.

Hoc quidem incommodum praecavetur in Ecclesia Orientali, ubi mos est infantes, statim post receptum baptismum, confirmandi. Eadem disciplina in usu quidem erat primis Ecclesiae saeculis etiam apud Latinos, et adhuc servatur ex legitima consuetudine penes quasdam nationes: communis tamen lex Ecclesiae Latinae, in citato can. 788 recepta, statuit ut huius sacramenti administratio differatur ad septimum circiter aetatis annum, quo, aequa praemissa catechesis instructione, pueri uberiores sacramenti sortiantur effectus.[2]

Porro ratio praecipua cur tam immodicus christicolarum numerus sine susceptione huius sacramenti de hac vita demigret, in eo est reponenda, quod iisdem in vitae discrimine constitutis ob Episcopi absentiam opportunitas non exhibetur hoc sacramentum suscipiendi.

Definitae doctrinae est solum Episcopum esse *ordinarium* confirmationis ministrum[3] (can. 782, § 1): proindeque Apostolica Sedes iugiter sedulo studuit, ut huius sacramenti collatio Episcopo, tamquam ius et officium ipsi proprium, quantum fieri potuisset, reservaretur. Haec vero S. Congregatio semper religiose cavit, ne detrimentum pateretur reverentia huic sacramento debita et offensionem piae plebis expectatio ob privationem personae Episcopi, neve illius administrationis conspicuus obfuscaretur splendor ac sollemnis, qui decet, minueretur apparatus.

Ast, necessitate bonoque fidelium id flagitante, non semel Apostolica Sedes passim indulgere compulsa est, ut Episcopo, qui in certis rerum et personarum adiunctis haberi non posset, simplex sacerdos in aliqua ecclesiastica dignitate constitutus sufficeretur, tamquam administer *extraordinarius* huius sacramenti (can. 782, § 2); qui congrua pompa eius administrationem perageret, praemonitis semper fidelibus Episcopum esse exclusivum ordinarium ministrum huiusce sacramenti illudque ab eo sacerdote conferri ex Apostolicae Sedis facultate[4] prout complura pontificia indulta luculenter ostendunt.[5]

[2] Cfr. Instructio S. C. de Sacr. edita die Pentecostes (20 maii) 1934, pro simplici sacerdote sacr. Confirmationis ex Sedis Apostolicae delegatione administrante (*A.A.S.*, vol. XXVII, pg. 11 seq.); Instructio S. C. de Prop. Fide 4 maii 17744; Instructio S. Officii m. julii 1888.

[3] Conc. Trident., sess. VII, *De confirmatione,* can. 3.

[4] Cfr. cit. Instr. S. C. de Sacr., III.

[5] Cfr. cit. Instr. S. C. de Sacr., I, n. 2; cit. Instr. S. C. de Prop. Fide; cit. Instr. S. Officii; Formulae S. C. de Prop. Fide.

This disadvantage is averted in the Oriental Church where the custom prevails of confirming infants immediately after the reception of baptism. Indeed the same discipline existed even among the Latins in the first centuries of the Church, which practice is preserved to the present day by lawful custom among some nations. However, the common law of the Latin Church, embodied in canon 788 cited above, has determined that the administration of this sacrament be deferred until about the seventh year of age, so that the children, after receiving suitable catechetical instruction, may derive richer benefits from this sacrament. (Cf. the Instruction for a simple priest who administers the sacrament of confirmation upon delegation from the Apostolic See, as issued on Pentecost Sunday, May 20, 1934—*AAS*, vol. XXVII, pg. 11 ff.; the Instruction of the Sacred Congregation for the Propagation of the Faith, May 4, 1774; Instruction of the Holy Office, July, 1888.)

Now, the principal reason why Christians in such an excessive number depart from this life without having received this sacrament must be attributed to the fact that, because of the absence of the bishop, the opportunity to receive this sacrament is not presented to them at this critical moment of life.

It is a defined doctrine of faith that the bishop alone is the ordinary minister of confirmation (canon 782, § 1; Council of Trent, seventh session, *on confirmation,* canon 3): therefore the Apostolic See has always zealously sought to reserve, in so far as it possibly could, the administration of this sacrament to the bishop as a right and duty proper to him. Indeed this Sacred Congregation has always scrupulously guarded against any and all loss to the reverence which is owed to this sacrament and against any and all grievance on the part of the pious faithful in consequence of being deprived of the person of a bishop as well as against any overshadowing of the striking splendor of its administration and any curtailment of the solemn ceremony which properly surrounds it.

Yet, whenever necessity and the good of the faithful demanded it, more than once the Apostolic See has been obliged to grant in different places that an ordinary priest, having some ecclesiastical dignity, be appointed as an extraordinary minister of this sacrament (canon 782, § 2) to substitute for a bishop who was unavailable in consequence of the given local or personal circumstance. He was to conduct the administration with fitting solemnity, always reminding the faithful that the bishop is the exclusive ordinary minister of this sacrament and that it is conferred by the priest in virtue of a faculty from the Apostolic See (cf. the above-mentioned Instruction of the Sacred Congregation of the Sacraments, part III), as is clearly evident from many pontifical indults. (Cf. Instruction of the Sacred Congregation of the Sacraments, part I, no. 2; the cited Instruction of the Sacred Congregation for the Propagation of the Faith; the cited Instruction of the Holy Office; the Formularies of the Sacred Congregation for the Propagation of the Faith.)

Ut igitur prospiciatur etiam spirituali conditioni tot infantium, puerorumque atque adultorum fidelium, qui ob gravem morbum in vitae discrimen adducantur, et certo certius mortem oppetant, quin sacro chrismate linantur, si observantia iuris communis quoad ordinarium ministrum adamussim urgeatur; necessarium visum est huic S. Congregationi remedium aliquod exquirere ac suppeditare hac gravissima de causa, ut tam notabili fidelium numero offeratur occasio Confirmationis suscipiendae.

Huius negotii momentum perpendens SSm̃us D. N. Pius Papa XII, animarum saluti plenius consulere studens, prae maxima, quam gerit, sollicitudine universalis Ecclesiae, committere dignatus est huic S. Congergationi, pro sua potestate in hac solvenda quaestione, ut rem diligenter ut impense expenderet in plenariis Comitiis, et resolutionem, quae opportuna sibi visa esset, Ipsi proponeret.

Sacra vero haec Congregatio, praehabitis votis plurium consultorum, doctrina prudentiaque praestantium, et ad trutinam revocatis insuper omnibus documentis et actis antea super disciplinam Confirmationis comparatis, totam rem sedulo examini subiecit Purpuratorum Patrum in pluribus Conventibus plenariis.

Mature autem perspecta, quae inde prodiit, sententia idem Summus Pontifex, in audientia Excm̃o huius Sacrae Congregationi Secretario die 6 Maii 1946 concessa, huic sacro Dicasterio mandavit ut decretum ederet quod disciplinam de Confirmatione administranda in peculiaribus adiunctis supra expositis digereret iuxta leges ab Ipso certa scientia et matura deliberatione probatas atque benigne declaratas.

Apostolico mandato ideo fideliter obsecundans haec Sacra Congregatio de Disciplina Sacramentorum praesentibus litteris, quae infra recensentur, statuenda decrevit:

1. Ex generali Apostolicae Sedis indulto, tamquam ministris extraordinariis (can. 782, § 2) facultas tribuitur conferendi sacramentum Confirmationis, in casibus tantum et sub conditionibus infra enumeratis, sequentibus presbyteris, iisdemque dumtaxat:

a) parochis proprio territorio gaudentibus, exclusis igitur parochis personalibus vel familiaribus, nisi et ipsi proprio, licet cumulativo, fruantur territorio;

b) vicariis, de quibus in canone 471, atque vicariis oeconomis;

c) sacerdotibus, quibus exclusive et stabiliter commissa sit in certo territorio et cum determinata ecclesia plena animarum cura cum omnibus parochorum iuribus et officiis.

2. Praefati ministri Confirmationis valide et licite conferre valent per se ipsi, personaliter, fidelibus tantummodo in proprio territorio degentibus, personis non exceptis in locis commorantibus a paroeciali iurisdictione sub-

In order, therefore, to take care of the spiritual welfare of so many infants, children and adult faithful who because of grave illness are constituted in danger of death, and more than likely will suffer death without being anointed with holy chrism if the observance of the common law regarding the ordinary minister of confirmation were strictly applied, this Sacred Congregation deemed it necessary to seek some remedy and in this most serious situation to make ample provisions, so that such a notable part of the faithful could be given the opportunity of receiving confirmation.

Reflecting on the importance of this matter, our most Holy Father, Pope Pius XII, desiring to provide more fully for the salvation of souls, in view of his very great concern for the Universal Church, deigned to authorize this Sacred Congregation, in accordance with its power to resolve this question, to ponder the matter faithfully and carefully in plenary sessions and to propose to Him the solution which it considered advisable.

Indeed, this Sacred Congregation, after it had obtained the opinions of a great number of consultors, of men outstanding for their learning and prudence, and after it had moreover investigated and weighed all the previous documents and records concerning the discipline which governs the administration of confirmation, submitted the entire matter to the painstaking and penetrating examination of the Cardinals in many plenary meetings.

After a careful and circumspect consideration of the submitted resolution, the same Sovereign Pontiff, in an audience granted on May 6, 1946, to the most excellent Secretary of this Congregation, ordered this Sacred Congregation to issue a decree which would determine the discipline to be followed in the administration of confirmation in the special circumstances discussed above, according to the norms which He Himself, with certain knowledge and after mature deliberation, approved and graciously promulgated.

Accordingly, in faithful obedience to this apostolic mandate, this Sacred Congregation for the Discipline of the Sacraments has through this present document decreed that the following provisions be established:

1. In virtue of a general indult of the Apostolic See, the faculty of conferring the sacrament of confirmation as extraordinary ministers (canon 782, § 2) is granted, in only those cases and under those conditions which receive mention below, to the following priests and to them alone:

a) to pastors who have their own proper territory; personal or family pastors are therefore excluded unless they possess their own proper territory, though it be cumulative;

b) to the vicars mentioned in canon 471 and to vicars econome (parochial administrators);

c) to priests to whom the full care of souls with all rights and duties of pastors is exclusively and in a fixed manner entrusted within a definite territory and along with a determined church.

2. The above-mentioned ministers can validly and lawfully confer confirmation themselves personally only upon the faithful who are sojourning in their territory, with no exception made for the persons who live in places withdrawn from the parochial jurisdiction. Therefore, seminaries, lodging

ductis; non exclusis, igitur seminariis, hospitiis, valetudinariis, aliisque omne genus institutis etiam religiosis quoquo modo exemptis (cfr. can. 792); dummodo hi fideles *ex gravi morbo in vero mortis periculo sint constituti, ex quo decessuri praevideantur.*

Si huiusmodi mandati limites iidem ministri praetergrediantur, probe sciant se perperam agere et sacramentum nullum conficere, incolumi praeterea manente statuto canonis 2365.

3. Hac facultate uti possunt tum in ipsa episcopali urbe tum extra ipsam, sive sedes plena sit sive vacans, dummodo Episcopus dioecesanus haberi non possit vel legitime impediatur quominus Confirmationem per se ipse valeat conferre, nec alius praesto sit Episcopus communionem habens cum Apostolica Sede, licet titularis tantum, qui sine gravi incommodo ipsi suffici queat.

4. Confirmatio conferatur servata disciplina per Codicem I.C. inducta et ad rem accommodata, nec non ritu adhibito ex Rituali Romano excerpto, quae fuse et ex integro infra transcribuntur: *gratis vero quovis titulo est conferenda.*

5. Si confirmandi rationis usum sint assecuti, praeter statum gratiae, aliqua dispositio atque instructio requiritur ut fructuose hoc sacramentum valeant suscipere. Ministri igitur est pro singulorum aegrotorum captu eos edocere de his, quae scitu sunt necessaria, intentionem aliquam suscitando percipiendi hoc sacramentum ad robur animae conferendum. Curari autem debet ab his, ad quos spectat, ut si dein convaluerint, opportunis institutionibus circa fidei mysteria, naturam atque effectum huius sacramenti diligenter instruantur.[6] (Cfr. can. 786.)

6. Ad normam can 798, collati sacramenti adnotationem minister extraordinarius in paroeciali confirmatorum libro peragat, ibidem inscribendo nomen suum ac nomina confirmati (et si eius subditus non sit, etiam illius dioecesis et paroeciae), parentum et patrini, diem et locum, adiectis demum verbis: *"confirmatio collata est ex Apostolico indulto, urgente mortis periculo ob gravem confirmati morbum."* Adnotatio facienda est etiam in libro baptizatorum ad normam can. 470, § 2.

Si confirmatus sit alienae paroeciae, quamprimum minister ipse de collato sacramento parochum confirmati proprium certiorem reddat per

[6] Cfr. S. Off., 10 apr. 1861 in Collect. S. C. de Prop. Fide, edit. a. MCMVII, vol. I, p. 663, n. 1213; Catechismus Romanus, *De Confirmatione.*

places, hospitals and every other kind of institution, even religious, no matter how exempt (cf. canon 792) are not excluded, provided that these faithful *because of a serious illness are constituted in a real danger of death from which it is foreseen that they will die.*

If these ministers go beyond the limits of this mandate, let them clearly understand that they are acting wrongly and do not confer the sacrament. Moreover, the provisions of canon 2365 retain their full force.

3. They can use this faculty both in the episcopal city itself as well as beyond it, whether the see is occupied or vacant, as long as the bishop of the diocese is unavailable or is lawfully prevented from administering confirmation himself and there is not present any other bishop who is in communion with the Apostolic See, even though he be only a titular bishop, and who without grave inconvenience could substitute for the bishop of the diocese.

4. Confirmation is to be administered in accordance with the requirements contained in the Code of Canon Law and adapted to the situation as well as with the rite taken from the Roman Ritual, both of which are reproduced below in their entirety. *It must be conferred free of charge and without recompense, no matter what the claim or title be.*

5. If those who are to be confirmed have attained the use of reason, then besides the state of grace on their part there is need of some disposition and instruction to enable them also fruitfully to receive this sacrament. Therefore it behooves the minister to give instruction to the sick in accordance with the capacity of each individual about those things which of necessity must be known, and to stimulate some intention for the reception of this sacrament with the view to obtaining strength for the soul. Care must be taken by those upon whom the responsibility rests that, if the sick persons recover, they receive thorough-going instructions in the mysteries of the faith as well as on the nature of the effect of this sacrament. (Cf. canon 786; also Instruction of the Holy Office, April 10, 1861, found in the Collection of the Sacred Congregation for the Propagation of the Faith, issued in 1907, Vol. I, p. 663, n. 1213; also the *Roman Catechism,* "On Confirmation.")

6. According to the norm of canon 798, the extraordinary minister is to enter a record of his conferring of the sacrament in the parish confirmation register, inscribing therein his own name and the names of the person confirmed (and in case the latter is not his own subject, also the diocese and the parish to which he belongs), the names of his parents and sponsor, the date and the place, with the added statement, "*confirmatio collata est ex Apostolico indulto, urgente mortis periculo ob gravem confirmati morbum,*" "the confirmation was administered in virtue of an apostolic indult, the person being in danger of death from grave illness." An annotation is to be made also in the baptismal register, in keeping with the norms of canon 470, § 2.

If the person who received confirmation belongs to another parish, the minister himself, as soon as possible, is to give notice of the administration

authenticum documentum, quod omnes notitias complectatur, de quibus supra.

7. Ministri extraordinarii tenentur praeterea singulis vicibus statim ad Ordinarium dioecesanum proprium authenticum nuntium mittere collatae a se Confirmationis, additis adiunctis omnibus in casu concurrentibus.

8. Ordinarii loci est ministros extraordinarios, de quibus supra, huius decreti praescriptiones meliore, quem censuerit, modo edocere, iisdemque singillatim explanare ut pares omnino inveniantur tam gravi negotio obeundo.

9. Eiusdem Ordinarii loci officium est quolibet anno, sub initio anni proxime insequentis, *relationem* mittere ad hanc S. Congregationem de numero confirmatorum, necnon de ratione a ministris extraordinariis suae dicionis in tam praeclaro munere perfungendo adhibita.

SSm̃us Dominus Noster Pius divina Providentia PP. XII, in Audientia Excm̃o Secretario huius Sacrae Congregationis die 20 Augusti 1946 concessa, decretum de quo supra approbare et Apostolica Auctoritate munire dignatus est, contrariis quibuslibet, etiam speciali mentione dignis, minime obstantibus; mandavitque ut idem decretum, in *Actorum Apostolicae Sedis commentario officiali* edendum, vim legis habere incipiat a die Ia Ianuraii 1947.

Datum Romae, ex aedibus Sacrae Congregationis de Disciplina Sacramentorum, die 14 Septembris anni 1946.

D. Card. Jorio, *Praefectus.*
F. Bracci, *Secretarius.*

L.S.

of the sacrament to the proper pastor of the recipient by means of an authentic document which contains all the data mentioned above.

7. Moreover, the extraordinary ministers are obliged, every time they use the faculty, to transmit at once to the proper diocesan ordinary an authentic notice of the confirmation which they have conferred, with all the circumstances affecting the case.

8. The local ordinary has the responsibility of informing the extraordinary ministers mentioned above, in the manner which he deems best, of the provisions of this decree, and to explain the same to them in detail, so that they may be fully prepared to perform this important function.

9. The same local ordinary also has the duty of sending to this Sacred Congregation at the beginning of the subsequent year an annual report on the number of persons confirmed as well as on the manner in which the extraordinary ministers under his jurisdiction discharged so distinguished a duty.

His Holiness by Divine Providence Pope Pius XII, in an audience granted to the most excellent Secretary of this Sacred Congregation on August 20, 1946, deigned to approve the foregoing decree and to confirm it with his Apostolic Authority, all things to the contrary notwithstanding, even those worthy of special mention, and he commanded that the same decree, to be published in the official publication of the Holy See, the *Acta Apostolicae Sedis,* have the force of law beginning with January 1, 1947.

Given at Rome, from the Offices of the Sacred Congregation on the Discipline of the Sacraments, on the 14th day of September, in the year 1946.

D. Cardinal Jorio, *Prefect.*
F. Bracci, *Secretary.*

(Seal)

APPENDIX II

Acta Apostolicae Sedis, XL (1948), 41

SACRA CONGREGATIO DE PROPAGANDA FIDE

DECRETUM

De Confirmatione Administranda IIs, Qui ex Gravi Morbo in Periculo Mortis Sunt Constituti

Post latum a Sacra Congregatione de Disciplina Sacramentorum decretum *Spiritus Sancti Munera* diei XIV Septembris an. 1946 (cf. *Acta Apostolicae Sedis,* vol. XXXVIII, 1946, p. 349) ad Sacrum hoc Consilium Christiano nomini propagando plures Ordinariorum missionum preces, ad easdem amplioresve facultates obtinendas, pervenerunt.

Quas Ssmus D. N. Pius Div. Prov. Papa XII, in Audientia diei XVIII huius mensis, referente infrascripto Cardinali Praefecto, benigne suscipere dignatus est.

Omnibus itaque Ordinariis locorum ab hac Sacra Congregatione de Propaganda Fide dependentibus potestatem Sanctissmus fecit, absque praeiudicio ceterorum indultorum quibus in re iam fruuntur, ut Sedis Apostolicae indulto (can. 782, § 2), tribuere valeant omnibus sacerdotibus sibi subditis curamque animarum gerentibus, facultatem sacram Confirmationem fidelibus sive adultis sive infantibus, intra fines missionalis circumscriptionis exstantibus et in mortis periculo constitutis, valide ministrandi; necnon licite in ipso loco residentiae Episcopi, absente tamen quolibet Episcopo vel legitime impedito; servataque formula a Rituali Romano statuta.

Praesens vero decretum eadem Sanctitas Sua confici publicique iuris fieri mandavit.

Datum Romae, ex Aedibus Sacrae Congregationis de Propaganda Fide, die XVIII mensis Decembris, anno Domini MCMXXXXVII.

P. Card. Fumasoni Biondi, *Praefectus.*
P. Costantini, *Arch. Theodos. in Arcadia, a Secretis.*

L.S.

APPENDIX II

Acta Apostolicae Sedis, XL (1948), 41

THE SACRED CONGREGATION FOR THE PROPAGATION OF THE FAITH

DECREE

ON THE ADMINISTRATION OF CONFIRMATION TO THOSE WHO ARE IN DANGER OF DEATH FROM A GRAVE ILLNESS

After the decree *Spiritus Sancti munera* was issued by the Sacred Congregation for the Discipline of the Sacraments on September 14, 1946 (cf. *Acta Apostolicae Sedis,* Vol. XXXVIII [1946], p. 349), this Sacred Council for the Propagation of the Christian name received many petitions from the ordinaries in mission territories asking for the same or more extensive faculties.

His Holiness by Divine Providence Pope Pius XII, in an audience on the 18th day of this month, at the instance of the undersigned Cardinal Prefect, deigned to receive these requests favorably.

Therefore, to all local ordinaries dependent upon this Sacred Congregation for the Propagation of the Faith, His Holiness bestowed the power, without prejudice to other indults which they already enjoy in this matter, to grant by indult of the Apostolic See (canon 782, § 2) to all the priests who are under their jurisdiction and have the care of souls the faculty of validly administering confirmation to the faithful, whether adults or infants, who actually are within the limits of the mission borders and in danger of death. They can also do this lawfully in the very place of residence of the bishop, provided that no bishop is present, or, being present, is lawfully impeded. The formula determined by the Roman Ritual must be followed.

His Holiness ordered that the present decree be duly drawn up and published.

Given at Rome, from the Offices of the Sacred Congregation for the Propagation of the Faith, the 18th day of December, in the year of our Lord, 1947.

P. Card. Fumasoni Biondi, *Prefect.*

P. Costantini, *Archbishop of Theodosiopalis in Arcadia, Secretary.*

(Seal)

APPENDIX III

Acta Apostolicae Sedis, XL (1948), pp. 422-423

SACRA CONGREGATIO PRO ECCLESIA ORIENTALI

DECRETUM

De Sacramento Confirmationis Administrando etiam Fidelibus Orientalium Rituum a Presbyteris Latini Ritus, Qui Hoc Indulto Gaudeant pro Fidelibus Sui Ritus

Cum, ex can. 782, § 4, C.I.C., presbyter Latini ritus, cui vi indulti competat facultas conferendi Sacramentum Confirmationis, illud valide conferre valeat solis fidelibus sui ritus "nisi in indulto aliud expresse cautum fuerit;" cumque, post primum et alterum universi terrarum orbis luctuosissimum bellum, permulti Orientalium rituum fideles in regionibus Latini ritus dispersi commorentur, qui quidem a prebyteris Latini ritus administrantur ac in eiusdem ritus usu adolescunt, ita ut saepenumero ad eumdem se pertinere putent, vel ad quem ritum reapse pertineant ignorent, non raro eiusdem Sacramenti collatio invaliditatis periculo exponebatur; idque praesertim in regionibus quibusdam, in quibus iidem locorum Ordinarii praedictum indultum presbyteris, curam animarum habentibus, concedunt.

Quod periculum magis profecto patuit post editum, die 14 mensis Septembris a. 1946, a S. Congregatione de Disciplina Sacramentorum Decretum "De Confirmatione administranda iis qui, ex gravi morbo, in mortis periculo sunt constituti."

Quapropter, Sacra haec Congregatio pro Ecclesia Orientali, consilio inito cum Sacra Congregatione de Disciplina Sacramentorum, ut bono spirituali fidelium rituum Orientalium, extra proprium territorium sub iurisdictione Ordinarii Latini ritus degentium, necnon reverentiae Sacramentis debitae rite consuleret, necessarium duxit Ssm̃um D.N. Pium Div. Prov. Pp. XII suppliciter exorare ut, quoties Latini ritus presbyteri, vi legitimi indulti, Confirmationis Sacramentum valide et licite adminstrare possunt fibelibus proprii ritus, idem dummodo constet ipsum immediate post Baptismum, uti mos est, iam non fuisse conlatum—conferre valeant fidelibus quoque rituum Orientalium, quorum spiritualis cura ipsis commissa permaneat, ad normam Constitutionis Apostolicae *Orientalium Dignitas* diei 30 mensis Novembris a. 1894, art. 9, quae statuit: "quicumque Orientalis extra patriarchale territorium commorans, sub administratione sit cleri latini."

APPENDIX III

Acta Apostolicae Sedis, XL (1948), 422-423

THE SACRED CONGREGATION FOR THE ORIENTAL CHURCH

DECREE

On the Administration of the Sacrament of Confirmation even to the Faithful of the Oriental Rites by Priests Of the Latin Rite Who Enjoy This Indult for the Faithful of Their Own Rite

Inasmuch as according to the fourth paragraph of canon 782 of the Code of Canon Law a priest of the Latin rite who has by indult the faculty to confer the sacrament of confirmation can validly confer it only on the faithful of his rite, "unless the indult expressly provides otherwise," and inasmuch as, after the dreadful first and second world wars, very many faithful of the Oriental rites live today scattered throughout lands of the Latin rite, where they are cared for by priests of the Latin rite and grow up in the practice of that rite, so that very often they think they belong to it or do not know to which rite they actually belong, it has frequently happened that the administration of this sacrament was exposed to the danger of invalidity, and particularly so in certain regions where the same local ordinaries grant the above-mentioned indult to priests engaged in the care of souls.

This danger became more clearly evident after the Sacred Congregation for the Discipline of the Sacraments on September 14, 1946, published its decree "on the Administration of Confirmation to those who are in danger of death from a grave illness."

Therefore, in order to protect the spiritual welfare of the faithful of the Oriental rites who are living outside their own territory under the jurisdiction of an ordinary of the Latin rite, as well as to protect the reverence properly due to the sacraments, this Sacred Congregation for the Oriental Church by agreement with the Sacred Congregation for the Discipline of the Sacraments deemed it necessary to humbly petition His Holiness by Divine Providence Pope Pius XII that, whenever priests of the Latin rite in virtue of a lawful indult can validly and lawfully administer the sacrament of confirmation to the faithful of their own rite, they can also administer it—provided it is clear that confirmation had not already been conferred after baptism, as is customary—to the faithful of the Oriental rites whose spiritual care is committed to them according to the norm of the Apostolic Constitution *Orientalium Dignitas,* issued on the 30th of November, 1894, of which article 9 provided that "every Oriental who is living outside of the patriarchal territory shall be under the administration of the Latin clergy."

Eadem, uti patet, valere pariter dicenda sunt quoties Confirmationis Sacramentum conferri possit ad normam memorati Decreti S. Congregationis de Disciplina Sacramentorum.

Quas preces, per infrascriptum Cardinalem huius Sacrae Congregationis pro Ecclesia Orientali a Secretis, in Audientia diei 28 mensis Februarii nuper elapsi, Summo Pontifici humiliter relatas, Sanctitas Sua benigne dignatus est adprobare; simulque iussit id publici iuris fieri praesenti Decreto.

Datum Romae, ex Aedibus Sacrae Congregationis pro Ecclesia Orientali, die 1ª mensis Maii an. 1948.

E. Card. Tisserant, *Ep. Portuen. et S. Rufinae,*
a Secretis.

I. Rosso, *Substitutus.*

L.S.

As is evident, the same must be said to hold as often as the sacrament of confirmation can be conferred in accordance with the norm of the abovementioned decree of the Sacred Congregation for the Discipline of the Sacraments.

This petition was humbly presented to the Supreme Pontiff by the undersigned Secretary of this Sacred Congregation for the Oriental Church in a recent audience held on the 28th day of February. His Holiness graciously deigned to approve it and at the same time ordered that by means of the present decree it be given its due publication.

Given at Rome, from the Offices of the Sacred Congregation for the Oriental Church, the first day of the month of May in the year 1948.

E. CARD. TISSERANT, *Bishop of Porto and Santa Rufina, Secretary.*

I. ROSSO, *Substitute.*

(Seal)

APPENDIX IV

DISCIPLINE OF THE CODE OF CANON LAW TO BE OBSERVED IN THE ADMINISTRATION OF CONFIRMATION BY VIRTUE OF THIS APOSTOLIC INDULT

[Latin text appears in the *Acta Apostolicae Sedis,* XXXVIII (1946), 354–356. The English translation of the canons is in large measure borrowed from the two volumes, *The Sacred Canons,* by Abbo-Hannan, with the kind permission of the publishers, B. Herder Book Co.]

Note.—The actual words of the text appear within quotation marks to distinguish them from the brief pastoral commentary which follows, whenever such commentary was deemed necessary or practical.

1. "A priest to whom this faculty has been granted must clearly understand that the sacrament of confirmation shall be conferred through the imposition of the hand accompanied by the anointing of the forehead with chrism and by the pronouncing of the words prescribed in the pontifical books approved by the Church (canon 780)."

The remote matter of confirmation is chrism, which is made from olive oil and fragrant balsam, blessed by the bishop. The olive oil is required *ex necessitate sacramenti,* the balsam is required at least *ex necessitate praecepti.*[1] It is common teaching that when confirmation is conferred with the use of oil alone it is doubtfully valid; in danger of death, however, the use of such oil could serve for a conditional administration, if no chrism were available.[2] Thus, since the oil of the sick (*oleum infirmorum*) is oil made of olives, if the priest went on a sick call without chrism and discovered that the person was not confirmed and there was no time to return because the person was very close to death, he could use the oil to confirm conditionally.[3] The use of the expression, "*si haec materia valet,*" is advisable but not necessary.[4]

[1] Cappello, *De Sacramentis,* I, n. 191, p. 167.

[2] Cappello, *De Sacramentis,* I, n. 191, p. 168. Noldin-Schmitt, *Summa Theologiae Moralis,* III, 89: ". . cum tamen sacramentum non sit certo invalidum, in articulo mortis, vel si quis alias semper careret hoc sacramento, deficiente chrismate, confirmatio cum alio oleo sub conditione conferri possit. . . ." "In adiunctis extraordinariis, scilicet in extrema necessitate et in defectu materiae certo validae, uti licet etiam materia dubie valida sub conditione. Ratio est quia bonum animae in extremo discrimine versantis exigit ut ei succurratur meliore quo fieri potest modo; aliunde vitatur periculum ne sacramentum frustretur, quia conditionate confertur, et si conditio non verificatur, nihil fit."—Pistoni, *De Confirmatione a Ministro Extraordinario,* n. 8, p. 9; also n. 52 (b), p. 55. Noldin-Schmitt cite St. Alphonsus as an authority, while Pistoni refers to Genicot.

[3] "En danger de mort, on peut employer l'huile des catéchumenès ou des infirmes pour confirmer sous condition, quoique la confirmation ne soit pas de nécessité de moyen pour le salut."—Naz, *Traité de Droit Canonique,* II,

The proximate matter is the anointing with chrism, through the sign of the cross made along with the imposition of the hand. All the authors agree that the anointing is necessary for validity,[5] and nearly all of them agree that it is essential that the anointing take place on the forehead in the form of a cross.[6] The imposition of the hand is certainly essential. Some good theologians maintain that the mere anointing of the forehead with the thumb is a real imposition of the hand. Others cast doubts on the validity of such a method. Hence the priest must follow out the rubrics to the letter.[7]

The form in the Latin Church consists in the words which accompany the anointing, namely, *"signo te signo crucis,* etc." Authors differ regarding which of the words are really essential.[8] Theoretically *"signo te"* could seem to suffice, though Lennerz, after a comparison of the Latin form with the Greek form *"signaculum doni Spiritus Sancti,"* concludes that *"signo te —confirmo te"* would be required for validity.[9]

Finally it should be noted that, whenever a Latin priest confirms a member of the Oriental rite in virtue of the special decree from the Sacred Congregation for the Oriental Church, he is to use the Latin form and follow the rubrics of the *Roman Ritual*.[10] The words of the form must be pro-

n. 67, p. 63. A. Bride in *L'Ami du Clergé,* 7e série, LXI (1951), 383, also confirms this conclusion. An observation of McCarthy concerning the use of chrism as well as the oil of catechumens in the conditional administration of extreme unction when the oil of the sick cannot be obtained in time seems apropos of the present discussion: "This view does not violate the principle that one cannot act in accordance with a probable opinion when the validity of the sacraments is in question. In our context this principle means that a priest may not use what is merely probably valid matter when certainly, or more certainly, valid matter is available. It does not mean that a priest may not give the recipient the possible benefit of the ministration of a sacrament with doubtfully valid matter when more certainly valid matter cannot be obtained in time. The proposition condemned by Pope Innocent XI reads: 'Non est illicitum in sacramentis conferendis sequi opinionem probabilem de valore sacramenti, relicta tutiore. . . .' The words *"relicta tutiore"* provide a basis for the point which we have made, namely, that the use of merely probably valid matter is not at all unlawful in cases of necesssity when certainly, or more certainly, valid matter is not available."—*Problems in Theology,* I: *The Sacraments,* p. 293.

4 Pistoni, *op. cit.,* n. 54, p. 56.

5 Cappello, *De Sacramentis* I, n. 192, p. 169.

6 Nabucho (*Pontificalis Romani Expositio Juridico—Practica,* Tom. I [Petropoli, Brasilia: Sumptibus Editora Vozes Ltda., 1945], p. 59) notes that otherwise the words "I sign you with the sign of the cross" would have no meaning.

7 Smiddy, *A Manual for the Extraordinary Minister of Confirmation,* p. 92.

8 Cappello, *op. cit.,* I, n. 194, p. 173.

9 *De Sacramento Confirmationis,* n. 160, pp. 97–98.

10 Canon 733, § 2: Unusquisque autem ritum suum sequatur. . . .

nounced vocally, without any substantial change or interruption, after the manner of consecrating, by the same minister who, as he anoints with chrism, must at least have the intention of doing what the Church does.

2. "This sacrament which imprints a character on the soul cannot be conferred a second time; but if there should exist a prudent doubt whether it was in fact conferred or whether it was validly conferred, it shall be conferred again conditionally (canon 732, § 1 and 2)."

There must be a prudent doubt whether the sacrament was previously conferred. This doubt can arise because of the lack of definite knowledge that the sacrament had been administered, or there may be a question of its valid administration. The first type of doubt will occur more frequently than the second. If possible, the priest should try to dispel this doubt by seeking specific information from the relatives. The person's family background, or his record of fidelity to religious duties, may serve as a corroboratory presumption in the establishing of moral certainty in regard to the previous confirmation or non-confirmation of the party.[11] If a reasonable doubt persists, the dying person should be favored and the sacrament conferred conditionally.[12] It suffices for the minister to form the condition mentally, though it would seem more fitting for him to express it verbally immediately before the anointing, for example, *"Joannes, si non es confirmatus, signo te, etc."*[13] Of course, if it is definitely established that the person was never validly confirmed, it goes without saying that the sacrament is to be conferred absolutely.

Unless the same sponsor can be obtained, which is most unlikely, a sponsor is not required when confirmation is conferred conditionally, since neither sponsor would contract the spiritual relationship.[14]

3. "The chrism which is used in the administration of this sacrament, even when conferred by a simple priest, must be such as has been blessed by a bishop in communion with the Apostolic See on the immediately preceding Holy Thursday; chrism blessed at an earlier date should not be used except in case of urgent necessity. If the supply of blessed oil should be greatly diminished in quantity, a smaller quantity of other unblessed oil may be added to it, and this may be done more than once (canons 781, 734, §§ 1 and 2). However, it is never lawful to administer confirmation without chrism, or to accept it from heretical or schismatical bishops. The anointing shall not be made with any instrument, but with the hand of the minister properly imposed on the head of the person to be confirmed (canon 781, § 2)."

11 Hannan, *The Jurist,* VII, (1947), 227.

12 Pistoni, *op. cit.,* n. 58, p. 58.

13 Connell, "The Recent Decree Empowering Priests to Confirm," *AER,* CXVI (1947), 259–260.

14 The situation would parallel the provisions of canon 763, which governs sponsors at conditional baptism.

It is necessary, at least by necessity of precept, that the chrism be blessed by a bishop.[15] The faculty of the ordinary priest is always limited by the requirement that he use chrism blessed by a bishop. The anointing cannot be done with an instrument; such a procedure would be invalid, since there would be no accompanying imposition of the hand.

4. "A priest of the Latin rite to whom, in virtue of an indult, this power has been imparted can validly confer confirmation only on the faithful of his own rite, unless contrary provision has been expressly made in the indult. It is a serious offense for priests of the Oriental rite who possess the power or privilege of conferring confirmation on infants of their rite at the time of baptism to confer it on infants of the Latin rite (canon 782, §§ 4 and 5)."

The decree of the Sacred Congregation for the Oriental Church, as issued on May 1, 1948, has for practical purposes abrogated the prohibition which restricted the priests of the Latin rite, so that it is no longer effective when they confirm in danger of death. For a fuller explanation consult article 3b of chapter VI in this dissertation, pp. 126 ff.

5. "A priest who possesses an apostolic indult is bound by the obligation of conferring this sacrament to those in whose favor the faculty has been granted when they properly and reasonably request it (canon 785, §§ 1 and 2)."

No comment is necessary, since this question is treated in great detail in article 2 of chapter VIII in this dissertation, pp. 158 ff.

6. "Although this sacrament is not absolutely necessary for salvation (*necessitate medii*), it is permitted to no one, when he has an opportunity to receive it, to pass it by; indeed, pastors shall see to it that the faithful shall receive it at a proper time (canon 787)."

The reader is reminded of St. Thomas' classic division of necessity. There are three kinds of necessity: absolute necessity, e.g., that God is, that a triangle has three angles; the necessity of coaction, that is, necesssity from an efficient cause, and necessity springing from one's aim or purpose. This is divided into a necessity without which one cannot be preserved *in esse*, e.g., food; the other, without which one would not have *bene esse*.[16] Baptism and penance are necessary for the *esse* in the spiritual life, whereas confirmation is necessary to the *bene esse* of the spiritual life. Thus it is not to be regarded lightly.

7. "Because of the very ancient usage of the Church, as in the case of baptism, so likewise in the administration of confirmation, a sponsor must be used, if it is possible to obtain one (canon 793)."

Though Cappello holds that from the words of the canon it seems that in practice the obligation of having a sponsor is light,[17] Coronata states that

[15] Coronata, *De Sacramentis*, I, n. 161, p. 119.

[16] In *IV Sent.*, dist. 7, q. 1, a. 1; also *Summa Theologiae*, IIIa, q. 72, a. 8, ad 4. Cappello, *De Sacramentis*, I. 207, pp. 190–191.

[17] *De Sacramentis* I, n. 210, p. 193.

the more common teaching favors the seriousness of the obligation.[18] The present writer feels that any reasonable difficulty in obtaining a sponsor would excuse from the need of his presence. As one commentator has noted, in danger of death, when time is an important consideration, it will often be out of the question to search for a suitable sponsor.[19]

The Sacred Congregation for the Propagation of the Faith declared on September 21, 1843, that the practice whereby a priest who confirms in virtue of an indult should also act as sponsor, even by way of proxy, is not to be tolerated.[20] Although the Sacred Congregation of the Rites on June 14, 1873 indicated (ad III) that a bishop when confirming could act as sponsor through the use of a proxy,[21] the prohibition against such a procedure on the part of a priest who confirms as an extraordinary minister still holds.[22]

8. "A sponsor should stand for only one person to be confirmed or at the most for two, unless another arrangement seems to the minister warranted by a justifying reason; moreover there shall be no more than one sponsor for each person to be confirmed (canon 794, §§ 1 and 2)."

9. "In order that a person may be a sponsor it is required (for validity):

"1) That he shall himself be confirmed, be possessed of the use of reason, and have the intention to discharge that function;

"2) That he shall not belong to a heretical or schismatical sect, or be excommunicated upon a condemnatory or declaratory sentence, or be infamous under legal infamy, or be barred from the exercise of authorized ecclesiastical acts, or be a deposed or degraded cleric (canon 765, n. 2);

"3) That he shall not be the father, the mother, or the spouse of the person to be confirmed;

"4) That he shall be designated by the person to be confirmed, or by the latter's parents or guardians, or, if these are not available, or if they refuse to act, by the minister or by the pastor;

"5) That he shall himself or through the use of a proxy physically touch the person being confirmed in the very act of confirmation (canon 795)."

The extraordinary minister should be very careful to ascertain previous reception of confirmation on the part of the sponsor, since this reception of confirmation is necessary for the validity of the sponsorship. In the haste of an emergency call one might too readily take this for granted. It may happen that the only ones present at the deathbed are the parents or the

[18] *Op. cit.*, I, n. 177, p. 135.

[19] Madden, *The Australasian Catholic Record,* XXXII (1955), 36. Connell ("art. cit.," *AER,* CXVI [1947], 262) says that a slight reason would excuse from the obligation. Cf. also Mahoney, *The Priest as Minister of Confirmation,* n. 113, p. 63.

[20] *Collectanea,* n. 969.

[21] *Fontes,* n. 6059.

[22] Mahoney, *loc. cit.;* Smiddy, *A Manual for the Extraordinary Minister of Confirmation,* pp. 89–90.

spouse. They cannot validly act as sponsors, although other relatives may. However, commissioned by the real sponsor, they could serve as proxy.

A reply of the Commission for the Authentic Interpretation of the Code, issued on July 30, 1934, determined that membership in an atheistic sect is to be considered, as regards all legal effects, the same as membership in a non-Catholic sect.[23]

Although some commentators seem to doubt the application of this reply to Communists, the writer has no hesitation in insisting that a Communist be not employed as a sponsor, for the reason, indeed, that his sponsorship would be invalid.[24]

10. "In order that a person may be lawfully admitted to the function of sponsor it is required:

"1) That he shall not be the same sponsor as the one used at baptism, unless a justifying reason, in the judgment of the minister, argues for the contrary, or confirmation is lawfully conferred immediately after baptism;

"2) That he shall be of the same sex as the person confirmed, unless, in individual cases, the contrary shall seem to the minister to be justified by a solid reason;

"3) That he shall have reached the fourteenth year of his age, unless for a justifying reason the minister judges otherwise;

"4) That he be not, on account of a notorious delict, excommunicated, or barred from the exercises of authorized ecclesiastical acts, or infamous under legal infamy, though not in consequence of a sentence, and that he be not affected by interdict or otherwise publicly marked by crime or factual infamy;

"5) That he shall know the rudiments of the faith;

"6) That he shall not be a novice or a professed member of a religious institute, except in a case of necessity, in which the express permission of at least the local superior has been obtained;

"7) That he be not in sacred orders, unless he has obtained the express permission of his proper ordinary (canon 796; nn. 3–7 inclusive are the provisions taken from canon 766)."

No comment on these conditions for lawful sponsorship seems necessary, except perhaps the observation of Smiddy on number 6. Although it never finds application when confirmation is administered at church ceremonies, it could prove a problem at the administration of confirmation in Catholic hospitals staffed by religious.[25]

[23] *AAS.* XXVI (1934), 494.

[24] Another declaration concerning Communism emanated from the Holy Office on July 1, 1949.—*AAS.* XLI (1949), 334. Further discussion on this point can be consulted in *Apollinaris,* XXII (1949), 57–70, "Annotationes ad Decretum S. Officii de Communismo," by Sirna; also in *Monitor Ecclasiasticus,* I (1949), 50–54, "Adnotationes" by Bidagor. The former specifically declares that formal Communists cannot validly act as sponsor, whereas the latter seems to support the contrary opinion.

[25] *Op. cit.,* p. 89.

11. "There arises from valid confirmation the bond of spiritual relationship between the person confirmed and the sponsor, as a consequence of which the sponsor is bound by the obligation to regard the confirmed person as perpetually entrusted to his concern and to provide for his Christian education (canon 797). The spiritual relationship arising from confirmation no longer constitutes a matrimonial impediment (canon 1079)."

Only one observation need be made, namely, that, unlike the situation in baptism (canon 768), the spiritual relationship is not contracted by the minister. A proxy does not contract spiritual relationship, but only the sponsor whom he represents.

12. "Provided that the interest of no one is prejudiced, to prove the fact of the conferring of confirmation, the testimony of one witness, who is above all suspicion, suffices, or the sworn testimony of the confirmed person himself, unless he was confirmed as an infant (canon 800)."

13. "A priest who has not the faculty either by law or by grant from the Roman Pontiff and dares to administer the sacrament of confirmation is to be suspended; should he presume to transgress the limits of the faculty which has been granted to him, he is by that very fact, i.e., *ipso facto*, deprived of the faculty (canon 2365)."

A full discussion of this provision is contained in article 3 of Chapter VIII in this dissertation, pp. 162 ff.

As is evident, there was no need of reference to canons 790 and 791, which refer to the time and place of confirmation.

APPENDIX V

THE RITE TO BE USED BY THE PRIEST IN HIS CONFERRING OF THE SACRAMENT OF CONFIRMATION IN VIRTUE OF THE APOSTOLIC INDULT ISSUED ON SEPTEMBER 14, 1946.

[Full Latin Text, *AAS,* XXXVIII (1946), 356–358.]

Note 1.—An English translation of the prayers can be used in such dioceses in the United States wherein the local ordinary has granted permission for the use of the *Collectio Rituum.* It appears in Title II, pp 35–39. The entire rite must be conducted in Latin, though the prayers in English may be said before or after the recitation of the Latin text.[1]

Note 2.—The Latin rubrics are italicized just as they appear in the *Ritus Servandus.* The English rubrics, which immediately follow, have been combined with the directions of liturgical commentators. The prayers appear in bold print.

Note 3.—To avoid distractions in the administration of the sacrament, if one should choose to follow the rite as it is herein included, all the footnotes, which are principally historical or explanatory in nature, have been placed at the conclusion of this section.

Praenotanda

1. The priest should try to be vested in cassock, surplice and white [2] stole when administering confirmation to a sick person in danger of death. If a surplice is not available, the stole will suffice.[3]

2. The priest shall bring with himself chrism from the supply blessed on the previous Holy Thursday,[4] a ritual with the rite of confirmation, pencil and paper to record the necessary information,[5] a container to hold the cotton and the bread crumbs which, together with the water used in the washing of the hands, must be burned and the ashes disposed of in the sacrarium.[6] If it is inconvenient to dispose of the cotton and crumbs in the sacrarium, they may be put in the fire in the house of the sick person.[7]

3. In the sick room a table covered with a white cloth should be prepared. On it there should be a crucifix, some cotton on a plate, a bowl of water with a towel, a piece of stale bread,[8] a candle and a glass of water with a spoon if Holy Viaticum is to be administered.

4. When confirmation is not the only sacrament to be administered, the proper sequence in the case of a baptized adult is penance (violet stole), confirmation (white stole), Viaticum (white stole), Marriage *in extremis,* if necessary (white stole), Extreme Unction (violet stole) and the apostolic blessing (violet stole).[9] For any good reason this order may be changed by the extraordinary minister, i.e., confirmation may be administered at a later

time if the priest who came to the sick call is not equipped for administering this sacrament.[10]

5. Before beginning the actual ceremony, the priest in a simple explanation, during which he might emphasize the great love which the Church shows for the spiritual welfare of her children, must inform those in attendance that the bishop alone is the ordinary minister of confirmation and that he himself will administer it only in virtue of a special privilege and power delegated to him by the Holy See.[11] The sacrament is not to be administered in the presence of heretics or schismatics, much less are they to be allowed to act as servers.[12]

6. The priest should instruct the sponsor to place his (her) right hand (ungloved) on the right shoulder of the person who is to be confirmed during the actual chrismal ceremony.[13]

7. Throughout the actual ceremonies the minister stands facing the recipient who, if possible, should keep his hands joined in a gesture of prayer. The server, nurse, relative or even sponsor of the sick person can hold the book for the celebrant. If several sick persons are to be confirmed at the same time, it suffices to pronounce the form of the sacrament and *Pax tecum* for each person in the singular. All the other prayers are said in the plural, in accommodation to the requisite cases and called for word-endings.

The Rite of Confirmation

Stans igitur versa facie ad confirmandum, iunctis ante pectus manibus dicit:

With his hands joined on his breast, the extraordinary minister says:

℣. Spiritus Sanctus superveniat in te et virtus Altissimi custodiat te a peccatis.

℟. Amen.

Deinde, signans se a fronte ad pectus signo crucis, dicit:

Making the sign of the cross on himself, he says:

℣. Adjutorium nostrum in nomine Domini.
℟. Qui fecit caelum et terram.

Joining his hands on his breast, he continues:

℣. Domine exaudi orationem meam.
℟. Et clamor meus ad te veniat.
℣. Dominus vobiscum
℟. Et cum spiritu tuo.

Tunc, extensis versus confirmandum manibus, dicit:

Extending both his hands toward the person to be confirmed, he says:

Oremus.

Omnipotens sempiterne Deus, qui regenerare dignatus es hunc famulum tuum (hanc famulam tuam) ex aqua et Spiritu Sancto, quique dedisti ei

remissionem *omnium* pecca*torum*: e*mit*te in eum (eam) septi*formem* *Spi*ritum tuum Sanctum Pa*ra*clytum de caelis. ℟. Amen.

℣. *Spi*ritum sapi*en*tiae et intel*lec*tus. ℟. Amen.

℣. *Spi*ritum con*si*lii et forti*tu*dinis. ℟. Amen.

℣. *Spi*ritum sci*en*tiae et pie*ta*tis. ℟. Amen.

Ad*imp*le eum (eam) *Spi*ritu ti*mo*ris tui, et con*si*gna eum (eam) signo Cru ✠ cis Christi, in vitam propitiatus ae*ter*nam.

Joining his hands together, he continues:

Per eundem *Do*minum nostrum Jesum Christum, *Fi*lium tuum: Qui tecum vivit et regnat in unitate *ejus*dem *Spi*ritus Sancti Deus, per omnia saecula saecu*lo*rum. ℟. Amen.

Postea sacerdos inquirit de nomine confirmandi, et, summitate pollicis dexterae manus Chrismate intincta, confirmat eum dicens:

N., Signo te signo Cru ✠ cis, *quod dum dicit, imposita manu dextera super caput confirmandi, producit pollice signum crucis in fronte illius, deinde prosequitur:* **et con*fir*mo te *Chris*mate sa*lu*tis. In nomine Pa ✠ tris et *Fi* ✠ lii et *Spi*ritus ✠ Sancti. ℟. Amen.**

He then reminds the sponsor to hold his (her) right hand on the right shoulder of the person to be confirmed. Then, after having inquired of the new name desired by the person to be confirmed, the priest dips his right thumb into the chrism, with it traces the sign of the cross on the forehead of the recipient while holding the other fingers of the right hand on the head of the person whom he is anointing and says:

N. [confirmation name of candidate is inserted in Latin in the vocative case] **SIGNO TE SIGNO CRU ✠ CIS ET CON*FIR*MO TE *CHRIS*MATE SA*LU*TIS.**[14]

He then removes his hand and, after the manner of a bishop, gives the triple blessing as he says:

IN NOMINE PA ✠ TRIS ET *FI* ✠ LII ET *SPI*RITUS ✠ SANCTI. ℟. AMEN.

Et leviter eum in maxilla caedit, dicens:

The minister gently strikes the candidate on the left cheek.[15]

Pax tecum.

There is no response.

Sacerdos, postquam frontem confirmandi linierit sacro Chrismate, eam gossypio diligenter abstergat.

Tergit postea cum mica panis, et lavat pollicem et manus super pelvim; deinde aquam lotionis cum pane et gossypio in vase mundo reponat et ad ecclesiam postea deferat, comburat, cineresque proiiciat in sacrarium.

Post lotionem ab ipso sacerdote dicitur:

Then the priest is to carefully wipe off with cotton the chrism from the forehead of the confirmed.

He then proceeds to purify his thumb with a small piece of bread and washes his thumb and hand over a basin. After he has washed and dried his hands, the priest says with his hands joined:

Confirma hoc, Deus, quod operatus es in nobis, a templo Sancto tuo, quod est in Jerusalem.

℣. Gloria Patri, et Filio et Spiritui Sancto. Sicut erat in principio et nunc et semper et in saecula saeculorum. ℟. Amen.

Confirma hoc, Deus quod operatus es in nobis, a templo Sancto tuo, quod est in Jerusalem.

Sacerdos, stans versus infirmum, iunctis ante pectus manibus, dicit:

Then facing the confirmed, with hands joined on his breast, he continues:

℣. Ostende nobis, Domine, misericordiam tuam.
℟. Et salutare tuum da nobis.
℣. Domine, exaudi orationem meam.
℟. Et clamor meus ad te veniat.
℣. Dominus Vobiscum. ℟. Et cum spiritu tuo.

Iunctis vero adhuc ante pectus manibus, dicit:

He continues to keep his hands joined and prays:

Oremus.

Deus qui Apostolis tuis Sanctum dedisti Spiritum, et per eos eorumque successores ceteris fidelibus tradendum esse voluisti; respice propitius ad humilitatis nostrae famulatum, et praesta ut ejus cor, cujus frontem sacro Chrismate delinivimus, et signo Sanctae Crucis signavimus, idem Spiritus Sanctus in eo superveniens, templum gloriae suae dignanter inhabitando perficiat: qui cum Patre et eodem Spiritu Sancto vivis et regnas Deus, in saecula saeculorum. ℟. Amen.

Deinde dicit:

Then the minister says:

Ecce sic benedicetur [omnis] homo, qui timet Dominum.

Et vertens se ad confirmatum,[16] *ac faciens super eum signum Crucis, dicit:*

He blesses the confirmed with a single sign of the cross, as he says:

Bene ✠ dicat te Dominus ex Sion, ut videas bona Jerusalem omnibus diebus vitae tuae, et habeas vitam aeternam. ℟. Amen.

The minister may recite the Credo the Pater and Ave with the patient or in his name. However, this is not required, since these prayers are not mentioned in the Ritus Servandus given in the AAS.

FOOTNOTES TO APPENDIX V

[1] "If the form of a sacrament is repeated in the vernacular, or is said previously for the sake of better understanding, the minister of the sacrament should realize that it is only for this purpose that the form is said in English. There should not be any intention of actually administering the sacrament when the vernacular form is recited. The confecting of the sacrament is to be accomplished by the Latin form and by no other." Danagher, "The New Vernacular Ritual," *Homiletic and Pastoral Review,* L (1955), 915.

[2] The ritual in the decree does not mention the color of the stole, though it should be white in the administration of confirmation. Cf. Martinucci, *Manuale Sacrarum Caeremoniarum in libros octos digestum* (3. ed., 4 vols., Ratisbonae-Romae-Neo-Eboraci: Pustet, 1911-1915 by I. B. M. Menghini), II, liber VII, cap. 2, p. 25.

[3] *AAS,* XXXVIII (1946), 356. The present writer suggests with reservations that under certain circumstances in this country the use of a clerical business suit with a white stole can be tolerated in the administration of confirmation in a non-sectarian or Protestant hospital or home. Smiddy (*A Manual for the Extraordinary Minister of Confirmation,* p. 81) notes that the language of the decree does not seem to be strictly preceptive on this point. However, since on numerous occasions the Sacred Congregation has insisted that it is unlawful to administer the sacraments without the proper vestments, which serve to reflect the solemnity which the Church wants associated with the sacrament of confirmation in the mind of the faithful, the priest should make an extra special effort to comply with the rubric and be vested in cassock, surplice and white stole.

[4] Cf. canons 734, § 1 and 781, § 1.

[5] A model card, as delineated by Smiddy (*op. cit.,* p. 98) will contain the following information: baptismal and family name, confirmation name, date and place of baptism, father's baptismal name, mother's maiden name, parish and diocese of the recipient, name of the sponsor, statement regarding the latter's confirmation, date of the confirmation.

[6] ". . . deinde aquam lotionis cum pane et gossypio in vase mundo reponat et ad ecclesiam postea deferat, comburat, cineresque proiiciat in sacrarium."—*AAS,* XXXVIII (1946), 357.

[7] Schulte-O'Connell, *Benedicenda,* The Rite Observed in Some of the Principal Functions of the Roman Pontifical and the Roman Ritual (New York: Benziger Brothers Inc., 1955), p. 231, footnote 40.

[8] Some salt and a slice of lemon will also be of help for the cleansing of the minister's thumb.

[9] Cf. Smiddy, *op. cit.,* p. 96; Connell, "The Recent Decree Empowering Priests to Confirm," *AER,* CXVI (1947), 262; Mahoney, "The Extraordinary Minister of Confirmation," *The Clergy Review,* XXVII (1947), 85.

[10] The traditional order of the administration of the sacraments seems to be that the administration of Holy Viaticum should precede that of extreme unction. Cf. *Rituale Romanum,* Title V, chap. 1, n. 2, which by way of instruction states the following: "In quo illud in primis ex generali Ecclesiae consuetudine observandum est, ut, si tempus, et infirmi conditio permittat, ante Extremam Unctionem, Poenitentiae et Eucharistiae Sacramenta infirmis praebeantur." Mueller-Ellis (*Handbook of Ceremonies for Priests and Seminarians* [revised ed., St. Louis, Mo.: B. Herder Book Co., 1956], p. 371) presume that extreme unction is administered immediately *after* holy Viaticum. However, the *Collectio Rituum* (1954) in the fourth chapter of Title III, which gives the order which is to be followed when the last rites are given without interruption, pp. 64–82, lists: confession (p. 67), the sacred anointing (p. 70), the administration of Viaticum (p. 76)

and the apostolic blessing for the hour of death (p. 79). This section follows the order of the 1950 German *Collectio.* O'Connell ("The New American Ritual," *The Clergy Review,* XL [1955], footnote 1, p. 209) comments that this order of procedure is in accordance with the earlier practice of the Church, since not extreme unction but Viaticum is regarded as the "last sacrament," and this is best prepared for by the anointing by which the *reliquiae peccati* are wiped away (Trent). It also has the advantage of allowing the patient undisturbed converse with his Eucharistic Lord.

Cappello (*De Sacramentis,* III, n. 88, pp. 53–54) treats of this matter under the question: "Utrum ante, an post poenitentiam et sacrum Viaticum, sit ministranda extrema unctio." He concludes that it is not a grave sin to adminster extreme unction before Viaticum, nor even a light one, if there exists a reasonable cause. He admits that some authors hold that there is no real regulation on this point. Accordingly there is no sin at all in the changing of the order. Since it is contained in a ritual which has the approval of the Sacred Congregation of Rites, surely it would be lawful to follow the order of administration contained therein.

11 *AAS,* XXXVIII (1946), 356.

12 *Loc. cit.* Cf. article 3 of chapter VII for detailed discussion on this point, pp. 148–149.

13 Originally the rubrics for confirmation prescribed that in the confirmation of adults the person to be confirmed was to place his foot on the right foot of the sponsor. However, on September 20, 1749, the Sacred Congregation of Rites declared that it sufficed for the sponsor to place his right hand on the right shoulder of the candidate. Cf. Gardellini *Decreta Authentica Congregationis Rituum ex Actis eiusdem Collecta* (3. ed., 5 vols., Romae: Typis S. Congregationis de Propaganda Fide, 1856–1859), II (1856), n. 4205, ad 1, p. 427.

The same procedure is to be followed even when an infant is being confirmed in danger of death.—*AAS,* XXXVIII (1946), 356.

14 Liturgical authors are divided as to the precise moment when the hand is to be removed from the head of the person who is being confirmed. Most of the liturgical books simply translate the anointing ceremony as given in the rituals.

A typical description is that of Martinucci: "Episcopus, sacram Confirmationem conferens, intinget pollicem in s. Chrisma, et manu extenta imposita super caput confirmandi, percontatus nomen eius ex patrino, unctionem in formam Crucis pollice efficiet in fronte, dicens N., signo te etc., dextera faciens triplex Crucis signum dum dicit, 'In nomine Patris, etc.' demum leviter percutiet eius genam sinistram et dicet 'Pax tecum,' cui non respondebitur 'et cum spiritu tuo.' *Manuale,* II, n. 38, p. 28.

Mueller-Ellis (*op. cit.,* p. 355) describe the ceremony thus: "*N., signo te signo crucis,* and while he says it, with his right hand laid upon the head of the person to be confirmed, he makes the sign of the cross on his forehead with his thumb and then continues, *et confirmo te, etc. . . .*".

Schulte-O'Connell (*Benedicenda,* p. 227) say after the word "*crucis*": "Then, making the sign of the cross three times over the candidate he continues, *In nomine Patris, etc.*" Ahearne-Lane (*Pontifical Ceremonies* [London and Dublin: Burns Oates and Washbourne. Ltd., 1942], pp. 316-317) are specific in their rubrical directions: "Placing his right hand on the candidate's head, the Bishop makes the sign of the cross with chrism on the forehead of each candidate saying, '*N. signo te signo crucis.*' The Bishop then raises his right hand and makes with it the sign of the cross three times over the candidate's head saying, '*et confirmo te chrismate salutis, etc.*'"

Connell ("art. cit.", *AER,* CXVI [1947], 263), on the other hand, teaches: "The anointing should be made in conjunction with the word *Crucis,* but the fingers should remain on the head until the word *salutis* has been pronounced.

Smiddy (*op. cit.*, p. 92) likewise adopts this opinion.

Nabuco (*op. cit.*, II, 49) is equally explicit in his directions: ". . dicens, praemisso nomine eius, 'N. signo te signo crucis' et adiungit 'et confirmo te chrismate salutis.' Deinde, amota manu, benedicit ter. . . ."

An authentic decree of the Congregation of Sacred Rites lays down two basic directions (Cf. Gardellini, *op. cit.*, IV (1958), n. 5186, pp. 171–172): "*n. 2.* Triplex signum crucis quod ab Episcopo confirmante fit super confirmatum dum profert verba, in nomine Patris, fieri ne debet pollice super frontem confirmati, aut manu simplicter sine frontis contactu super personam confirmati? *Ad 2.* Iuxta Pontificale dum frontem Chrismate iniungit dicere debet signo te signo crucis super frontem ipsam pollice producens; quo facto manu extensa versus confirmatum incipit, in nomine patris, etc. ter signum crucis efformans more solito."

This decree, however, is not completely explanatory or decisive, since it takes account only of the action which is to accompany "signo te signo crucis"; it then accounts for the actions which begin with the words, "in nomine etc." In what position is the hand to be held during the "confirmo etc."? The present writer, as is evident from the rubrical directions asserted in the text, adopts as more symbolical the view that the hand is to be removed after the words, *"chrismate salutis."*

[15] Neither the *Pontifical* nor the *Ritual* indicates on which cheek the blow is to be administered. Many authors say the left, and that, of course, certainly seems to be the more convenient practice to follow. One writer, however, says that the right cheek should receive the blow, then adds that many bishops follow this procedure. *L'Ami du Clergé* (LIII (1936), 442–445) presents an interesting and fairly well documented history of the liturgical origin of the slap given at confirmation. The author concludes (p. 445) that it takes the place of the kiss of peace which in the early days of the Church the bishop gave to the person confirmed.

[16] This rubric is taken verbatim from the *Ritual*, where it is presumed that up to this time the priest has been facing the altar. In the present situation it is not needed, since the priest is already facing the candidate.

APPENDIX VI

COPY OF THE ORIGINAL RESCRIPT FOR HOSPITAL CHAPLAINS

Romae, die 18 novembris, 1948.

SACRA CONGREGATIO
DE SACRAMENTIS
N. 5869/48.

BEATISSIME PATER,

Archiepiscopi et Episcopi Statuum Foederatorum Americae Septentrionalis, ad pedes S.V. provoluti, humiliter postulant derogationem Decreto "Spiritus Sancti munera" die 14 septembris a. 1946 a S. Congregatione de Sacramentis edito, ita ut in domibus sic nuncupatis maternitatis vel pro nosocomiis pro mulieribus parturientibus vel brephotropheis suarum dioecesium, Confirmationis sacramentum valide et licite conferre valeat puerulis ibi receptis, qui in adiunctis ab eodem Decreto recensitis reperiantur, Cappellanus earumdem domorum.

Petitionis ratio est difficultas maxima pro parocho loci, aliis ministerii sui gravato muneribus, Confirmationem fere passim conferendi, attento praesertim magno infantium infirmorum numero in enunciatis domibus commorantium.

EX AUDIENTIA SS.mi diei 25 octobris, 1948.

Sanctissimus Dominus Noster Divina Providentia Pius Papa XII, referente infrascripto huius S. Congregationis Pro-Praefecto, relatis precibus benigne annuere dignatus est, ea tamen lege ut Confirmationis sacramentum, in adiunctis de quibus in praefato Decreto, personaliter conferatur puerulis a Cappellano domibus de quibus in precibus *stabiliter* addicto, et si plures in una domo constituti sint Cappellani, ab eorumdem primo, ceteris prorsus exclusis.

Cappellano autem hac facultate uti licebit tantum si Episcopus dioecesanus haberi nequeat, aut legitime impediatur quominus per se ipse Confirmationem conferat; nec alius praesto sit Episcopus, communione gaudens cum Sede Apostolica, licet titularis tantum, qui sine gravi incommodo ipsi suffici queat. Itidemque si parochus loci, in iisdem adiunctis, haberi et ipse nequeat, vel legitime impediatur quominus sacramentum istud conferat. In absentia autem Cappellani, aut in eius impossibilitate per se ipsum confirmandi, nullus alius, praeter Episcopum vel loci parochum, idem sacramentum valide conferre valet. Servatis, in reliquis, terminis et clausulis memorati Decreti.

Contrariis quibuslibet minime obstantibus.

Praesentibus valituris ad *annum*, a data huius rescripti computandum.

B. CARD. ALOISI-MASELLA, *Pro-Praefectus*
F. BRACCI, *Sec.*

L.S.

APPENDIX VII

AN EXEMPLAR OF THE RENEWAL OF THE INDULT

N. 458/51

SACRA CONGREGATIO
DE SACRAMENTIS

BEATISSIME PATER,

Archiepiscopi et Episcopi Statuum Foederatorum Americae Septentrionalis, ad pedes S. V. provoluti, humiliter postulant prorogationem rescripti Sacrae Congregationis de Sacramentis ex Audientia SS.mi diei 25 octobris 1948, No. 5869/48, vi cuius in domibus sic noncupatis [sic] maternitatis vel nosocomiis pro mulieribus parturientibus vel brephotropheis suarum dioecesium, puerulis ibi receptis Confirmationis Sacramentum conferre valeat earumdem domorum Capellanus, vel si plures sint, eorum primus, iisdem causis perdurantibus.

* * * * *

EX AUDIENTIA SS.mi diei 22 Januarii 1951.

Sanctissimus D. N. Pius Papa XII audita relatione Card. Pro-Praefecti S. C. de Sacramentis, attentis expositis, gratiam prorogationis benigne impertitur *ad triennium,* servatis in reliquis forma ac tenore praecedentis rescripti.

F. BRACCI, *Sec.*

L.S.

Advertatur: Ordinarii curent ut prorogatio indulti tempore utili postuletur: secus si confirmatio collata fuerit tempore interiecto inter exspirationem praecedentis indulti et renovationem eiusdem irrita foret.

BIBLIOGRAPHY

Sources

Acta Apostolicae Sedis, Commentarium Officiale, Romae, 1909–1929; Civitate Vaticana, 1929–

Acta et Decreta Sacrorum Conciliorum Recentiorum, Collectio Lacensis, 7 vols., Friburgi Brisgoviae, 1870–1892.

Acta Sanctae Sedis, 41 vols., Romae, 1865–1908.

Annuario Pontificio per l'Anno 1957, Città del Vaticano: Tipographia Poliglotta Vaticana, 1957.

Anacleta Juris Pontificii, Recueil des dissertations sur divers sujets de droit canonique, de liturgie, de théologie et d'histoire, 28 vols., Romae, Parisiis, Bruxellis, 1855–1891.

Bouscaren, T. Lincoln, *The Canon Law Digest,* 3 Vols. and Supplements through 1956, Milwaukee: Bruce & Co.; 1934–1949–1953–1954–1955–1956–1957.

Codex Iuris Canonici Pii X Pontificis Maximiiussu digestus, Benedicti Papae XV auctoritate promulgatus, Praefatione, Fontium Annotatione et Indice Analytico-Alphabetico ab Emo Petro Card. Gasparri Auctus, Romae: Typis Polyglottis Vaticanis, 1917; reimpressio, 1934.

Codicis Iuris Canonici Fontes, cura Emi Petri Card. Gasparri editi, 9 vols., Romae (postea Civitate Vaticana): Typis Polyglottis Vaticanis, 1923–1939. (Vols. VII-IX, ed. cura et studio Emi Iustiniani Card. Serédi.)

Codificazione Canonica Orientale, Fonti Serie I, 13 fasc., Serie II, 18 fasc., *Fontes,* Series III, Vols. I, II, III, V, VI, VII, Città del Vaticano: Tipografia Poliglotta Vaticana, 1930–

Collectanea S. Congregationis de Propaganda Fide, 2 vols., Romae: Typographia Polyglotta S.C. de Propaganda Fide, 1907.

Collectanea Constitutionum, Decretorum, Indultorum ac Instructionum Sanctae Sedis ad Usum Operariorum Apostolicorum Societatis Missionum ad Exteros, Parisiis: Typis Georges Chamerot, 1880.

Concilium Tridentinum: Diariorum, Actorum, Epistularum, Tractatuum Nova Collectio, edidit Societas Goerresiana, 13 vols., Friburgi Brisgoviae: B. Herder, 1901-

Corpus Iuris Canonici, editio Lipsiensis II, post Aemelii Ludovici Richteri curas instruxit Aemilius Friedberg, Lipsiae: Ex officia Bernahrdi Tauchmitz, 1879-1881; ed. anastatice repetita, 1928.

Decretales D. Gregorii Papae IX, suae integritati una cum glossis restitutae, cum privilegio Gregorii XIII, Pont. Max., et Aliorum Principum, Romae, 1582.

Decretum Gratiani emendatum et notationibus illustratum cum glossis, Gregorii XIII, Pont. Max., iussu editum, 2 vols., Romae, 1582.

Denzinger, Henricus—Bannwart, Clemens—Umberg, Joannes-Rahner, Carolus, *Enchiridion Symbolorum, Definitionum et Declarationum de Rebus Fidei et Morum,* 30. ed., Friburgi Brisgoviae: Herder, 1955.

Gardellini, Aloisius, *Decreta Authentica Congregationis Rituum ex Actis eisdem Collecta,* ab anno 1588, num. 1, ad annum 1877, num. 5715, 3. ed., 5 vols, Romae: Typis S. Congregationis de Propaganda Fide, 1856-1859.

Jaffé, Philippus, *Regesta Pontificum Romanorum ab condita Ecclesia ad annum post Christum natum MCXCVIII,* 2. ed., correctam et auctam auspicilis G. Wattenbach, curaverunt S. Loewenfeld, F. Kaltenbrunner, P. Ewald, 2 vols., Lipsiae, 1885-1888.

Leonis XIII Pontificis Maximi Acta, 23 vols., Romae: ex Typographia Vaticana, 1881-1905.

Mansi, Joannes, *Sacrorum Conciliorum Nova et Amplissima Collectio,* 53 vols. in 60, Parisiis, 1901-1927.

New Testament of Our Lord and Savior Jesus Christ, The, translated into English from the original Greek by Francis Spencer, O.P., edited by Charles Callan, O.P. and John McHugh, O.P., New York: Macmillan Co., 1945.

Old Testament, The, first published by the English College at Douay, *A.D.* 1609 in *The Holy Bible,* translated from the Latin Vulgate, New York: P. J. Kenedy & Sons.

Pallottini, S., *Collectio Omnium Conclusionum, et Resolutionum Quae in Causis Propositis apud Sacram Congregationem S. Concilii Tridentini Interpretum Prodierunt ab eius Institutione Anno MDLXIV ad MDCCLX, Distinctis Titulis Alphabetico Ordine per Materias Digestas,* 18 vols., Romae, 1868-1895.

Pii IX Summi Pontifics Acta, 9 vols., Romae, 1854-1878.

Potthast, Augustus, *Regesta Pontificum Romanorum inde ab anno post Christum natum MCXCVIII ad annum MCCCIV*. 2 vols. Berolini, 1874-1875.

Sylloge praecipuorum documentorum recentiorum Summorum Pontificum et S. Congregationis de Propaganda fide necnon aliarum SS. Congregationum Romanorum ad Usum Missionariorum, Typis Polyglottis Vaticanis, 1939.

Theiner, Augustinus, *Acta Genuina SS. Oecumenici Concilii Tridentini sub Paulo III, Julio III et Pio IV, PP. MM.*, 2 vols., Zagabriae (Croatiae), 1874.

Thesaurus Resolutionum Sacrae Congregationis Concilii, 167 vols. Urbini, 1739-1740; Romae, 1741-1908.

Waddingus, Lucas, *Annales Minorum seu Trium Ordinum a S. Francisco Institutorum,* 27 vols., 3. ed., curavit Joseph Maria Fonseca, Ad Claras Aquas (Quarrachi), 1931-1934.

REFERENCE WORKS

Abbo, John A.—Hannan, Jerome D., *The Sacred Canons,* revised ed., 2 vols., St. Louis: B. Herder Co., 1957.

Ahearne, Pierce—Lane, Michael, *Pontifical Ceremonies,* London and Dublin: Burns Oates and Washbourne, Ltd., 1942.

Albertus Magnus, *Opera Omnia,* 38 vols., Vivès: Parisiis, 1890–1899.

Alzog, John, *Manual of Universal Church History,* translated from the 9. German edition by J. Pabisch and T. Byrne, 3 vols., Cincinnati: Robert Clarke & Co., 1874.

Aquinas, Thomas, St., *Opera Omnia,* 25 vols., New York: Musurgia Publishers, 1948–1949.

Bastnagel, Clement V., *The Appointment of Parochial Adjutants and Assistants,* The Catholic University of America Canon Law Studies, no. 58, Washington, D. C.: The Catholic University of America, 1930.

Benedictus XIV (Prospero Lambertini), *De Synodo Dioecesana,* 2. ed., 2 vols., Romae, 1806.

Bennington, J. Clement, *The Recipient of Confirmation,* The Catholic University of America Canon Law Studies, no. 267, Washington, D. C.: The Catholic University of America Press, 1952.

Beste, Udalricus, *Introductio in Codicem,* 3. ed. Collegeville, Minn.: St. John's Abbey Press, 1946.

S. Bonaventura, Opera Omnia, 9 vols., Vol. IV, ad Claras Aquas prope Florentinam, 1889.

Cappello, Felix, *Tractatus Canonico-Moralis de Sacramentis,* 5 vols., Vol. I, 6. ed. Taurini-Romae: Marietti, 1953; Vol. III, ed. tertia emendata et aucta, Taurini-Romae: Marietti, 1949; Vol. IV, ed. tertia accurate recognita et aucta, Taurini-Romae: Marietti, 1951.

Cayré, F., *Manual of Patrology and History of Theology,* translated by H. Howitt, 4 books in 2 vols., Paris-Tournai, Rome: Desclée & Co., 1936–1940.

Cicognani, Amleto, *Canon Law,* authorized English translation, 2. ed. revised, Philadelphia: The Dolphin Press, 1935.

Ciesluk, Joseph E., *National Parishes in the United States,* The Catholic University of America Canon Law Studies, no. 190, Washington, D. C.: The Catholic University of America Press, 1944.

Coleman, John J., *The Minister of Confirmation,* The Catholic University of America Canon Law Studies, no. 125, Washington, D. C.: The Catholic University of America Press, 1941.

Conte a Coronata, Mattheus, *Institutiones Iuris Canonici, De Sacramentis Tractatus Canonicus,* 3 vols., ed. altera emendata et aucta, Vol. I, Taurini: Marietti, 1951.

Conway, William, *Problems in Canon Law,* Dublin: Browne & Nolan, Limited, 1956, distributed in this country by Newman Press, Westminster, Maryland.

DeBaysio, Guido, *Rosarium seu in Decretorum Volumen Commentaria,* Venetiis, 1577.

DeClercq, Charles, *Conciles des Orientaux Catholiques,* v. XI of *Histoire des Conciles d'après les Documents Originaux,* Paris: Librairie LeTouzey et Ané, 1949–1952.

Dictionnaire de Droit Canonique, commencé sous la direction de A. Villien et E. Magnin, continué sous la direction de A. Amanieu, publié sous la direction de R. Naz, Parisiis: Letouzey et Ané, 1924–

Dictionnaire de Théologie Catholique, 15 vols. with General Tables, Paris: Letouzey et Ané, 1903–

Diedericks, Michael F., *The Jurisdiction of the Latin Ordinaries over Their Oriental Subjects,* The Catholic University of America Canon Law Studies, no. 229, Washington, D. C.: The Catholic University of America Press, 1946.

Doronzo, Emmanuel, *De Baptismo et Confirmatione,* Milwaukee: Bruce Publishing Co., 1947.

Duchesne, Louis, *Origines du Culte Chrétien, Étude sur la liturgie Latine avant Charlemagne,* 3. ed., Paris: Thorin et Fils, 1902.

Dvornik, François, *Le Schisme de Photius, Histoire et Légende,* Paris: De-Latour-Maubourg, 1950.

Fagnani, Prospero, *Commentaria in Quinque Libros Decretalium,* 5 vols. in 4, Venetiis, 1709.

Ferraris, Lucius, *Prompta Bibliotheca Canonica, Iuridica, Moralis, Theologica, nec non Ascetica, Polemica, Rubricista, Historica,* ed. novissima, 9 vols., Romae, 1885–1899.

Gasparri, Petrus, *Tractatus Canonicus De Matrimonio,* ed. nova ad mentem Codicis I.C., Typis Polyglottis Vaticanis, 1932.

Gillis, James R., *The Effects of the Sacrament of Confirmation,* A dissertation submitted to the Faculty of Theology of the Pontifical Institute "Angelicum," Rome, Washington, D. C., 1940.

Golden, Henry F., *Parochial Benefices in the New Code,* A dissertation submitted to the Faculty of the Sacred Sciences of the Catholic University of America, 1921.

Guérin, Paul, *Concile Oecuménique du Vatican,* Bar-le-Duc: Louis Guérin, 1872.

Hefele, Charles—LeClercq, Henri—DeClercq, Charles, *Histoire des Conciles d'après les Documents Originaux,* traduite en français par Dom H. Leclercq, 11 vols., in 21, Paris: Librairie Letouzey et Ané, 1907-1952.

Hinschius, Paul, *Decretales Pseudo-Isidorianae,* Lipsiae, 1835.

Hoffman, Lawrence J., *Clergy Conferences: Canon 131,* The Catholic University of America Canon Law Studies, no. 383, Washington, D. C.: The Catholic University of America Press, 1957.

Hostiensis, Cardinalis (Henricus de Segusio), *Commentaria in Quinque Decretalium Libros,* 6 vols. in 4, Venetiis, 1581.

Hughes, Philip S., *A History of the Church,* 3 vols., New York: Sheed & Ward, 1934–1947 (Vols. I and II, revised ed., 1949).

Innocentius IV, *Commentaria in V Libros Decretalium,* Venetiis, 1570.

Kelly, Bernard M., *The Functions Reserved to Pastors,* The Catholic University of America Canon Law Studies, no. 250, Washington, D. C.: The Catholic University of America Press, 1947.

Lennerz, Henricus, *De Sacramento Confirmationis,* 2. ed., Romae: 1949.

Lewis, Charlton T., *A Latin Dictionary for the Schools,* Oxford: The Clarendon Press, 1901.

Mahoney, E. J., *The Priest as Minister of Confirmation,* The Decree "Spiritus Sancti" 14 September 1946 with a Commentary, London: Burns Oates & Washbourne Ltd., 1952.

Martinucci, Pius—Menghini, I. B., *Manuale Sacrarum Caeremoniarum,* in libros octos digestum, 3. ed., 4 vols. Ratisbonae-Romae-Neo-Eboraci: Pustet, 1911–1915.

McCarthy, John, *Problems in Theology, I: The Sacraments,* Dublin: Browne and Nolan, Limited, 1956, Westminster, Md: The Newman Press.

Michiels, Gommarus, *Normae Generales Iuris Canonici,* 2. ed., 2 vols., Parisiis-Tournai-Romae: Desclée, 1949.

Migne, Jacques Paul, *Patrologiae Cursus Completus, Series Graeca,* 161 vols., Parisiis, 1857–1866.

———, *Patrologiae Cursus Completus, Series Latina,* 221 vols., Parisiis, 1844–1855.

———, *Theologiae Cursus Completus,* 28 vols., Paris, 1863–1866.

Mostaza, Antonio Rodriguez, *El Problema del Ministro Extraordinario de la Confirmación,* estudio historico-teologico-canonico, Salamanca, 1952.

Mueller, John Baptist—Ellis, Adam C., *Handbook of Ceremonies for Priests and Seminarians,* revised ed., B. Herder Book Co.: St. Louis, 1956.

Nabuco, Joachim, *Pontificalis Romani Expositio Juridico-Practica,* "Functiones Pontificales Extraordinariae," Tomus I—*De Personis,* Petropoli-Brasilia: Sumptibus editora Vozes Ltda., 1945.

Naz, Raoul (Editor), *Traité de Droit Canonique,* 4 vols., Parisiis: Letouzey et Ané, 1948–1949, Vol. II, 1948.

Neill, Thomas P.—Schmandt, Raymond, *History of the Catholic Church,* Milwaukee: Bruce Publishing Co., 1957.

Noldin, H.—Schmitt, A., *Summa Theologiae Moralis iuxta Codicem Iuris Canonici,* 26. ed. 3 vols., Oeniponte-Lipsiae: Felician Rauch, 1940.

O'Doherty, Michael, *The Scholastic Teaching on the Sacrament of Confirmation,* The Catholic University of America Studies in Sacred Theology (Second Series), no. 23, Washington, D. C.: The Catholic University of America Press, 1949.

Pistoni, Joseph. *De Confirmatione a Ministro Extraordinario,* Città del Vaticano: Libreria Editrice Vaticana, 1947.

Quasten, Johannes, *Patrology,* 2 vols., Westminster, Maryland: The Newman Press, Spectrum Publishers (Utrecht-Brussels), 1950–1953.

Quinn, John S., *The Extraordinary Minister of Confirmation According to the Most Recent Decrees of the Sacred Congregations,* Dissertatio ad Lauream in Facultate Juris Canonici Pontificiae Universitatis Gregorianae, Romae, 1951.

Regatillo, Eduardus, *Ius Sacramentarium,* 2. ed., Santander: Sal Terrae, 1949.

Rituale Romanum, Pauli V Pontificis Maximi jussu editum aliorumque Pontificum cura recognitum atque auctoritate sanctissimi D.N. Pii Papae XI ad normam codicis Juris Canonici accommodatum, editio juxta typicam, Romae-Tournai-Parisiis: Desclée et Socii.

Roelker, Edward G., *Principles of Privilege According to the Code of Canon Law,* The Catholic University of America Canon Law Studies, no. 35, Washington, D. C.: The Catholic University of America, 1926.

Schmidt, John Rogg, *The Principles of Authentic Interpretation in Canon 17 of the Code of Canon Law,* The Catholic University of America Canon Law Studies, no. 141, Washington, D. C.: The Catholic University of America Press, 1941.

Schroeder, H. J., *Disciplinary Decrees of the General Councils to the Council of Trent,* St. Louis: B. Herder Co., 1937.

Schulte, A. J.—O'Connell, J. B., *Benedicenda,* The Rite Observed in Some of the Principal Functions of the Roman Pontifical and Roman Ritual, New York: Benziger Bros., 1955.

Sheehy, Robert F., *The Sacred Congregation of the Sacraments, Its Competence in the Roman Curia,* The Catholic University of America Canon Law Studies, no. 333, Washington, D. C.: The Catholic University of America Press, 1954.

Smiddy, Thomas, *A Manual for the Extraordinary Minister of Confirmation,* Milwaukee: The Bruce Publishing Co., 1949.

Suarez, Franciscus, *Opera Omnia,* 28 vols., Parisiis, 1856–1861.

Temporary Diocesan Statutes of the Byzantine Apostolic Exarchy of Philadelphia, Pa., U.S.A., Paterson: St. Anthony's Guild Press, 1955.

Tournely, Honoratus, *Cursus Theologicus,* 14 vols., Venetiis, 1755–1765.

Turner, William, *History of Philosophy,* Ginn & Co., 1929.

Vademecum for Priests Serving the Military Vicariate of the United States of America, 1957.

Van Hove, A., *Commentarium Lovaniense in Codicem Iuris Canonici,* Volumen I, Tomus V, *De Privilegiis—De Dispensationibus,* Mechliniae-Romae: H. Dessain, 1939.

Vermeersch, A.—Creusen, J., *Epitome Iuris Canonici,* 7. ed., 3 vols., Mechliniae-Romae: H. Dessain, Vol. I, 1949, Vol. II, 1954.

Wernz, F.—Vidal, P., *Ius Canonicum ad Codicis Normam Exactum,* 7 vols. in 8, Vol. II, 1943; Vol. VII, 1937, Romae: Apud Aedes Universitatis Gregorianae.

Zerba, Caesar, *Commentarius in Decretum "Spiritus Sancti Munera,"* Libreria Editrice Vaticana: Typis Polyglottis Vaticanis, 1947.

Zubizarreta, Valentinus, *Theologia Dogmatico-Scholastica ad Mentem S. Thomae Aquinatis,* Vol. IV, *De Sacramentis in Communi et in Particulari ac De Novissimis,* editio quarta, El Carmen: Vitoria, 1949.

ARTICLES

Alonso, Sabino Moran, "Commentario al Decreto de la S. Congregación de Sacramentos sobre la confirmación de Moribundos," *Revista Española de Derecho Canonico,* I (1947), 158–170.

Alvarez, S. Menendez, "De Extraordinario Confirmationis Ministro iuxta Recentiora praesertim S. Sedis Documenta," *Angelicum,* XXIV (1947), 168–194.

Bastnagel, Clement V., "Is a Parish for Colored People a 'National' Parish?" *The Ecclesiastical Review,* CVIII (1943), 382–384.

———, "Parochial Vicars and the Faculty to Confer Confirmation," *The Jurist,* VII (1947), 174–179.

———, "Confirmation of Orientals by Latin Priests," *The Jurist,* IX (1949), 87–90.

Beck, George Andrew, "The School and the Parish," *The Clergy Review,* XL (1955), 577–584.

Bergh, E., "Administration de la Confirmation aux Fidèles dangereusement Malades," *Nouvelle Revue Théologique,* LXIX (1949), 82–87.

Bidagor, Raymundus, "Adnotationes," *Monitor Ecclesiasticus,* I (1949), 50–55.

———, "Casus cum canone 209 Codicis I.C. connexi seu de Iurisdictione ab Ecclesia suppleta," *Periodica,* XLV (1956), 257–283.

Bride, A., "Questions de science ecclésiastique, consultation diverses," *L'Ami du Clergé,* LXI, 7ᵉ série (1951), 383.

———, "Questions de science ecclésiastique, consultations diverses," *L'Ami du Clergé,* LXI, 7ᵉ série (1951), 772–773.

———, "Erreur Commune et Suppléance de Juridiction," *Revue de Droit Canonique,* IV (1954), 3–49; "pouvoir de confirmer," 36–40.

Cappello, Felix M., "Annotationes—Decretum de Confirmatione," *Periodica,* XXXV (1946), 380–389.

Comyns, Joseph J., "The Relation of the Religious Pastor to the Local Ordinary," *The Jurist,* XV (1955), 186–204.

Connell, Francis J., "Answers to Questions—A Pastor's Right to Confirm," *The American Ecclesiastical Review,* CXVII, (1947), 221–222.

———, "The Recent Decree Empowering Priests to Confirm," *The American Ecclesiastical Review,* CXVI (1947), 241-265; an offprint with its own proper pagination was issued by The Catholic University of America Press, 1947.

———, "Answers to Questions—Confirmation Administered by a Pastor," *The American Ecclesiastical Review,* CXIX (1948), 148-149.

———, "Answers to Questions—The Pastor's Right to Confirm," *The American Ecclesiastical Review,* CXXII (1950), 60-61.

———, "Answers to Questions—Validity of Confirmation by a Priest," *The American Ecclesiastical Review,* CXXVI (1952), 466–467.

———, "Answers to Questions—Some Pastoral Problems," *The American Ecclesiastical Review,* CXXIX (1953), 399–400.

———, "Answers to Questions—A Priest's Right to Administer Confirmation," *The American Ecclesiastical Review,* CXXXII (1955), 206.

———, "Answers to Questions—Confirmation by a Substitute Chaplain," *The American Ecclesiastical Review,* CXXXII (1955), 352.

Conway, William, "Notes and Queries—New Decree on Confirmation and Danger of Death," *The Irish Ecclesiastical Record,* 5. series, LXIX (1947), 228–230.

———, "Notes and Queries—Obligation to Avail of New Confirmation Faculties," *The Irish Ecclesiastical Record,* 5. series, LXIX (1947), 346–348.

———, "Notes and Queries—Confirmation Decree: One of the Conditions," *The Irish Ecclesiastical Record,* 5. series, LXIX (1947), 432–435.

———, "Notes and Queries—Obligation to Administer Confirmation," *The Irish Ecclesiastical Record,* 5. series, LXIX (1947), 535–538.

———, "Notes and Queries—Confirmation in Danger of Death," *The Irish Ecclesiastical Record* 5. series, LXX (1948), 540.

———, "Notes and Queries—Chaplains of Institutions and Confirming Power," *The Irish Ecclesiastical Record,* 5. series, LXXII (1949), 361–362.

———, "Notes and Queries—Confirmation and Curate in Charge of a Vacant Parish," *The Irish Ecclesiastical Record,* 5. series, LXXIX (1953), 61–62.

———, "Notes and Queries—Confirmation in Danger of Death," *The Irish Ecclesiastical Record,* 5. series, LXXXVII (1957), 51–52.

Crehan, Joseph, "Ten Years' Work on Baptism and Confirmation: 1945–1955," *Theological Studies,* XVII (1956), 494–515.

Crosignani, J., "De Extraordinario Confirmationis Ministro," *Divus Thomas,* XXIV (1947), 87–92.

Damen, Cornelius, "Annotationes," *Appollinaris,* XXII (1949), 75–77.

———, "Annotationes," *Apollinaris,* XXII (1949), 78–79.

Danagher, John J., 'Questions Answered—Danger of Death for Confirmation," *The Homiletic and Pastoral Review,* LV (1955), 703–705.

———, "The New Vernacular Ritual, Part I," *The Homiletic and Pastoral Review,* LV (1955), 912–919.

Delchard, A., "Décret du 18 décembre 1947. De confirmatione administranda iis, qui ex gravi morbo in periculo mortis sunt constituti," *Nouvelle Revue Théologique,* LXX (1948), 531–533.

Didier, J. C., "Le Pouvoir de confirmer, pour un simple prêtre, est-il pouvoir d'ordre ou de juridiction?" *L'Ami du Clergé,* LXVII, 7ᵉ série (1957), 646–648.

Donovan, Joseph P., "Answers to Questions—May Negro Falling from Airplane into White Parish be Confirmed?" *The Homiletic and Pastoral Review,* XLVIII (1948), 61–62.

———, "Answers to Questions—What Can a Pastor Do in the Matter of Confirming the Dying?" *The Homiletic and Pastoral Review,* XLVIII (1948), 379–380.

———, "Questions Answered—Have Assistants the Faculty to Administer Confirmation?" *The Homiletic and Pastoral Review,* XLIX (1949), 417–418.

———, "Questions Answered—Practical Cases Arising from the Recent Indult Empowering Priest to Confirm," *The Homiletic and Pastoral Review,* XLIX (1949), 248–249.

———, "Questions Answered—Can This Priest Confirm in Danger of Death?" *The Homiletic and Pastoral Review,* L (1950), 286–288.

Dooley, Eugene, "The Canonical Status of Parishes Held by Religious in the United States," *The Jurist,* XV (1955), part I, pp. 225–251, part II, pp. 393–421.

Ellard, Gerald, "How Fifth Century Rome Administered Sacraments," *Theological Studies,* IX (1948), 3–19.

Ellis, Adam E., "Notes on Canon Law, Confirmation," *Theological Studies,* VIII (1947), 118–122.

Fernandez, Jacinto Martinez, "Algunos Ministros Extraordinarios de la Confirmación," *Revista Española de Derecho Canonico,* II (1947), 645–661.

Ferretto, Joseph, "In Normas et Facultates pro Sacerdotibus in Spiritualem Navigantium Maritimorum et Emigrantium Curam Incumbentibus Adnotationes," *Apollinaris,* XXVIII (1955), 75–103.

Hannan, Jerome D., *The Denver Register,* January 24, 1947, p. 1.

———, "Decretum de Confirmatione—Commentary," *The Jurist,* VII (1947), 226–233.

Herman, Aemilius, "Pontificia Commissio ad Redigendum Codicem Iuris Canonici Orientalis—Adnotationes," *Monitor Ecclesiasticus,* IV (1952), pp. 421–428.

Kuttner, Stephan, "New Studies on the Roman Law in Gratian's Decretum," *The Jurist Seminar,* XI (1953), 12–50.

Leeming, Bernard, "The Confirmation of Dying Infants," *The Clergy Review,* XL (1955), 641–657.

Madden, James, "Confirmation in Danger of Death," *The Australasian Catholic Record,* XXXII (1955), 34–36.

Mahoney, E. J., "The Extraordinary Minister of Confirmation," *The Clergy Review,* XXVII (Jan.–June, 1947), 80–87.

———, "Questions and Answers—Confirmation: Grave Sickness," *The Clergy Review,* XXVII (Jan.–June, 1947), 344–347.

———, "Questions and Answers—Confirmation: territorial Limits," *The Clergy Review,* XXVII (Jan.–June, 1947), 347–348.

———, "Questions and Answers—Confirmation: Exclusion of Heretics," *The Clergy Review*, XXVIII (July–Dec., 1947), 40–42.

———, "Questions and Answers—Confirmation: Bishop Unobtainable," *The Clergy Review*, XXVIII (July–Dec., 1947), 42–45.

———, "Questions and Answers—Confirmation: Bishop Unobtainable," *The Clergy Review*, XXVIII (July–Dec., 1947), 336–337.

———, "Questions and Answers—Confirmation: Textual Variations of the Rite," *The Clergy Review*, XXVIII (July-Dec., 1947), 337–338.

———, "Questions and Answers—Confirmation: Privation of Faculty," *The Clergy Review*, XXVIII (July–Dec., 1947), 407–408.

———, "Questions and Answers—Confirmation: Apparent Death," *The Clergy Review*, XXX (July–Dec., 1948), 340–341.

———, "Questions and Answers—Confirming a Dying Heretic," *The Clergy Review*, XXXI (Jan.–June, 1949), 338–341.

———, "Questions and Answers—Confirmation: A Missionary Priest," *The Clergy Review*, XXXIV (July–Dec., 1950), 110–112.

———, "Questions and Answers—Obligation of Confirming the Dying," *The Clergy Review*, XXXV (Jan.–June, 1951), 326–329.

———, "Questions and Answers—Priest Minister of Confirmation-Administrator," *The Clergy Review*, XXXVI (July–Dec., 1951), 124–126.

———. "Questions and Answers—Minister of Confirmation," *The Clergy Review*, XXXVII (1952), 428–430.

McCarthy, John, "Notes and Queries—The Nature of a Priest's Power to Confirm," *The Irish Ecclesiastical Record*, LXX (1948), 347–350.

———, "Notes and Queries—Excusation of a Priest from the Obligation of Conferring Confirmation," *The Irish Ecclesiastical Record*, 5. series, LXX (1948), 350–351.

———, "Notes and Queries—The Obligation of a Priest to Administer Confirmation," *The Irish Ecclesiastical Record*, 5. series, LXXXI (1954), 204–208.

McReavy, L. R., "Questions and Answers—Proximate Matter of Confirmation, An Added Rubric," *The Clergy Review*, XL (1955), 283–286.

———, "Questions and Answers—Hospital Chaplain and Confirmation," *The Clergy Review*, XLI (1956), 486–487.

———, "Questions and Answers—Confirmation in Danger of Death: Vicarius Substitutus," *The Clergy Review*, XLII (1957), 104–107.

Montague, G., "Extraordinary Minister of the Sacrament of Confirmation in Danger of Death," *The Irish Ecclesiastical Record*, 5. series, LXIX (1947), 59–61.

———, "Notes and Queries—Rite to be Used by the Extraordinary Minister of Confirmation," *The Irish Ecclesiastical Record*, 5. series, LXIX (1947), 543–544.

O'Connell, J. B., "The New American Ritual," *The Clergy Review*, XL (1955), 203–216.

Onclin, W., "L'Administration du Sacrement de la Confirmation en Cas de Danger de Mort," *Ephemerides Theologicae Lovanienses,* XXV (1949), 332–355.

Paventi, Xaverius, "Adnotationes," *Monitor Ecclesiasticus,* II (1950), 57–58.

Quigley, Joseph A. M., "The Extraordinary Minister of the Sacrament of Confirmation," *The Jurist,* XIV (1954), 194–212.

Regatillo, Eduardo F., "El Ministro Extraordinario de la Confirmación, *Sal Terrae,* XXXVI (1948), 166–181.

Sirna, Joseph, "Annotationes ad Decretum S. Officii de Communismo," *Apollinaris,* XXII (1949), 57–70.

Souarn, R., "De Presbytero Orientali Confirmationis Ministro," *Jus Pontificium,* XI (1931), 133–143.

Thomas, John, "Nationalities and American Catholicism," chap. VIII, *The Catholic Church, U.S.A.,* edited by Louis Putz, Chicago: Fides Publishers Association, 1956, pp. 155–176.

Tynan, Michael, "Confirmation at Eleven Plus—A View from Ireland," *The Clergy Review,* XLI (1956), 201–206.

Umberg, I. B., "Sacramenta Acatholicis Nonnisi Condicionate Conferenda," *Periodica,* XXXVII (1948), 97–102.

Wassmer, Thomas A., "The Power to Confirm," *The American Ecclesiastical Review,* CXXXVI (1957), 246–264.

Zerba, Caesar, "In Margine al Recente Decreto della S. C. dei Sacramenti circa il Conferimento della Cresima ai Moribundi," *Osservatore Romano,* October 31, 1946, reproduced in *The Irish Ecclesiastical Record,* 5. series, LXIX (1947), 160–166, with English translation, 257–264.

———, "Annotationes ad Decretum *Spiritus Sancti munera,* d. 14 sept., 1946," *Apollinaris,* XIX (1946), 236-245.

"Annotationes," *Ephemerides Iuris Canonici,* II (1946), 341–342.

"Questions de science ecclésiastique, consultations diverses," *L'Ami du Clergé,* LIII, 6ᵉ serie (1936), 308–312.

"Liturgie," *L'Ami du Clergé,* LIII, 6ᵉ serie (1936), 442–445.

"New Decisions," *Review for Religious,* VI (1947), 26–27.

Periodicals

American Ecclesiastical Review, The, Vols. I-XXXII, Philadelphia, 1889–1905: from 1905: *The Ecclesiastical Review,* Vols. XXXIII-CIX, Philadelphia, 1905–1943; from 1944: *The American Ecclesiastical Review,* Washington, D. C.: Vol. CX, 1944–

L'Ami du Clergé, Langres, 1878–

Anacleta Iuris Pontificii, Romae, 1855–1869; Parisiis, 1872–1891.

Angelicum, Romae, 1924–

Apollinaris, Romae, 1928–

Australasian Catholic Record, The, Manly, N. S. Wales, Australia, 1923–

Clergy Review, The, London, 1931–

Divus Thomas, Friburg, 1923–

Ephemerides Iuris Canonici, Romae, 1945–
Ephemerides Theologicae Lovanienses, Brugis, 1924–
Homiletic and Pastoral Review, The, New York, 1900–
Irish Ecclesiastical Record, The, Dublin, 1864–; 5. series, 1913–
Jurist, The, Washington, D. C., 1941–
Jus Pontificium, Romae, 1921–1940.
Monitor Ecclesiasticus, Romae, 1949–
Nouvelle Revue Théologique, Tournai, 1869–
Osservatore Romano, Città del Vaticano, Sept. 5, 1849–May 27, 1852; July 1, 1861–
Periodica de Religiosis et Missionariis, Brugis, 1905–1919; *Periodica de Re Canonica et Morali, utilia praesertim Religiosis et Missionariis*, Brugis, 1920–1927; *Periodica de Re Morali, Canonica, Liturgica*, Brugis, 1927–1936, Romae, 1937–
Review for Religious, Topeka, Kansas, 1942–1956; St. Louis, Mo., 1957–
Revista Española de Derecho Canonico, Salamanca, 1946–
Revue de Droit Canonique, Strasbourg, 1951–
Sal Terrae, Santander, 1912–
Seminar, annual extraordinary number of *The Jurist*, Washington, D. C., 1943–1956.
Theological Studies, Woodstock, Md., 1940–

ABBREVIATIONS

AAS—*Acta Apostolicae Sedis, Commentarium Officiale*
AER—*The American Ecclesiastical Review*
Collectanea—*Collectanea S. Congregationis de Propaganda Fide*
C.Tr.—*Concilium Tridentinum: Diariorum, Actorum, Epistularum, Tractatuum Nova Collectio*
Denzinger-Rahner, *Enchiridion*—*Enchiridion Symbolorum Definitionum et Declarationum de rebus fidei et morum,* 30. ed.
ETL—*Ephemerides Theologicae Lovanienses*
Fontes—*Codicis Iuris Canonici Fontes*
Hinschius—*Decretales Pseudo-Isidorianae*
Jaffé—*Regesta Pontificum Romanorum ab condita Ecclesia ad annum post Christum natum MCXCVIII*, 2. ed.
Mansi—*Sacrorum Conciliorum Nova et Amplissima Collectio*
MPL—Migne, *Patrologiae Cursus Completus, Series Latina*
NRT—*Nouvelle Revue Théologique*
Thesaurus—*Thesaurus Resolutionum Sacrae Congregationis Concilii*

ALPHABETICAL INDEX

BIOGRAPHICAL NOTE

Henry Joseph Dziadosz was born August 13, 1923, in Meriden, Conn. After graduating from the St. Stanislaus Parochial School, he entered the Meriden High School, from which he was graduated in 1941. In the fall of that year he entered the St. Thomas Seminary in Bloomfield, Conn., where he completed two years of his classical studies. Having been awarded a Basselin scholarship, he entered the Catholic University of America to pursue his philosophical studies, which he completed in 1945 with the reception of the Master of Arts degree. He also pursued his theological studies at the Catholic University and received the degree of the Licentiate in Sacred Theology in 1949. He was ordained in St. Joseph's Cathedral in Hartford, Conn., on May 26, 1949. After several years of parish work, he was appointed by the Most Reverend Bernard J. Flanagan, D.D., J.C.D., first Bishop of the diocese of Norwich, created August 6, 1953, to pursue graduate study at the School of Canon Law of the Catholic University of America, where he received the Degree of the Baccalaureate in Canon Law in June, 1956, and the Degree of the Licentiate in Canon Law in June, 1957.

CANON LAW STUDIES *

392. Adams, Rev. Donald E., A.B., J.C.L., The truth required in the *preces* for rescripts.
393. Bégin, Rev. Raymond F., A.B., S.T.L., J.C.L., Natural law and positive law.
394. Clancy, Rev. Walter B., A.B., J.C.L., The rites and ceremonies of sacred ordination.
395. Cox, Rev. Ronald J., S.T.L., J.C.L., A study of the juridic status of laymen in the writing of the medieval canonists.
396. Demers, Rev. Francis L., O.M.I., A.B., J.C.L., Temporal administration of the religious house in a non-exempt clerical pontifical institute.
397. Dziadosz, Rev. Henry J., M.A., S.T.L., J.C.L., The provisions of the Decree "Spiritus Sancti munera": the law for the extraordinary minister of confirmation.
398. Gerhardt, Rev. Bernard C., A.B., S.T.L., J.C.L., Interpretation of rescripts.
399. Hackett, Rev. John H., A.B., J.C.L., The concept of public order.
400. Murphy, Rev. Richard J., O.M.I., S.T.L., J.C.L., The canonico-juridical status of a communist.
401. O'Connor, Rev. David, M.S.SS.T., J.C.L., Parochial relations and cooperation of the religious and secular clergy.

* For a complete list of the available numbers of this series apply to the Catholic University of America Press, 620 Michigan Avenue, N.E., Washington (17), D.C., for a general catalogue.

www.ingramcontent.com/pod-product-compliance
Lightning Source LLC
LaVergne TN
LVHW050248080826
844660LV00012B/610

* 9 7 8 0 8 1 3 2 2 5 5 7 9 *